BAPTIZED
INFLATION

BAPTIZED INFLATION

A Critique of
"Christian" Keynesianism

Ian Hodge

Institute for Christian Economics
Tyler, Texas

Printed in the United States of America
ISBN 0-930464-08-7
Library of Congress Catalog Card Number 86-081800

Typesetting by Thoburn Press, Tyler, Texas

Published by
Institute for Christian Economics
P.O. Box 8000
Tyler, Texas 75711

Dedicated to those who make life delightful
Jessie,
Matthew, Rachel and Peter

YOUR $3 DISCOUNT VOUCHER

John Maynard Keynes is the most influential economist of the twentieth century. This speaks poorly of the twentieth century. The creaking world economy is based on the ideas and policies recommended by Keynes.

Keynes was not just an economist. He was also a dedicated homosexual, and a member of a powerful British secret society filled with homosexuals that Keynes himself recruited. It was so dangerous that Beatrice Webb, co-founder of the Fabian Society, worried that it would influence her disciple, Bertrand Russell, who was a member of it.

Most college-level economics textbooks are Keynesian. Most graduate programs in economics and even business schools are still dominated by Keynesian economists (although this is at last beginning to change—not always for the better).

You or someone you know may be shelling out a small fortune each semester to send a student to a Christian college, where he or she is being indoctrinated by "Christian" Keynesians. It may seem strange to you that Christian colleges teach Keynesianism. It may seem odd. Peculiar. Even a little . . . well . . . queer. But they do.

Hard to believe? So are the books written by Prof. Douglas Vickers, a self-conscious Keynesian economist and also a professed Christian. Dr. Vickers has spent the last decade blasting Christian reconstruction in general and my *Introduction to Christian Economics* in particular.

Now, Australian Ian Hodge has written a devastating reply to Vickers and Keynes. The myths of Keynesian economics are exposed in clear, no-jargon language. It's called *Baptized Inflation*.

It's a bombshell. Campus liberals will be outraged. Hodge shows that the whole Keynesian system is a snow job, a pile of lies and nonsense piled high and deep (Ph.D.), a system so idiotic that anyone with a smattering of common sense would reject it as utter nonsense.

Douglas Vickers devoted his career to defending it. Worse, he has devoted the last ten years to defending it in the name of biblical ethics.

Normally, the book retails for $12.50. It's worth every cent. No college student should leave home without reading it. But as an introductory offer, you can buy it for $9.50, if you send in this handy-dandy order form. (Yes, the picture on the order form appears on the cover of the book.)

I wrote the Foreword. Those who have read it say it's like the "old" Gary North, not the mild-mannered, soft-spoken diplomat of today. They may be right.

Dominion Press · 7112 Burns St., Fort Worth, Texas 76118

☒ **Yes**, I want a copy of Ian Hodge's *Baptized Inflation*. Enclosed is my check for $9.50, plus one dollar for postage and handling.

T. G. Allen
Diamond Shamrock-IIAPco
name
P.O. Box 650202
address
Dallas, TX 75265-0202
city, state, zip

P.S. I want ___1___ extra copies at $9.50 each, and no postage and handling fees. I enclose one check for a total of $ _21.00_ .

see Note   CODE: CLN116

TABLE OF CONTENTS

FOREWORD
by Gary North

Discretion will guard you, understanding will watch over you, to deliver you from the way of evil, from the man who speaks perverse things; from those who leave the paths of uprightness, to walk in the ways of darkness; who delight in doing evil, and who rejoice in the perversity of evil; whose paths are crooked, and who are devious in their ways (Proverbs 2:11-15, New American Standard Version).

Back in 1968, economist Douglas Vickers received a shock, or so I would imagine. He discovered that he had spent his entire academic career defending the work of a homosexual pervert. The pervert's name was John Maynard Keynes. Until that fateful year, when Michael Holroyd published his two-volume biography of Lytton Strachey, one of Keynes' "companions," the academic world had not known of Keynes' sexual preferences, or at least had no proof. A few economists knew, and his biographer, Sir Roy Harrod, certainly knew.[1] But before then, his friends who knew had remained discreet. However, by 1968, the world had thrown discretion to the wind. Holroyd's revelation created a stir, but not a sensation, among economists. (Besides, by 1968, the "Keynesian revolution" was well on its way out of fashion—a fact which Dr. Vickers may not have been willing to admit then, or recognize even today, but which the better economists knew in 1968, and virtually all younger economists have known for at least a decade.)

In 1985, Richard Deacon's book appeared which deals with the Cambridge University secret society, the Cambridge Apos-

---

1. I interviewed F. A. Hayek in July of 1985, and I asked him about this. Hayek and Keynes had been academic rivals in the 1930's in England, and Hayek was on good terms with Keynes socially. He assured me that Harrod had known.

tles.[2] It revealed that this group was controlled by homosexuals throughout the early decades of the twentieth century, and that their most prestigious members in this era—John Maynard Keynes, G. Lowes Dickenson, G. E. Moore, and Lytton Strachey —were all dedicated homosexual perverts. So blatant was their public commitment to sodomy that Fabian socialist Beatrice Webb was concerned in 1911 when her protégé Bertrand Russell returned to Cambridge to teach, for he had been an Apostle as a student there in 1892, and she feared that he might get involved with them again: ". . . we have for a long time been aware of its bad influence on our young Fabians."[3]

The Apostles was not simply some undergraduate club. Members continued to attend meetings for decades. In Keynes' fourth year at Cambridge, he became Secretary, yet there was only one undergraduate member.[4] Like the powerful Yale University secret societies, Skull and Bones (George Bush, William Buckley, etc.) and Scroll and Key, membership was gained as an undergraduate, but the links continued throughout life.

Deacon's summary is important for what follows in this book: "Homosexuality probably reached its peak in the Society when Strachey and Maynard Keynes formed a remarkable partnership in conducting its affairs. Here were two minds both devoted to achieving power and influence in their respective ways. Keynes himself was the chief protagonist of the homosexual cult, obsessed with the subject to an abnormal degree for one with a good intellect and wide interests. So obsessed, in fact, that when, years later, he married the Russian ballet dancer, Lydia Lopokova, the news was received with outraged horror among such friends. Some of them never forgave him; others maliciously speculated what was the real reason for the marriage. It slowly dawned on them that this was all part of Keynes's power game.

" 'The Apostles repudiated entirely customary conventions and

---

2. Richard Deacon, *The Cambridge Apostles: A history of Cambridge University's élite intellectual secret society* (London: Robert Royce Ltd., 1985).

3. *Ibid.*, p. 62.

4. *Ibid.*, p. 79.

traditional wisdom,' declared a smug and at the same time delighted Keynes. 'We were in the strict sense of the term Immoralists.'"[5]

Apostles' philosopher G. E. Moore had once announced in a paper read to the group: "In the beginning was matter, and matter begat the devil, and the devil begat God."[6] How terribly clever! How revealingly perverse. He then went on to say that first God had died, then the devil, and now only matter remains.[7] (That Moore is regarded as one of the half dozen major philosophers of this century testifies to the pathetic moral and intellectual character of this century.)

It was within this moral and religious cesspool that Keynes emerged as co-master, along with Strachey. As in every cesspool, the large chunks rise to the top. Keynes was a very large chunk. "A product of Eton, where he displayed a great contempt for his examiners even though they regarded him highly, he brought to Cambridge a high degree of arrogance and assertion of personal superiority over his contemporaries. Surprisingly, this told in his favour rather than against him. Just as the mindless, sadistic public [English private] school bully held sway among the hearties, so did the intellectual bully (which was what Keynes was) dominate when he came to Kings [College, Cambridge]."[8]

"Keynes was an ideal partner for Strachey. The two men were devoted to the same sexual cult and had the same contempt for conventional thought. But there was a difference between the two men. In Strachey's case this was more a question of perversity for its own sake than any carefully thought out philosophy. Keynes was reacting positively against the Puritan ethic: he hated Puritanism in any form and not the least in the form it had taken at Cambridge. Both men, however, regarded homosexuality as the supreme state of existence, 'passing Christian understanding,' and being superior to heterosexual relationships."[9]

---

5. *Ibid.*, p. 64.
6. *Ibid.*, p. 69.
7. *Ibid.*, p. 70.
8. *Ibid.*, p. 78.
9. *Ibid.*, p. 64.

Keynes vs. the Puritan Ethic

What has this got to do with Keynes' ideas on economics? A lot, argues Deacon: "Keynes's hatred of Puritanism is important in the light of his economic theories. He was to become the man who has gone down in history as the most outstanding economist and architect of social progress of the past seventy years, though some would dispute such an assessment. But it was his hostility to the puritan ethic which stimulated and lay behind his economic theories — spend to create work, spend one's way out of depression, stimulate growth. It was also his hatred of Puritanism which caused him in early life to devote rather more time to pursuing homosexual conquests than to economics. More positively, his papers to the Society were in the main nothing whatsoever to do with economics. One such paper, often cited, was on the subject of 'Beauty.'"[10]

Strachey wrote to Keynes: "We can't be content with telling the truth — we must tell the whole truth, and the whole truth is the Devil. It's madness of us to dream of making dowagers understand that feelings are good, when we say in the same breath that the best ones are sodomitical."[11]

Keynes' economic principles matched his moral principles: he didn't believe in them. He denied that fixed economic principles even exist.[12] When, in 1930, he switched from his earlier free

---

10. *Idem.*

11. *Ibid.*, p. 65.

12. Keynes announced in testimony before a 1930 economic commission: "All the same I am afraid of 'principle.' Ever since 1918 we, alone amongst the nations of the world, have been the slaves of 'sound' general principles regardless of particular circumstances. We have behaved as though the intermediate 'short periods' of the economist between our [one?] position of equilibrium and another were short, whereas they can be long enough — and have been before now — to encompass the decline and downfall of nations. Nearly all our difficulties have been traceable to an unaltering service to the principles of 'sound finance' which all our neighbours have neglected. . . . Wasn't it Lord Melbourne who said that 'No statesman ever does anything really foolish except on principle'?" Cited by D. E. Moggridge, *The Return to Gold, 1925: The Formation of Economic Policy and its Critics* (Cambridge: At the University Press, 1969), p. 90. See Hodge's discussion in Chapter 7, "Economic Law."

trade position and became a promoter of protective tariffs against foreign imports, he thereby adopted the ancient, erroneous, and long-refuted policies of mercantilism. These were the trade policies founded on the principle of "beggar thy neighbor." But Keynes had long since decided to do a lot worse than just beggar his neighbor.

Vickers' Deliberate Vagueness

How much of a shock Dr. Vickers suffered when he found out this unsavory fact about his hero, I cannot say. Being a self-professed Christian, he could not have been pleased to find that the founder of the economic school of thought of which he was an obscure member, the "new economics," or "Keynesian orthodoxy school," had spent his life committing this foul crime against God. But Dr. Vickers went on bravely, still proclaiming the wisdom of his intellectual master. He did not bother to warn his Christian readers about Keynes' debauched lifestyle in his book-long defense of Keynesian economics in the name of Jesus, *Economics and Man* (1976). He did feel compelled to admit that "It would be a theological mistake, of course, to imagine that Keynes's own work was influenced by a confessedly Christian perspective. Quite the contrary, as we shall see in our brief comments at a later point on the philosophical predilections and presuppositions of certain famous economists." Philosophy, indeed! So much for the forthright admissions in *Economics and Man*.[13]

Don't misunderstand me. I'm not saying that Douglas Vickers is a limp-wrist economist. A limp-prose economist, unquestionably, but not limp-wrist. He just had the misfortune of not recognizing economic perversion early in his career, so he found himself in questionable intellectual and moral company when the world discovered that Keynes was a specialist in non-economic perversion, too.

I never wrote a refutation of Vickers' book. I was asked to. In

---

13. Douglas Vickers, *Economics and Man* (Nutley, New Jersey: Craig Press, 1976), p. 39.

the first two years after *Economics and Man* was published, occasionally — very, very occasionally — some young man would write to
me and ask me if I had answers to Dr. Vickers' arguments. I
always assumed that I didn't really need answers to those arguments. Sometimes I would ask the inquirer just which argument
offered by Dr. Vickers had impressed him, and not once did anyone tell me precisely which idea he found thought-provoking.
This is understandable, because Dr. Vickers' prose makes it virtually impossible to follow any of his arguments. Couple this with
the fact that Keynes' *General Theory* was almost equally incoherent,
and the reader has a problem. (So did Dr. Vickers' publisher.)

I saw no reason to try to find a publisher for a book refuting a
man who was academically unknown, at the end of his tenured-
level career,[14] a member of a tiny Calvinist denomination, with no
followers except for a tiny coterie inside that denomination made
up of academic types who were fearful in those days (and even
these days) of appearing conservative. Not that they actually read
Economics and Man; nobody reads it. But they pretend to have read
it, and they make others think that they have understood it, just to
keep up appearances. They have to: in thirteen years, *Economics
and Man* is the only book-length study published by anyone, any-
where, which tries to refute the dreaded Christian reconstructionists. The liberals and full-time pietistic retreatists just cannot
stand the thought of Christian reconstruction, and they feel duty-
bound to line up behind any scholar who will take us on. Sadly for
them, the only soul willing to take up the challenge was poor,
jargon-burdened Douglas Vickers, with his tattered Keynesian
banner flying in the breeze. (I'd like to tell you the symbol the
Keynesians have inherited from their master, but this is a family-
oriented book.)

I knew that *Economics and Man* was unlikely ever to go into a
second printing. What I never imagined was that a decade after
its publication, it has yet to sell out the first edition. It is one thing

---

14. He later received a full professorship at the University of Massachusetts, a
taxpayer-financed institution whose most famous former students are Dr. Bill
Cosby, a comedian, and "Dr. J," Julius Erving, a famous basketball player.

to write a one-printing dud, but this is ridiculous! Maybe *Baptized Inflation* will enable Craig Press to unload those last 250 copies.

Hodge vs. Hodge Podge

In short, it just wasn't worth my time to write a response. So I forgot about *Economics and Man*—certainly an easy thing to do. Then, in 1985, Ian Hodge sent me the manuscript of *Baptized Inflation*. It was so delightful tnat I couldn't resist publishing it, now that I have my own outlets for books. Here is a book which not only destroys Dr. Vickers' arguments, but does so in a lively style, with plenty of documentation, and with arguments so clear that even a Harvard economist can follow them.

This book is similar to David Chilton's critique of Ronald Sider, *Productive Christians in an Age of Guilt-Manipulators*. It is not only a critique, but a positive statement of just what biblical free market economics is all about. It does little good to publish critiques of obscure, unreadable books, unless the critique provides insights into what is right. There is so much error in this world, especially in the Ph.D.-holding, self-certifying, risk-free, tax-supported academic world, that the only excuse for responding to any segment of it is that out of the refutation will come positive knowledge of the truth. That is what the reader will get when he reads *Baptized Inflation*.

Hodge answers all of the Keynesians' favorite myths: that the free market cannot clear itself of unsold goods; that monetary inflation is a positive benefit to society; that the gold standard is a "barbarous relic"; that Keynes somehow "refuted" Say's Law; that monetary demand creates economic production; that saving isn't necessarily a productive thing; that we can "spend ourselves rich"; that the free market needs a "visible hand" of a central planning bureaucracy to make it fair, efficient, and "Christian"; that "deficits don't matter"; that the free market is inherently unstable (random); that the free market is also inherently stable (with significant unemployment); and on and on.

The book also makes plain Dr. Vickers' real concern: that Christians might begin to take seriously the Bible, especially biblical law, and use the plain teachings of the Bible to reconstruct the field of economics. That would be terrible, Dr. Vickers assures us in *Economics and Man*. Better to use the teachings of a God-hating, principle-hating, State-loving homosexual pervert as our guide to economic wisdom, Dr. Vickers proclaims. He staked his career on that premise, and lost. Ian Hodge shows just how badly he lost.

Hodge's book is uncompromising. It pulls no punches. It does not profess to be a "gentlemanly exchange of opinions." It recognizes that Dr. Vickers has proclaimed falsehood in the name of truth, economic perversion in the name of academic scholarship, and antinomianism in the name of biblical principle. Dr. Vickers' *Economics and Man* is a defense of the "received wisdom" of the Keynesian revolution — an academic revolution which has led the whole world to the brink of economic catastrophe: an international orgy of debt, inflation, and broken promises by the State.

Hodge also realizes that the fate of civilization hangs in the balance in our day, and that Dr. Vickers has his thumb on the scales — on the side of evil. Hodge recognizes that the economic recommendations made by Dr. Vickers and his far more influential Keynesian academic peers have pushed the world into evil, and therefore toward God's righteous judgment. Like an Old Testament prophet confronting a fourth-level false prophet of some rebellious king of Israel, Ian Hodge points the finger at Douglas Vickers and warns him: "Thus saith the Lord!"

I wonder if Dr. Vickers will listen. False prophets never did in the Old Testament.

Dr. Vickers isn't used to such "undignified" discussions. Tough providence for him. He has become an evangelist for a pervert, a defender of lies, and a scoffer at biblical law, all in the name of Jesus. He deserves everything this book gives him.

Now, a word of warning to the reader. This book bogs down in several sections, not because Hodge can't write clearly, but because he quotes Dr. Vickers verbatim. You will not believe just how bad published writing can be until you struggle with a paragraph or two from *Economics and Man*. Like any sane person, you will be tempted to quit. "I don't have to put up with this; life is too short," you may think to yourself. But Hodge had no choice: if he had just summarized what Dr. Vickers actually teaches, no one would believe him. Readers would conclude that nobody could hold such preposterous views. So Hodge felt compelled to quote Dr. Vickers verbatim, just to prove that the man really does teach utter nonsense. This makes Hodge's book rough going in places. But be patient; once he has quoted Dr. Vickers, he then proceeds to disembowel him. It is a delight to read. If you enjoyed David Chilton's crushing of Ronald Sider's head, and Greg Bahnsen's humiliating of Dr. Vickers' friend Meredith Kline, you'll enjoy Hodge's dissection of Douglas Vickers' "Christian" economics.

Should I be so hard on Dr. Vickers? Should Hodge? If we were not in a war for the minds of the Christian community, and if the stakes were not the survival of Western civilization, it wouldn't be worth the trouble. But I believe that Hodge's book can serve as a warning to younger scholars not to sell their intellectual birthrights as Christians for a mess of humanist academic pottage. To pull any punches when the stakes are this high would be tantamount to pulling out of the fight — a fight which Dr. Vickers started in 1976 when he went into print to tell Christian people not to take seriously the *revealed* economics of the Bible. This book is his reward.

Epistemological Child Molesters

I have already received the standard response from the standard professor at what is a standard Christian college. In a letter written on college stationery, he tells me to apologize to Dr. Vickers for what I regard as a rather mild and semi-humorous remark I made about Dr. Vickers' economic thought. What I said in an advertisement was that with the publication of this book, Dr. Vickers would be "dead meat."

This juicy phrase was made by a character in a popular film, *Rocky III*. The "heavy" of the movie was a boxer, played by a ferocious-looking black actor named "Mr. T," who was the challenger to the heavyweight champion, Rocky, in the fight for the championship. To unnerve Rocky before the fight, the Mr. T character says that once he gets into the ring with Rocky, Rocky will be dead meat. Rocky had trained in the first movie by punching frozen sides of beef inside a commercial freezer-locker. The challenger was referring back to what Rocky had done to the beef: punched it "senseless." It had been dead meat; now it would be Rocky's turn.

The phrase "dead meat" became instantly popular to describe someone who is completely outclassed in any form of competition. In the academic world, this means someone who is exposed in print for his ignorance, incompetence, or even intellectual dishonesty. I think this describes quite well what Ian Hodge does to Douglas Vickers in this book.

The concerned letter-writer says that I owe Dr. Vickers an apology for such a "crude description." Judge for yourself the accuracy of this description after you read what it is that Dr. Vickers has taught students for four decades, and what he has taught Christians for a decade in the name of Jesus. Judge for yourself the coherence of his writing and the nature of his conclusions. Pay close attention to Hodge's arguments. I read and reread the manuscript. "Dead meat" describes Dr. Vickers' condition — describes it to a T.

The letter-writer is a friend of Vickers, which may explain some of his concern. Most of all, however, he is a professor at a neo-evangelical (read: spiritually compromised) college. He resents all this nastiness. He wants polite discussions. We must not be overly critical. We must not use ridicule. We must not be like Luther in his battles with the Pope, or Augustine in his battles with Pelagius. No, we must all be good sports. More than that: _Christian_ good sports.

I will be far more impressed with this sort of nonsense when Christian reconstructionists start getting offers of professorships at neo-evangelical colleges. These tenured scholarly types want reconstructionists to keep our comments polite, as if we were members of good standing in the campus faculty club, when in fact we have been universally blackballed by the existing power brokers inside the so-called Christian colleges. "Put us on the team, fellows, and we might just become good sports!" (Probably not, though. We would probably do our best to pull off what the liberals who dominate the faculties have done so well: screen out our opponents from day one, and staff the institutions with people who believe as we do. But at least we would be open about it. At least we are willing to admit that an ideological war is going on, and Western civilization is at stake. At least we admit that we are street fighters. We prefer to stab our opponents in the belly, publicly; the campus liberal establishment specializes in stabbing them in the back, privately. We do it in print; they do it in closed-session faculty meetings.)

My correspondent says, "I find this terribly offensive." Well, then, I guess he got the idea. *I am doing everything I can to offend classroom humanists who parade themselves as Christians, and who live off the donations of naive Christians who trust their children to these ideological child seducers.* They are stealing the minds of our children, and they have been doing it for two generations. They are doing everything they can to make left-wing, welfare State-promoting voters out of our children. I am trying to catch the attention of parents and donors. I care not a whit for the sensibilities of the Ph.D.-holding classroom compromisers. My job is to expose them, but more to the point, to do what I can to get their funds cut off.

Fighting to Win

We who call ourselves Christian reconstructionists are fighting a war for Western civilization: to save it, and then restore it to its original Christian underpinnings. We are therefore fighting a war for the kingdom of God. We are opposed by the classroom humanists who call themselves Christians. We have outraged them by suggesting that Christian college instructors should teach every discipline strictly in terms of the revelation of the Bible — yes, even if the Bible does not agree with classroom notes that were taken at State U. back in 1968, or even in 1938.

The classroom compromisers are not used to any kind of opposition. They have ridden roughshod over two generations of college students who fear being flunked out of school if they voice opinions counter to the New Deal economics of their professors. The professors have had a free ride, especially Christian college professors. Until the Christian reconstructionists started pounding on them, nobody paid any attention to them except an occasional conservative donor, and he didn't have an earned Ph.D. from an accredited state university. Now that the free ride has ended for a few of them, the frightened mice are banding together in helpless outrage. "You can't do these things!" Yes, we can.

After all, Jesus did. I am presently writing a manuscript that I intend to call, *Thou Hypocrite! Jesus' Tactics of Direct Confrontation.* He called the Pharisees whited sepulchers. He called them hypocrites. He called Herod, a civil magistrate, a fox, and a female fox at that. He did everything He could to embarrass his opponents in front of their formerly helpless followers. Jesus was one of the most effective verbal street fighters in history, and He was crucified for it. Yet today's academic wolves in sheep's clothing pretend that He was president of the International Association of Wimps.

The Academic Seduction of the Innocent

These classroom compromisers are the products of a century of classroom humanism. They have immersed themselves in the humanistic methodologies of the secular universities that granted them their advanced academic degrees. They have done everything within their power to screen out students and rival faculty members who come before them and announce that every academic discipline must be reformed, top to bottom, in terms of what the Bible says. They will not allow such people to teach at *their* colleges. They will not grant them tenure. They resent the fact that others say in public that they, the compromisers, have sold their spiritual birthrights for a mess of tenure.

They worry most of all when they think about the very real possibility that most of the donors to their colleges are probably closer in their opinions to the reconstructionists than to the campus faculty club. Why, the donors might . . . they just might . . .

cut off the donations! And then what would happen to people who earn their livelihood by reading ten-year-old lecture notes to students for 12 whole hours a week? What would happen to their four months of paid vacations a year?

They go into the classrooms and teach liberation theology (Marxism) as if it were not a call for bloody revolution; yes, even if they are paid to teach eighteenth-century English literature. They teach the wonders of socialism, as if it were not the foundation of universal tyranny and poverty. They call for ever-larger doses of the welfare State, as if it had not destroyed three generations of families, especially black families, in the United States.[15] But call attention to what they are doing in tenured security with donors' money, and they become outraged. "You can't do that!" Yes, we can.

Like adulterers who are caught in the act by a private investigator hired by an outraged spouse, they protest loudly that the investigator failed to knock at the motel door before walking in and taking photographs. The photographer was terribly impolite by entering without knocking, which therefore is supposed to let the adulterers off the hook. "See here," the startled man says, as he gets into his trousers, "this barging-in business is totally uncalled for. We are all adults here." (Indeed, we are.) As he is buttoning up his shirt, he reminds the photographer, "Things just aren't done this way in refined circles." Finally, as he is putting on his tweed jacket with the leather patches on the elbows, he lowers the boom. "I can assure you, sir, that you're never going to see one of your articles in *The Journal of Comparative Obscurity*, of which I am an associate editor."

Then, after the private eye has published full-color photographs of the man and his adulterous companion, with the headline, "Adulterers Caught in Tryst," he receives an outraged letter from one of the man's academic colleagues. "We are offended by such a caption," the letter says. "Your photographs were in ex-

---

15. Charles Murray, *Losing Ground: American Social Policy, 1950-1980* (New York: Basic Books, 1984).

tremely bad taste, and furthermore, the headline was in very
large print, which is *not* scholarly, and it should have read, 'Close
Acquaintances in a Friendly Hug.' You owe them both an apology." There is a P.S., too: "I notice that no respectable scholarly
press was willing to publish this scurrilous attack, which *proves*
that you are way out of line." No, it only indicates that the editors
of the scholarly presses are not innocent bystanders. They guard
the hall of the motel while the couple is otherwise engaged; they
try to head off photographers.

These mild-mannered drones are defenders of the revolutionary destroyers of Western civilization. They think they will all be
safe and sound when this civilization falls. They act as though
they believe that their tweed jackets are bulletproof. They think
the revolutionary conflicts going on today are the equivalent of a
monthly debate in the faculty lounge. They are even naive
enough to imagine that the agreed-upon position statements of
the latest faculty club meeting are relevant to anyone, anywhere,
anytime soon. They think that the great issues of the world will be
settled in the pages of scholarly journals.

They are wrong. The only position statements that can make
it through the faculty committees in today's Christian liberal arts
colleges are watered-down conclusions that were dropped as un-
workable (or no longer useful in a program of planned deception)
by the liberal intelligentsia ten years earlier. If you doubt me, wait
until you read Ian Hodge's account of what happened to Dr. Vickers' "revolutionary new ideas" long before Dr. Vickers went into
print with *Economics and Man*. The delightful fact is that Dr. Vickers still hasn't figured out what his younger humanist peers did to
him. They did to him what he did to his elders decades ago. They
left him behind in the dust, or the academic economists' equivalent of dust, stochastic equations.

Over the Falls With the Mainstream

Herbert Schlossberg, whose *Idols for Destruction* is a footnoted,
gentlemanly, academically acceptable hand grenade against modern campus liberalism, has the trust of the neo-evangelical aca-

demics. (Little do they suspect!) He speaks in subdued and scholarly tones while he slices them, throat to groin. We in the Christian reconstruction movement regard him as our major wedge into Christian academia, for he brings many of our anti-establishment, anti-liberal conclusions to this spiritually parched desert, and in a format that is academically acceptable. But sometimes we make him a bit nervous.

He has commented on one aspect of the Christian reconstructionist writers: their "outsider" status. He believes that for our movement to gain more influence, we must join the publishing mainstream. "One thing that will have to change for that to happen is the style with which these sharpies skewer their opponents. That kind of invective is just not *done* in polite publishing circles."[16] He should have added, "at least in the United States." In Britain, knock-down, drag-out scholarly battles are quite common. A. J. P. Taylor, perhaps the most prolific historian of our time, is famous for his devastating scholarly book reviews, which are notable for their shark-like sensitivity to weakness. "To have been Taylored" well describes the victims. It is an educational experience, both for the reader and the victim.

Schlossberg has misunderstood our strategy. We have a comprehensive program. We tailor (or Taylor) our writing to fit the intended audience. We write sweetness-and-light books for some audiences, disguising ourselves as mild-mannered reporters. But when it comes time to take off the kid gloves in order to pulverize some pompous academic bozo who has devoted his career to spewing out humanist wood, hay, and stubble in the name of Jesus, we take off the gloves and pulverize him. Our motto is simple: *Take no prisoners!*

If our style is not considered polite in certain academic circles, then to avoid being manhandled, it would be wise for these epistemological child molesters to stay out of print, hidden from public

---

16. Schlossberg, "Evangelical Awakenings," a review of David Chilton's *Productive Christians in an Age of Guilt Manipulators*, in *The American Spectator* (April 1986), p. 35.

view in their tenured classroom security. If they go into print, as Douglas Vickers did, they can expect "the treatment." Meanwhile, let them pick up the battered, semi-conscious body of their colleague, dress him in a new tweed jacket, and tell everyone that he only suffered minor cuts and bruises at the hands of unspeakable reconstructionist ruffians.

By the way, those who are unfamiliar with Christian academia need to be made aware of another aspect of these public beatings. Once the skewered colleague is out of earshot, his fellow scholars sit around reading reconstructionist materials, chortling among themselves. "They really caught him on that one, didn't they? Ho, ho, ho." They may resent us, but they enjoy seeing their colleague publicly deflated, yet they can hardly admit their delight publicly. This is one reason why they buy our books, although in plain brown wrappers. They like to see an occasional beating. Like the rest of us, they like to see stuffed shirts get the stuffing knocked out of them once in a while. They are not complete ignoramuses; they recognize that the victim really is an intellectual lightweight. They have had to sit through his boring monologues in faculty club meetings on numerous occasions. Furthermore, they are not altogether free from envy: the enjoyment of watching some "superior" sort get knocked off his pedestal. He got a book into print; *they* never have. But no one inside the faculty lounge would admit this moral weakness, even to himself. Nevertheless, they buy our books. Their colleague, even with his new tweed jacket, never again looks quite the same in their eyes. He suspects as much, too. That is why I enjoy publishing a book like this one.

The best example of this is Ronald J. Sider, whose *Rich Christians in an Age of Hunger* was the rage on neo-evangelical campuses, 1977-1982. He got the usual free ride. Then ICE published David Chilton's *Productive Christians in an Age of Guilt-Manipulators* in 1981, and a second edition in 1982. Sider was stunned. The free ride was over. He wrote a second edition in 1984, promising on the cover that he had replied to his critics. In fact, he replied to none of his published critics, especially Chilton. Within a few months, Chilton had written and ICE had published the third edition of

Productive Christians, reviewing Sider's desperate and ineffective squirming in his second edition, page by page. Sales of Sider's second edition stalled, indicating that the Sider fad is just about over. When he failed to reply to Chilton, pretending that Chilton hadn't beaten him to a pulp, he removed himself from the intellectual contest. Schlossberg noted in his review of Chilton's book that Sider had failed to reply. Sider will never recover his academic reputation, to the extent that he ever had one. He knows that if he can get anyone to publish a third edition, which is unlikely, Chilton will simply beat him up again. Who needs it?

Vickers knows this, too. The free ride is over. Hodge does the unforgivable in the world of liberal academia: he quotes Dr. Vickers in context, verbatim. When you read these passages, you will better understand how cruel Hodge is. In short, if you enjoyed the final scenes in the "Rocky" movies, you'll enjoy *Baptized Inflation*. When you're finished, I'm sure you'll agree: *Douglas Vickers is indeed dead meat.*

PREFACE

The idea for this book was prompted by a number of circumstances. During 1979 I read my first economics book since leaving school in 1964. For the first time economics now made sense, thanks to the remarkable clarity Gary North gave to the topic in his book *An Introduction to Christian Economics*. This book was such a delight that I followed his advice and purchased many of the books the author recommended.

Not to appear biased, however, I also obtained books which presented an alternative perspective. In the Christian field there was not much choice. In fact, the choice is virtually the same in 1986 as it was in 1979: Gary North, Ronald Sider, and an Australian economist named Douglas Vickers. Dr. Vickers, in contrast to Dr. Sider (a historian of European Anabaptism), is a professional economist, and therefore one will find much more of the "dismal science" theory in his book *Economics and Man* than in those which Dr. Sider has authored. But it is dismal for one reason: Dr. Vickers is a promoter of popular economic theory, and by popular I mean the theory of John Maynard Keynes. The theories of Keynes pervade the schools and universities, and therefore the economics profession in general. Economic advisers to business and government are usually advising from a Keynesian perspective, although in business there is pragmatic abandonment of Keynesian theories *because they do not work*. It is in the practical world of business that economic theory gets its real testing, not the hallowed walls of Congress, where economic theory can be overruled by legislative act (at least temporarily).

In fact, I can say quite truthfully that it was Dr. Vickers who

made me a follower of the free market system. It was his attempt
to portray Keynesian nonsense as serious economic thinking
which caused me to accept the ideas of North and Rushdoony as
having much more logic and coherence than could be found in Dr.
Vickers' book. (Thanks, Doug!)

During 1980 I made the mistake of attempting to introduce
discussion on Christian economics into a Reformed theological
college I was attending. It was a mistake, as I have subsequently
realized, because there was no interest among staff or students to
know whether there might be a specifically biblical theory of economics. It was as if the intellectual effort needed to make such an
analysis of Scripture was too great. (I have witnessed a similar intellectual laziness among many pastors, elders, and deacons.)
Besides, I was informed, Dr. Vickers had the answers to anything
that Gary North, R. J. Rushdoony, and others might happen to
say. I should read Vickers' book, I was told both by staff and students, especially in the case of one who had been a former economics teacher, and get "straightened out" on my economics.

Fortunately, I had already made that effort and ploughed my
way through Dr. Vickers' book. (Ploughing is especially necessary
when the soil is hard, and believe me, the soil in this case was *very*
hard.) One of the brightest students in that college during that
period actually made an effort to read Dr. Vickers' book, but gave
up in defeat after the first chapter. He admitted he did not understand it, and nothing I could say at that time convinced him of the
possibility that he could not understand it *because it did not make
sense*. He preferred to believe that there was something lacking in
his own intelligence.

The idea and outline for this book began during that period I
spent in what is known as a Protestant monastery: Theological
College, a recluse where staff and students escape from the real
world and the realities of life. This manuscript is an attempt to
put Dr. Vickers' book into perspective and highlight some of the
inherent difficulties Keynesian economic theory presents in contrast with the Word of God. Most of what appears in this book
comes from marginal notes I made on my first reading of Dr.

Vickers, which I had undertaken in 1979. Subsequent readings (plural!) have not caused me to alter the content of any of my initial notes, and in some cases they have been expanded and additional comments made.

I am very grateful to those who have made the publication of this book possible. To my wife Jessie, and children Matthew, Rachel and Peter, who have been without husband and father in order that this manuscript could come to fruition. To Noel Weeks and Peter Wolnizer who read the manuscript and offered helpful advice. A very special thanks to Dr. Gary North and the staff at the Institute for Christian Economics who have not only been willing to publish the manuscript, but also provide practical assistance and editorial skills to make this project possible. Whatever shortcomings exist, however, must remain my own.

Ian Hodge
Engadine, NSW
Australia

Even more serious may be the failure of the basic postulate underlying Keynesian economic *policy:* the "economist-king," the objective, independent expert who makes effective decisions based solely on objective, quantitative, unambiguous evidence, and free of both political ambitions and of political pressures on him. Even in the 1930's, a good many people found it difficult to accept this. To the Continental Europeans in particular, with their memories of the post-war inflations, the "economist-king" was sheer *hubris* — which in large measure explains why Keynes has had so few followers on the Continent until the last 10 or 15 years. By now, however, few would take seriously the postulate of the non-political economist who, at the same time, controls crucial political decisions. Like all "enlightened despots," the Keynesian "economist-king" has proven to be a delusion, and indeed a contradiction in terms. If there is one thing taught by the inflations of the last decade — as it was taught by the inflations of the 1920's in Europe — it is that the economist in power either becomes himself a politician and expedient (if not irresponsible), or he ceases to have power and influence. It is simply not true, as is often asserted, that economists do not know how to stop inflation. Every economist since the late 16th century has known how to do it: Cut government expenses and with them the creation of money. What economists lack is not theoretical knowledge, it is political will or political power. And so far all inflations have been ended by politicians who had the will rather than by economists who had the knowledge.

Without the "economist-king," Keynesian economics ceases to be operational. It can play the role of critic, which Keynes played in the 1920's, and which Milton Friedman plays today. In opposition, the Keynesian economist, being powerless, can also be politics-free. But it is an opposition that cannot become effective government. The Keynesian paradigm is thus likely to be around a long time as a critique and as a guide to what not to do. But it is fast losing its credibility as a foundation for economic theory and as a guide to policy and action.

Peter Drucker*

---

*Drucker, "Toward the Next Economics," *The Public Interest* (Special Issue, 1980), p. 12.

INTRODUCTION

We have been driven into a widespread system of arbitrary and tyrannical control over our economic life, not because "economic laws are not working the way they used to," not because the classical medicine cannot, if properly applied, halt inflation, but because the public at large has been led to expect standards of performance that as economists we do not know how to achieve. . . . I believe that we economists in recent years have done vast harm — to society at large and to our profession in particular — by claiming more than we can deliver. We have thereby encouraged politicians to make extravagant promises, inculcate unrealistic expectations in the public at large, and promote discontent with reasonably satisfactory results because they fall short of the economists' promised land.

Milton Friedman (1971)[1]

Economic recession and its products — growing unemployment, decreasing production, falling commodity prices, together with the potentially imminent collapse of the international financial system — have become increasingly important topics of concern for everyone. What will happen to *my* money in *my* local bank if Poland, or Mexico, or Brazil, or the Philippines, or one of several other countries defaults on its payment to Western, and especially U.S., private commercial banks?

Some commentators incline to the opinion there is no problem, or if a problem does exist, it is not really very serious. Two

---

1. Presidential address, American Economic Association, reprinted in the *American Economic Review* (May 1972), pp. 17-18.

young business executives were heard to declare their faith in our government by acknowledging that economic difficulties did exist, but at the same time they were sure that "the government" would get them out of the mess. Such faith should not—and shall not—go unrewarded! On the other hand, the statistical game played by most governments creates confusion in the mind of the average person because such profoundly conflicting statistical data are presented. The economy is declining; now it's on the rise; inflation of 5%, once thought to be out of control at that rate, is now considered acceptable after having reached heights of 10% or more; unemployment is rising; job opportunities have increased as never before; business is booming as people spend; sorry, correct that, they are saving instead of spending; we're into another recession. No wonder we are a little confused.

The perspective of this book is that *there really is something radically wrong with the present economic climate*. What is today occurring is not merely flying in the face of sound economic principles, but is also contrary to common sense and what most of us know by intuition. For example, we all know that if we borrow something from someone, one day we will have to make repayment, unless we are perverse. "The wicked borroweth, and payeth not again" (Ps. 37:21a). (Some economists, however, are perverts—this book deals with the most famous pervert of them all, John Maynard Keynes—so it is not surprising that they recommend perverse policies.) We might like to think we can postpone such repayment indefinitely, but deep down we all have the conviction it will be made. It is a matter of *when*, not *if*. Yet the premier economists of our day—Keynesian, monetarist, supply-side—have all either explicitly or implicitly accepted the dictum that "deficits don't matter (at least in the short run)," and that "temporary" increases in government debt may be helpful in stimulating the economy. There has not been a single book by an academically certified economist of any school of thought in over five decades which informs us of just exactly how a nation can repay its debt without suffering either mass depression, mass inflation, or both: first mass inflation, then mass depression. In fact, I am unaware of a single scholarly study by an economist *in this century* which provides a theoretical case (let alone a *moral* case) for the complete repayment of government debt, bringing all government debt to zero.[2]

Why not? First, because economists pretend to be morally neutral, so they do not acknowledge the essential immorality of permanent debt. It is a form of slavery: "The rich ruleth over the poor, and the borrower is servant to the lender" (Prov. 22:7). The economists ignore this. Second, they do not discuss the complete repayment of government debt because of a distinct economic problem that modern policies of government debt management have created. All government debt structures today are partially "monetized." This means that the nation's central bank has created credit money out of thin air (or computer blips) to buy billions' worth of government bills or bonds. This has increased the money supply of every nation, and it has introduced the infamous "boom-bust" cycle. Once begun, monetary inflation leads to inflationary booms and panic recessions. The question for which no economist or politician has published a politically acceptable (or even an economically plausible) answer is this one: How can the government repay 100% of its debt without drastically shrinking the money supply when it buys back the central bank's bonds? Since monetary inflation and then price inflation came when the central bank bought the bonds, monetary deflation and then price deflation will come when the government buys them back (retires them).[3] If the debt is repaid, the nation goes into a deflationary

---

2. There are books by certain "Social Credit" writers that advocate this, but so far, there has never been an academically trained or university-certified economist in the "Social Credit" movement, and we have waited fifty years. Before that, the "greenbackers" (printing press inflationists) in the United States promoted ideas similar to "Social Credit," but there was never an economist in their camp, either.

3. There is one solution, but it may be worse than the cure. If the central bank decreases reserve requirements for commercial banks in order to offset the reduction in the central bank's monetary base — its holdings of government debt — then there need not be deflation. But then the commercial banks are given even greater freedom to pump up the money supply by expanding loans which they create out of nothing. Thus, the nation will experience a new wave of monetary inflation and another round of the boom-bust trade cycle. What we need is *zero*

depression, unless the central bank is allowed to start buying up private firms' debt certificates. But this just extends the problem of permanent debt to the private sector. *So the now-monetized government debt is never scheduled to be repaid.*

Nevertheless, instinctively we all know that it must be repaid. The economists tell us that we are wrong, that our instincts have no scientific validity. Yet year by year, the central banks' inflationary policies ratchet prices ever upward. Year by year, the commercial banks face the threat of ever-larger loan defaults by Third World nations and hard-pressed domestic farmers. Year by year, the economic theorists forecast events that do not come to pass.

A Loss of Confidence

What is wrong? The economists cannot say. They are baffled. Nevertheless, they keep offering their opinions. The public keeps hoping that they will come up with solutions soon, and the incumbent politicians keep hoping that these solutions, when implemented, will not lead to their defeat at the next election. The public and the politicians are acting in terms of faith in economists — a faith that has little or no evidence to justify itself. Increasingly, it is a waning faith. (Question: "What's the difference between a dog which has just been run over by a car, and an economist who has just been run over by a car?" Answer: "There are skid marks in front of the dog.")

Academic economic theories do not perform well any more. Economist Peter Drucker says that Keynes was a great economist, yet he writes of Keynes' "magic": "The Keynesian 'policies,' in spite — or perhaps because — of their elaborate apparatus of mathematical formulae and statistical tables, are spells. Because of this, the fact that they failed once, in the [United States'] New Deal, means that they have failed forever. For it is of the nature of

---

government debt and *100% reserve* commercial banking. To get there, a nation either has to go straight to mass deflation and depression, or first go through universal debt repudiation by mass inflation, and *then* deflation, meaning the substitution of a new currency system, which most Continental European nations have gone through several times since World War I.

a spell that it ceases altogether to be effective as soon as it is broken once."[4] He wrote these words in the year Keynes died, 1946. He wrote them two decades prematurely, as far as the economics profession was concerned, but Drucker is always way ahead of the pack. His point is now correct: *the Keynesian magic is dead.* But the spells and incantations are still being tried. Sometimes economists give the policies new names, such as "supply-side economics." The results are the same: more government spending and larger budget deficits.

Christian Economics

Amidst all this confusion, the Christian has a particular obligation to develop a distinctively biblical economics that will provide the answers to the world's difficulties. Political economy, or economics as it is now known, had been of little interest to Christians until Gary North and R. J. Rushdoony brought the subject to the attention of the Christian public with their important analyses, which they offered from a self-consciously biblical perspective.[5] Since the appearance of their two major early works in 1973, *Introduction to Christian Economics* and *Institutes of Biblical Law*, other authors have contributed books from a similar perspective.[6] The

---

4. Peter Drucker, "Keynes: Economics as a Magical System," *Virginia Quarterly Review* (Autumn 1946); reprinted in Drucker, *Men, Ideas & Politics* (New York: Harper & Row, 1971), p. 247.

5. Gary North, *An Introduction to Christian Economics* (Nutley, New Jersey: Craig Press, 1973); *The Dominion Covenant: Genesis* (Tyler, Texas: Institute for Christian Economics, 1982), volume one of an intended multi-volume economic commentary on the Bible. Volume two is to be in three parts: *Moses and Pharaoh: Dominion Religion vs. Power Religion* (1985), *The Sinai Strategy: Economics and the Ten Commandments* (1986), and the forthcoming book, *Tools of Dominion: The Case Laws of Exodus*, all published by the Institute for Christian Economics. Rousas John Rushdoony, *The Institutes of Biblical Law,* (Nutley, New Jersey: Craig Press, 1973); *The Myth of Overpopulation* (Fairfax, Virginia: Thoburn Press, [1969] 1978); *Politics of Guilt and Pity* (Fairfax, Virginia: Thoburn Press, [1970] 1978); *The Roots of Inflation* (Vallecito, California: Ross House Books, 1982).

6. E. L. Hebden Taylor, *Economics Money and Banking: Christian Principles* (Nutley, New Jersey: Craig Press, 1978); Tom Rose, *Economics: Principles and Policy From a Christian Perspective* (Milford, Michigan: Mott Media, 1977); John Jefferson Davis, *Your Wealth in God's World: Does the Bible Support the Free Market?* (Phillipsburg, New Jersey: Presbyterian & Reformed, 1984).

head of Margaret Thatcher's Conservative Party "think tank," Prof. Brian Griffiths, an economist at the City University of London, is also a Christian. He acknowledges privately that he had never imagined that there could be such a thing as a specifically Christian economics until he read Gary North's *Introduction to Christian Economics* in the late 1970's. He has now written Christian-oriented materials on economics.[7]

This perspective could be categorized, broadly, as one of a "free market" or *laissez-faire* economy, although it would be a grave error to omit mentioning that these authors insist that Scripture be brought to bear on what has been traditionally known under these titles. For these authors, "free market" does not mean anarchy, since Scriptural principles provide the moral and legal framework within which a *laissez-faire* approach is adopted, and from which Western capitalism originated.[8] Christian economic thinking demands a rejection of economic theories that do not stand the test of three standards: the Bible, internal consistency, and historical verification. It therefore demands a rejection of Keynesian economics.

The "Flexible" Legacy of Keynes

Modern economics is the economics of John Maynard Keynes, the son of a Cambridge University economist, John Neville Keynes. (The name is pronounced "Canes," as in candy canes.) The younger Keynes has been the most influential economist of this century and, as Gary North reminds us, this speaks poorly of this century. It matters little where we study economics outside of the Iron Curtain; we can be sure that at least some of the theories of Keynes will be presented and actively promoted as being the panacea for the ills

---

7. Brian Griffiths, *Morality and the Market Place: Christian Alternatives to Capitalism and Socialism* (London: Hodder and Stoughton, 1982); *The Creation of Wealth* (London: Hodder & Stoughton, 1985).

8. By the term *laissez-faire* is meant the general principle of non-intervention in the economy by coercive organizations such as government-protected trade unions. It includes non-intervention by government officials except for the punishing of those who indulge in theft, fraud, or coercion.

of society. (Even Milton Friedman has said that, methodologically speaking, "we are all Keynesians now.")

In the search for a solution to the perceived problems, however, Keynesianism has come in for more than its fair share of criticism, both from the "right" and more recently the "left."[9] Keynesianism, it seems, does not work, or at least has not worked well recently. Nevertheless, the solutions to society's economic problems offered by most economists, especially those in the bureaucracy and in tenured university positions, have called for even more Keynesianism. Examples of this can be cited in great number, from all over the Western world.

Consider the question of tariffs. These barriers to voluntary trade between people of different geographical areas have been promoted in the United States and elsewhere in times of rising wealth and also in times of recession. Some interest groups are hurt during one phase of the trade cycle, who then call for protection from "cut-throat competition," and different groups are hurt in the other phase of the cycle, who then call for protection from "cut-throat competition." (What these special-interest groups really want is to protect consumers from "cut-throat *opportunities*" offered by foreign sellers.)[10] Yet we are always assured by all groups that they are only calling for "temporary" tariffs. Similarly, most of those politicians who promote free trade will do so only on the basis of "temporary" conditions. If conditions change, the voters are assured, the imposition of tariffs will be considered.

This tradition of promoting both the accurate and inaccurate conclusions of economic theory in the name of temporary expediency or historical circumstances was reinforced by Keynes. He would promote bad economic theory as enthusiastically and as confidently in one period as he had previously promoted sound economic conclusions. Specifically, he shifted from advocating low tariffs in the 1920's to a pro-tariff position in 1931. The shift was made purely in terms of expediency; economic theory was

---

9. Michael Bleaney, *The Rise and Fall of Keynesian Economics: An investigation of its contribution to capitalist development* (London: Macmillan, 1985).

10. Gary North, "Cut-Throat Opportunities," *The Freeman* (June 1982).

always regarded by Keynes as a lamb to be sacrificed on the altar of expediency. His devoted apologist, Prof. Robert Lekachman, has written that "Keynes readily shifted ground on tariffs in the Macmillan Committee *Report* and elsewhere out of a sober consideration of British interests. Not entirely consistently, he preferred these interests to a doctrine of free trade, which he continued to value highly on intellectual grounds."[11] *Not entirely consistently:* ah, the wonders of scholarly verbal restraint! What Keynes did was to sell out the interests of British consumers (who would otherwise have purchased additional foreign goods), as well as foreign purchasers of British goods (who needed export sales to Britain in order to earn British pounds sterling, in order to import British goods), and he did so in the name of "British interests," meaning the "old boy" network of uncompetitive British manufacturers.

Another acolyte in the Keynesian church, E. A. G. Robinson, has also politely commented on Keynes' notorious lack of consistency: "A careful study of Keynes will, I believe, show him to have been remarkably consistent in his strategic objectives, but extraordinarily fertile in tactical proposals for achieving them. Like a resourceful tactician, he would probe, try to find the enemy's weak points; if repulsed he would quickly fall back and regroup and put in another attack elsewhere."[12] What a marvelous phrase: "fertile in tactical proposals." He might have called it "Keynes' finger in the wind," but that would have implied crass opportunism. It might have revealed the truth, namely, that economic ideas were treated by Keynes as little more than pawns on a chessboard, and *he regarded the whole British economy as his personal chessboard.* He was ready to sacrifice these "pawns"—consistent ideas —for the sake of some overall "game plan." But what kind of "game plan" for the economy can be constructed on the foundation of an economic theory which denies the existence of reliable

---

11. Robert Lekachman, *The Age of Keynes* (New York: Random House, 1966), p. 52.

12. E. A. G. Robinson, "John Maynard Keynes, 1883-1946," in Robert Lekachman (ed.), *Keynes' General Theory: Reports of Three Decades* (New York and London: Macmillan, 1964), pp. 61-62.

cause-and-effect relationships (tendencies) in economic affairs? And what kind of legal order results from such unpredictable shifts of political opinion? What kind of protection for private property can anyone expect?

I cannot resist citing Robinson's next sentences, published in 1964, at the tail end of the post-War faith in the Keynesian experiment, within months of the period when Keynesian policies at last began to erode the world economy in successive waves of price inflation: "But in the end his victory was complete. Full employment of resources has become the national objective; some would say it has obscured other objectives. Ordered flexibility of exchange rates has become the agreed world system. Low interest rates have become the official policy to the extent that former advocates now begin to fear."

Within 18 months, the American inflation began. Ten years after these words were published, Keynes' personal invention, the Bretton Woods system of managed currency exchange rates, had collapsed; free market (flexible) exchange rates were setting currency prices moment by moment. Two decades later, unemployment had become a worldwide phenomenon at rates higher than any experienced since 1940. "Real" interest rates — market rates minus expected price inflation — had become abnormally high, and stayed high. In short, *the entire Keynesian experiment has collapsed.* As Hegel (and Marx, following Hegel) once remarked, the owl of Minerva flies only at dusk: men finally adopt some "comprehensive and complete" explanatory system at the precise moment when this system or historical epoch is about to break down.[13]

Vickers' Defense of Keynes

You would not imagine that any Christian economist would still (or ever!) be an advocate of Keynesian economics, but you would imagine wrong. Douglas Vickers, one-time Professor of

---

13. Perhaps the classic "owl" book was Walter Heller's *New Directions in Political Economy* (New York: Norton, 1966). Heller had been Chairman of the Council of Economic Advisors under Presidents Kennedy and Johnson. The book announced the arrival of a new era of economist-directed prosperity.

Economics at the University of Western Australia, and more recently at the University of Massachusetts, is a dedicated Keynesian. His book *Economics and Man* was written as " 'a prelude' to a more exhaustive Christian critique"[14] in which he endeavors to set forth what he believes to be a Christian perspective on the subject. To date, his prelude has not been followed by that promised "exhaustive Christian critique," although he hired a "vanity" (author-financed) publisher to get into print *A Christian Approach to Economics and the Cultural Condition*,[15] a book much shorter than *Economics and Man*, and which is little more than a re-statement of the ideas presented in his earlier work. (His inimitable style is easily recognized on the dust jacket's fly leaf: "Throughout his argument, Douglas Vickers adopts a carefully delineated scriptural perspective, and textual support for the structure and conclusions of the work is adduced." Bear in mind that a book's fly leaf is supposed to grab the book browser's attention and get him to buy the book. In short, this is the place for an author — who has to write his own fly leaf when he hires a vanity press — to prove his readability. Presumably, this is the most lively writing that Dr. Vickers is capable of producing. I must admit, it *is* a good deal livelier than what we find inside the book.)

In his writings, Dr. Vickers has "had to dissent at several points from the recent work of certain Christian scholars whose writing in economics is calculated, I have judged, to misdirect rather than assist the nascent concern for social and economic problems on the part of Reformed theologians and the Christian public."[16] These "certain scholars" are, primarily, R. J. Rushdoony and Gary North, but also includes others who are incorrectly labeled "neo-Dooyeweerdians."[17]

---

14. Douglas Vickers, *Economics and Man* (Nutley, New Jersey: Craig Press, 1976), p. viii.

15. Smithtown, New York: Exposition Press, 1982.

16. Vickers, *Economics and Man*, pp. viii-ix.

17. *Ibid.*, p. ix; cf. p. 353-57. Herman Dooyeweerd was a Dutch professor of law who wrote a massive four-volume set, *A New Critique of Theoretical Thought* (Philadelphia: Presbyterian & Reformed, 1953-57). It is even more filled with

The Blackout

More recently, Dr. Vickers has had opportunity to review E. L. Hebden Taylor's *Economics Money and Banking* (1978), a book explicitly written in the tradition of North and Rushdoony. (In the late-1960's, Taylor was a conservative Dooyeweerdian.) Dr. Vickers was given this opportunity by the editors of the *Westminster Theological Journal*, the scholarly publication of Westminster Theological Seminary, an officially Calvinistic institution. This journal systematically suppressed all reviews of Rushdoony's books after 1961, except for a marginally favorable review of *The Institutes of Biblical Law* which was virtually forced on the editor by John Frame, a Westminster faculty member, and it has never reviewed a book by North, who attended Westminster, whose first book appeared in 1968.[18] For a quarter of a century, the editors of this scholarly journal have played the familiar academic game of "pretend our competition will go away soon, and pray that their ideas will not spread in our circles."[19] Taylor, however, is not considered one of the leaders of the Christian Reconstruction movement, and perhaps this was why an exception was made to the long-standing blackout. Smaller fish are safer to fry when the great white sharks are still in the vicinity. Besides, a fried smaller fish may be able to

---

jargon than Dr. Vickers' books, although it has the merit of being massively researched and a serious scholarly contribution. I suspect that Dooyeweerd's followers treat him as "the Founder," and the *New Critique* as "the Book." Most of his self-proclaimed followers are completely unfamiliar with economics, and can best be described as medieval guild socialists. Dr. North has criticized the Dooyeweerdian school repeatedly since 1967, and he reprints his 1967 essay, "Social Antinomianism," in *The Sinai Strategy*.

18. They did allow him to publish a two-and-a-half page abstract of his doctoral dissertation on Puritan economic thought in the November 1972 issue.

19. It is interesting that Rushdoony's essays and reviews occasionally appeared in the *Westminster Theological Journal* from the early 1950's until the November 1967 issue, when he wrote a generally favorable review of Hebden Taylor's *The Christian Philosophy of Law, Politics and the State* (Nutley, New Jersey: Craig Press, 1967), in which he referred to the Netherlands' Anti-Revolutionary Party as the Moderately-Revolutionary Party (p. 101). Westminster Seminary relied heavily on contributions by Dutch-American conservative Christians. Rushdoony never gained access to the *Journal* again.

be palmed off on the uninformed public as fried shark, and both the fisherman and his publisher can then look like fearless daredevils.

What did Dr. Vickers say about Taylor's book? He followed Westminster's "party line" concerning all so-called Christian Reconstruction publications, namely, that *suppression is the better part of valor*. The book "needs careful attention because of its thoroughgoing and fatal error. It is a kind of 'economics' which should not be given hospitality by the Christian church."[20] There are so many details in Taylor's book which "crowd on the reader," says Dr. Vickers, that to "mention of any of them is in danger of causing loss of the calm evaluative perspective that is needed."[21] Keep calm, keep cool, and above all, *keep silent*.

Warmed-Over Keynesianism

Dr. Vickers is unquestionably verbally calm in his writings. He has adopted a style of expression which also produces calm in his readers — indeed, I would describe this state of mind as near-catatonic. Anyone who smokes in bed while reading one of Dr. Vickers' economics books takes his life in his hands. But the more important question is this one: Is Dr. Vickers' book fair? I contend that it is not. My book is an analysis of the writings, and the economic theories, that Dr. Vickers proposes. His theories are self-consciously Keynesian. He openly professes his allegiance to the work of John Maynard Keynes, whose "subtle and capacious mind" shook "us from the blinkers of the classical postulates [and] brought something of morality back into economics."[22] He does admit that Keynes was not "informed by a confessedly Christian perspective," and therefore Dr. Vickers does not "commit [himself] to all that Keynes said on either economic thought or economic policy simply because we have found him reaching for a demonstrably significant analytical proposition."[23] Keynes achieved,

---

20. *Westminster Theological Journal*, Vol. XLII (Fall 1979), p. 236.
21. *Ibid.*
22. Vickers, *Economics and Man*, p. 350; cf. p. 212.
23. *Ibid*, p. 39.

however, "a significant logical and methodological reconstruction in economics" thereby giving "us a new way of looking at things" so that we now have a "more complete understanding of the structure and functioning of the economic system. . . ."[24]

In *Economics and Man* Dr. Vickers has as his purpose, *first*, to set forth a Keynesian system of Christian economics and, *second*, to redirect the "misdirected" efforts of North and Rushdoony who have allowed "considerable confusion . . . to enter economic argument from a purportedly Christian perspective. It was in order to contribute to a correction of that perspective that we have developed the entire argument of this book in the manner and in the order we have adopted."[25]

Conclusion

This book is written from the belief that it is Dr. Vickers, not North and Rushdoony, who has contributed to the "considerable confusion" in the debate about Christian economics. I cannot claim to be calm and evaluative always, for I am overwhelmed on occasions that so many things which do not make sense — common or otherwise — are taken for granted and passed off as "serious" economic scholarship on a more than gullible Christian public. However, I have endeavored at all times to provide answers to those ideas that Vickers would have us believe are Christian and economic.

There are no "brute" facts — facts independent from other facts, and independent from God's authoritative revelation. All knowledge resides in God, and since He knows everything exhaustively, all facts exist in God-given and God-interpreted relationships. Man's knowledge, on the other hand, is forever finite. He struggles to put facts into some coherent whole, or else he rebels against the idea and accepts the concept of brute factuality, where meaning (relationship of ideas) does not and cannot exist. However, because man *is* limited in knowledge and does exist in

---

24. *Ibid.*, pp. 103, 212.
25. *Ibid.*, p. 241.

time and space, his thoughts do not come all at once. It is not possible for man to think of everything at once. This requires the splitting of knowledge into sequence. But there needs to be an integrating theory to put the split fragments back together. The Bible provides such a framework; Keynesian economic theory does not.

1

KEYNES, VICKERS, AND VAN TIL

No one has done more, on either side of the Atlantic, to preserve the kernel of the logic of Keynes's position than his Cambridge [England] disciple, Joan Robinson, and we can acknowledge a valuable element of truth in her observation that Keynes, having shaken us from the blinkers of the classical postulates, brought something of morality back into economics. . . . And while his own confessed philosophic predelections explain the absence from his influence of any distinctively Christian concern for the deeper explanation of things which only a Christian perspective can provide, nevertheless Keynes did direct our attention effectively to the inevitable instabilities of the aggregative economic system, and, on the level of pragmatic affairs, and down in the earthy arena of economic policy formulation, to the need for compensatory economic action. Here, then, was the point of departure for a Christian economics.[1]

The contribution of Christian philosopher Cornelius Van Til to twentieth-century Christian thought has centered on the fact that there is no such thing as neutrality in the debate between those who are for and those who are against the Christian faith. All thought inescapably rests on certain presuppositions, meaning assumptions that are taken for granted before organized thought can even begin. Even the skeptic's claim that "we can't be sure about anything" is a contradiction, in that it rests on the premise that we can be sure about this much, at least.

---

1. Vickers, *Economics and Man*, pp. 350-51.

To deny the existence of presuppositions is to denigrate human reason. It is to omit one of the most basic facts of existence. In addition, all presuppositions which do not take the God of Scripture as the ultimate reference point end in making human reason impossible. "Nothing is known unless there is first the presupposition of knowledge, and on no other ground is such a presupposition possible than the Christian theistic one. We *know* a real world because we believe by faith that God created it. From our first breath as a babe, we assume the reality of that world and the trustworthiness of our knowledge and experience."[2] In his rebellion against the Creator, man will deny *all* knowledge just to deny that one basic inescapable fact: the existence of God.

The interesting aspect of Van Til's influence outside of his more narrow academic field of apologetics is that two schools of economic thought have developed that both give homage to Van Til. One school is better known, for it is indeed a "school." There is more than one member. This is the "Christian reconstructionist" group: Gary North, R. J. Rushdoony, and their followers. The other school is in fact a one-man band: Douglas Vickers.

Christian Reconstruction

North and Rushdoony come to the field of economics, Bibles in hand, and with the writings of the Austrian School (Ludwig von Mises, F. A. Hayek, Murray Rothbard, Israel Kirzner) and Chicago School economists ("Friedmanites" or "monetarists") in reserve. They pick and choose from the conclusions of these free market scholars, but always in terms of the Bible, and more specifically, in terms of Old Testament law.

The approach of these "reconstructionists" is unquestionably revolutionary. No economists in history have ever set out to create a specifically Biblical economics, meaning an economic system governed by the revelation of the Bible. There have been scholastic economics, natural law economics, moral economy, political

---

2. Rousas John Rushdoony, *The Word of Flux* (Fairfax, Virginia: Thoburn Press, 1975), p. 98, emphasis in original.

economy, and other variants, but for the first time in history, a group of (necessarily) self-taught scholars are calling for a reconstruction of economic thought by means of Biblical revelation.

This appeal has fallen on deaf ears within the economics profession, which is understandable. Economics was the first "autonomous" social science. Economists were the first scholars who set about self-consciously to separate the content and categories of their technical discussions from all appeals to religion and morality. This separation began in the seventeenth century, and it has never been healed.[3] Seventeenth-century economists believed that while religious and moral debates can never be settled by appeals to reason, technical economic debates can be. This faith is still integral to modern economics. It is still just as utopian; the economists are legendary for their inability to agree on anything. "Where there are five economists, there will be six opinions," goes one barb. "Lay all economists end to end, and they would never reach a conclusion," goes another. Nevertheless, there is no academic school of economics which is not specifically and self-consciously "value-free" in its official methodology, except for the Marxists, who proclaim their commitment to proletarian values, which they predict will be the only values "after the Revolution."

Vickers the Disciple

Like the reconstructionists, Douglas Vickers also comes with a bible in hand, but his bible is John Maynard Keynes' *General Theory of Employment, Interest, and Money* (1936). Yet in an earlier work, Dr. Vickers acknowledges his debt to Van Til. He pays homage to Van Tillian apologetics, and he can therefore make the statement: "Man in sin is, in a phrase, the slave and the dupe of the devil."[4] If man in sin is the slave and dupe of the devil, then we might legitimately ask: Can such a man produce anything of value?

---

3. William Letwin, *The Origins of Scientific Economics* (London: Methuen; New York: Doubleday, 1963).

4. Douglas Vickers, *Man in the Maelstrom of Modern Thought* (Phillipsburg, New Jersey: Presbyterian and Reformed Publishing Co., 1975), p. 20.

This is not the place for a theological argument about the doctrine of common grace and the creative possibilities of unregenerate minds. Nevertheless, we can and should note that without the light of Scripture, God's authoritative revealed Word to man, the unregenerate mind can only grasp truth by means of theft. He possesses true knowledge only insofar as he operates inconsistently with his own presuppositions. We might paraphrase Van Til's argument as follows: "What man knows 'autonomously' isn't true, and what he knows truly isn't known autonomously." We should therefore have a healthy skepticism to anything which the unbeliever might propose. The more "devilish" he is, the less we should expect from him, other things being equal (as the economists love to say). *The more immoral he is, the less "common grace" we should expect him to display.* This is what Van Til has taught for many decades.[5] Yet in his economic methodology and also in his conclusions, Dr. Vickers has adopted the economics of John Maynard Keynes, as self-conscious an immoral public figure as the academic world had seen in his generation, or today's.

It is somewhat surprising, to say the least, that Dr. Vickers is willing to give credence to the theories of Keynes. Given the qualifications he has made, to declare that Keynes has given us anything like the correct approach to economic issues is to place a great deal of faith in an unbelieving mind. We should argue, in fact, that *no* faith can be put in any human being, unbeliever *or* believer, until such time as his ideas have been tried and tested in the light of Biblical teaching.

The Character of Keynes

Recent biographies of Keynes have provided evidence not only to his philosophical meanderings, but his debauched and re-

---

5. "Common grace will diminish still more in the further course of history. With every conditional act the remaining significance of the conditional is reduced. God allows men to follow the path of their own self-chosen rejection of Him more rapidly than ever toward the final consummation." Cornelius Van Til, *Common Grace* (Philadelphia: Presbyterian and Reformed [1947] 1954), p. 83. Reprinted in *Common Grace and the Gospel* (Presbyterian and Reformed, 1974), p. 83.

pulsive lifestyle.[6] We also see in the forthrightness of this biography the progressive debauchery of, and therefore progressive toleration of debauchery by, the general public. Sir Roy Harrod's 1951 biography was careful not to come right out and say what Keynes was, although his language indicates that he was well aware of Keynes' sexual preferences.[7] He was content to write such concealed summaries as: "From the outside he seemed all urbanity, suavity, self-possession. He appeared to some to be almost inhuman, so mechanical was the precision with which he achieved every objective. Yet underneath that urbanity he had an ardent, passionate nature. He had a great fund of affection which he wished to lavish and have reciprocated. . . . One concentrates a stronger stream of affection upon one's particular friends."[8] Knowing what we know now about Keynes passion, especially his fondness for Tunisian boys (especially when available at discount hotels),[9] this prose in retrospect is enough to encourage a good, healthy puke.

The academic world did not know of Keynes' debaucheries until Michael Holroyd discussed them in his biography of Lytton Strachey, a "Bloomsbury Circle" bright light, and one of Keynes' homosexual partners. Keynes was a homosexual whose activities in this regard included other well-known British subjects. But as Skidelsky observes, their reasons for such activity were a little different from those expressed by the current "gay rights" movement, which asks for mere acceptance of their lifestyle. "They

---

6. Robert Skidelsky, *John Maynard Keynes*, Volume 1, *Hopes Betrayed, 1883-1920* (London: Macmillan, 1983).

7. See, for example, Harrod's reference to Keynes' relationship with B. W. Swithenbank: "He and Maynard became intimates." He then reproduces a letter from Keynes to Swithenbank which began, "O Swithen, Swithen," and includes the words, "if I write I must needs gush. . . ." Harrod, *The Life of John Maynard Keynes* (New York: Norton, [1951] 1982), p. 68. Or, referring to Strachey, "If Maynard fell for him at once, that was by virtue of his own clever judgment . . ." (p. 86). I like this one, too: "To intellectual companionship was added a deeper communion of spirit" (p. 90).

8. *Ibid.*, pp. 89-90.

9. Michael Holroyd, *Lytton Strachey*, 2 vols. (New York: Holt, Rinehart and Winston, 1968), II, p. 80.

[Keynes & Co. — I. H.] thought that love of young men was a higher form of love. They had been brought up and educated to believe that women were inferior — in mind and body. If from the ethical point of view . . . love should be attached only to worthy objects, then love of young men was, they believed, ethically better than love of women."[10] In other words, Keynes and his partners were not just expressing a sexual preference. Theirs was an *ethical* and philosophical position. The Christian must affirm, in contrast, that perversion is perversion, irrespective of the apparent justification for the act.

Keynes' ethics were a product of his own rebellious mind. Similarly were his views on economics. His writings carefully delineate his fundamental philosophy and everything he did was done from a philosophic viewpoint.[11] One of his fellow members of the Apostles group, as they were known at Cambridge University, was G. E. Moore, who published a philosophical work on ethics entitled *Principia Ethica*. In commenting on this work, Keynes declared that "one of the greatest advantages of his [i.e., Moore's] religion was that it made morals unnecessary — meaning by 'religion' one's attitude to oneself and the ultimate and by 'morals' one's attitude towards the outside world and the intermediate."[12] Keynes thus believed and practiced the *autonomy of human thought*. Nowhere does the concept of divine revelation enter his thoughts, nor does he perceive the need for such revelation. After all, if man is god, man makes his own rules and ethical principles. Wrote Keynes:

We entirely repudiated a personal liability on us to obey general rules. We claimed the right to judge every individual case on its merits, and the wisdom to do so successfully. This was a very important part of our faith, violently and aggressively held, and for the outer world it was our most obvious and dangerous characteristic. We repudiated entirely customary morals, conventions and traditional wisdom. We were, that is

---

10. Skidelsky, *Keynes,* pp. 128-129.
11. *Ibid.,* p. 133.
12. *The Collected Writings of John Maynard Keynes,* X, 436, quoted in *ibid.,* p. 141.

to say, in the strict sense of the term, immoralists. The consequences of being found out had, of course, to be considered for what they were worth. But we recognized no moral obligation on us, no inner sanction, to conform or obey.[13]

The admission that they were "immoralists" is evidence that Keynes knew that he and his colleagues were breaking with conventional morality. This conventional morality was essentially Christian morality which had influenced the British Isles for almost 2,000 years. In addition, however, men do not sin in ignorance. They have before them, as Romans 1:18-23 reminds us, the *evidence* that God exists. Men are created in the image of God and therefore *know* with certainty what they are doing. No man disobeys God in ignorance; it is always willful and deliberate rebellion against a sovereign God.

Deliberate Obscurity

Having established some background to the character of Keynes, it should not surprise us that his economic writings are not at all what some would have us believe. Keynes' major contribution to economic thought, his presentation of his "new" economics in *The General Theory*, is one of the most difficult books to read. It frequently borders on the incoherent. Its style is abominable, in sharp contrast—indeed, suspiciously sharp contrast—to his lucid *Essays in Biography* and his first best-seller, *The Economic Consequences of the Peace*. This assessment of the style of the *General Theory* is shared not just by his critics. Listen to these comments about *The General Theory* publication by well-known Keynes disciple and Nobel Prize-winning economist Paul Samuelson:

It is a badly written book, poorly organized; any layman who, beguiled by the author's previous reputation, bought the book was cheated of his five shillings. . . . It abounds in mares' nests of confusions. . . . In it the Keynesian system stands out indistinctly, as if the author were hardly aware of its existence or cognizant of its properties. . . .

---

13. *Collected Writings*, X, 446, quoted in *ibid.*, pp. 142-143.

Flashes of insight and intuition intersperse tedious algebra. An awkward definition suddenly gives way to an unforgettable cadenza. . . . I think I am giving away no secrets when I solemnly aver—upon the basis of vivid personal recollection—that no one else in Cambridge, Massachusetts, really knew what it was all about for some twelve to eighteen months after its publication. Indeed, until the appearance of the mathematical models of Meade, Lange, Hicks and Harrod, there is reason to believe that Keynes himself did not truly understand his own analysis.[14]

This comment concerning Keynes' ignorance of the implications of his own system comes from one of the founders of the "Keynesian synthesis," and a representative of a school of thought which claimed Keynes' name. What he is *really* saying is that Keynes never adopted the rigorous methodological, textbook-type approach to economics that his disciples adopted. There is no evidence that Keynes ever acknowledged members of this school of economics as his legitimate intellectual heirs. F. A. Hayek recalls his final meeting with Keynes in 1946: "Later a turn in the conversation made me ask him whether he was not concerned about what some of his disciples were making of his theories. After a not very complimentary remark about the persons concerned he proceeded to reassure me: those ideas had been badly needed at the time he had launched them. But I need not be alarmed: if they should ever become dangerous I could rely upon him that he would again quickly swing round public opinion—indicating by a quick movement of his hand how rapidly that would be done. But three months later he was dead."[15]

On top of this, at the end of his life, Keynes could suggest that

---

14. Quoted in Daniel Bell's essay, "Models and Reality in Economic Discourse," *The Public Interest* (Special Edition, 1980), pp. 62-63. This special edition was devoted to a reassessment of Keynesian economics. The general consensus appears that the Keynesian ideas have not achieved their stated goals of lower unemployment. For pragmatic reasons, there has been a shift away from the older Keynesian ideas.

15. F. A. Hayek, "A Review of *The Life of John Maynard Keynes*, by Roy F. Harrod"; published in *The Journal of Modern History* (June 1952); reprinted in Hayek, *Studies in Philosophy, Politics and Economics* (Chicago: University of Chicago Press, 1967), p. 348.

doses of "classical medicine" (free market economics) might well prevent the need for import restrictions and exchange controls. Once more in his career, he had shifted completely from his earlier recommendations. Keynes seemed aware that he really did not have the answers to the economic ills of his day and age.[16]

Vickers as Vicar

Given the fact of Keynes' background, the admission that Keynes lacked understanding of the long-term implications and consequences of his own work, and the fact that he eventually favored some "classical medicine," it is surprising to find that Dr. Vickers can promote Keynes and his ideas with such vigor. Admittedly, Dr. Vickers has included his own qualification that Keynes was not informed from a distinctively Biblical perspective, but he then proceeds to defend those views as if they were Biblical. The fundamental ideas that Dr. Vickers promotes have their origin in Keynes. We may certainly recognize that Dr. Vickers attempts to baptize those ideas with Christian thinking, but when it all boils down, they are precisely that: baptized *secular* ideas. They are secular *because* they do not have a basis in the Word of God. Given that Keynes liked to display his disproofs of Christianity,[17] it is incumbent on Dr. Vickers to demonstrate precisely how this debauched homosexual pagan somehow rewrote economic theory to conform more closely to Christian principles. He has an obligation to spell out exactly where this deviant deviated from the economic perspective of the Bible. To neglect this —and Dr. Vickers has devoted his entire professional career to just such a program of systematic neglect—is to convey the impression that Keynes was closer to Biblical truth than humanist free market defenders are, but more to the point, closer to the Biblical truth than Gary North or Rousas Rushdoony, neither of whom is a God-hating homosexual pervert.

---

16. W. H. Hutt, *The Keynesian Episode: A Reassessment* (Indianapolis, Indiana: Liberty Press, 1979), p. 20.

17. Skidelsky, p. 123.

In short, the burden of proof rests on Dr. Vickers' shoulders.

Nearer to the truth are the words of Scripture. "The fool hath said in his heart, There is no God" (Ps. 53:1). The trouble is, the fool has a habit of sharing his foolishness with the rest of the world. "A fool layeth open his folly" (Prov. 13:16). The question is, has Douglas Vickers made his academic bed alongside of fools?

The Enthusiasm of Safe "Revolutionists"

How can we explain Vickers' commitment to Keynesianism? As I hope this book will show, it is not Keynes' logic or clarity which motivated economists to join the "Keynesian revolution," since *The General Theory* is neither logical nor clear. It is also not the success of his policies in recent years. It has more to do with the original enthusiasm of a group of aging academics who remember fondly their own participation in a now-distant world of exciting change. The "old ways" were being abandoned in the 1940's; young economists had an opportunity to rebuild their world, even if it was only an academic world. This sense of revolutionary innovation was basic to Keynes' thinking, Harrod reports.[18] Keynes wrote to George Bernard Shaw in 1935, while he was writing *The General Theory*: "To understand my state of mind, however, you have to know that I believe myself to be writing a book of economic theory which will largely revolutionize — not, I suppose, at once, but in the course of time — the way the world thinks about economic problems."[19] This same sense of participating in revolution was also an important aspect of the young men who followed him. Canadian-American-British economist Harry Johnson[20] once described the coming of the Keynesian revolution — which he really does not believe was a revolution, but

---

18. Harrod, *Life of Keynes*, p. 88.

19. *The General Theory and After, Part I, Collected Writings*, Vol. XIII (London: Macmillan, 1973), p. 492.

20. Johnson delivered the presidential address at the 1971 meeting of the Cambridge Apostles: Richard Deacon, *The Cambridge Apostles: A history of Cambridge University's élite intellectual secret society* (London: Robert Royce Ltd., 1985), p. 173.

rather a declaration of independence[21] — as a five-step process.

1. Attack on orthodoxy: a free market economy does *not* tend automatically toward full employment.

2. Appearance of newness, yet maintaining many of the older tradition's ideas, but giving new names to everything.

3. Difficulty of understanding the theory, especially for men trained in the earlier tradition.

4. A new methodology: partial aggregation, mathematics, empirical relevance.

5. A handle for studying economic relationships: the consumption function.

Johnson's third point is most relevant to my discussion, and I quote it at length: "Third, the new theory had to have the appropriate degree of difficulty to understand. This is a complex problem in the design of new theories. The new theory had to be so difficult to understand that senior academic colleagues would find it neither easy nor worthwhile to study, so that they would waste their efforts on peripheral theoretical issues, and so offer themselves as easy marks for criticism and dismissal by their younger and hungrier colleagues. At the same time, the new theory had to appear both difficult enough to challenge the intellectual interest of younger colleagues and students, but actually easy enough for them to master adequately with a sufficient investment of intellectual endeavor. These objectives Keynes's *General Theory* managed to achieve: it neatly shelved the old and established scholars, like Pigou and Robertson, enabled the more enterprising middle- and lower-middle-aged like Hansen, Hicks, and Joan Robinson to jump on and drive the bandwagon, and permitted a whole generation of students (as Samuelson has recorded) to escape from the slow and soul-destroying process of acquiring wisdom by osmosis from their elders and the literature into an intellectual realm in

---

21. Harry G. Johnson, "Keynes's *General Theory*: Revolution or War of Independence?" *Canadian Journal of Economics* (1976); in Elizabeth S. Johnson and Harry G. Johnson, *The Shadow of Keynes: Understanding Keynes, Cambridge and Keynesian Economics* (Chicago: University of Chicago Press, 1978), ch. 18.

which youthful iconoclasm could quickly earn its just reward (in its own eyes at least) by the demolition of the intellectual pretensions of its academic seniors and predecessors. Economics, delightfully, could be reconstructed from scratch on the basis of a little Keynesian understanding and a lofty contempt for the existing literature—and so it was."[22]

It was this *sense of overthrowing one's elders almost overnight* which motivated the younger men. They mastered—or pretended to master—the deliberately complex definitions and formulas in Keynes' *General Theory*, and they rewrote economics to conform to his primary proposal, which was simple enough: the State can spend an economy into prosperity by taxing and spending and (ultimately) by printing money. It was the age-old hope of "stones into bread," as Mises has observed.[23] It fitted neatly into the plans of the politicians in almost every nation in the late 1930's.

The great irony today is that another group of bright, young, mathematically minded economists has appeared. They are doing to the graying Keynesian full professors what the incumbents did to their predecessors four to five decades ago. The new group is called the "rational expectations" school. They conclude that government planning does not accomplish its declared goals because individuals act to thwart the planners. This is basically the theme of Mises and Hayek, going back to the 1920's, but the younger men dress up their arguments in lots of mathematics. Also, unlike Mises and Hayek, they do not call for a roll-back of government; they just argue that nothing the government does is likely to work out as the planners have predicted.

This is a revolutionary idea these days. The older Keynesians resent the idea, and they resent even more the fact that these young whippersnappers are now beginning to gain the attention

---

22. Harry G. Johnson, "The Keynesian Revolution and the Monetarist Counter-Revolution," *American Economic Review* (1971); in *ibid.*, pp. 188-89. This devastating analysis did not appear in the original essay in the *AER*.
23. Ludwig von Mises, "Stones Into Bread," in Henry Hazlitt (ed.), *Critics of Keynesian Economics* (Princeton, New Jersey: Van Nostrand, 1960).

of the most energetic undergraduates. A "scientific revolution"[24] is in the making. Susan Lee describes the tactics of the younger men; it is strikingly parallel to the tactics of the original Keynesians in their youth. This process might well be called "the revenge of the invisible hand":

Sour Grapes?

Rational expectations ("ratex") has become fairly commonplace for modeling economic behavior. Still controversial, however, are its sleek mathematics and other assumptions. For example, according to their critics, ratexians claim the economy will operate with all resources fully employed and that markets will clear (sellers equal buyers at any given price) unless government, inadequate information or bad laws interfere.

Thus, critics argue that ratexians have no contact with reality — with a world of unemployment or unsold houses. As one nonratexian economist puts it: "Sure, they make elegant models. They just ignore messy policy applications."

The Keynesian old guard, in particular, feels threatened by the new mathematical tools that have rendered their skills obsolete. They complain that the techniques make for good Ph.D. theses and fast starts in publishing academic articles, but little else. Robert Solow, for instance, compares the appeal the esoteric math has for younger economists with the appeal that developing the hydrogen bomb had for scientists. "Both are technically so sweet," he says.

Also, the old guard pooh-poohs the enthusiasm that rational expectations generates among younger economists. Paul Samuelson shrugs: "Given the low self-esteem in the economics profession, any theory is going to get a hearing." Others sigh that "the young have no sense." So they have been temporarily beguiled by the opportunity to thumb their noses at their teachers.

Some of this carping and sniffing is just a normal reaction when the old makes way for the new. Stanford's John Shoven observes that the increasingly sophisticated math has left the profession with "a bit of a generation gap." That's a nice way of saying the older chaps feel obsolete. Chief ratexian Robert Lucas of the University of Chicago puts it this

---

24. Thomas Kuhn, *The Structure of Scientific Revolutions* (2nd ed.; Chicago: University of Chicago Press, 1970).

way: "It hurts to see people come in with new tools when you thought you knew everything."[25]

But what is Dr. Vickers' role in all this? He was one of those young men once upon a time. He was swept into the revolution in far-away Australia, on the fringes of the academic world. But he was a Christian, and he did not want to abandon his faith. So he did what evolutionists and Freudians and other members of academic guilds have done in the past: he attempted to fuse two unreconcilable positions. He tried to baptize the Keynesianism of his youth. He did not decide to reconstruct the errors of youth; he decided to persuade Christian scholars to accept his baptized Keynesianism in the name of "Christian relevance." He tried to herd them on board at precisely the time that the academic world's faith in the Keynesian paradigm had begun to fade. The owl of Minerva once again was flying at dusk.

The "Red Curates"

I am reminded of an earlier revolutionary generation, the era of the French Revolution and immediately following. In those days, the revolutionaries needed the support of clerics. They even adopted the language of the Bible to enlist support. As Prof. Billington says: "Already in his *Plebian Manifesto,* Babeuf had begun to develop a sense of messianic mission, invoking the names of Moses, Joshua, and Jesus, as well as Rousseau, Robespierre, and Saint-Just. He had claimed Christ as 'co-athlete' and had written in prison *A New History of the Life of Jesus Christ.* Most of the conspirators shared this belief in Christ as *sans-cullotte* at heart if not a prophet of revolution. The strength of the red curates within the social revolutionary camp intensified the need to keep Christian ideas from weakening revolutionary dedication."[26]

Who were these "red curates"? They were priests who attempted to fuse Jesus and "the Revolution." These men "found an almost

---

25. Susan Lee, "The un-managed economy," *Forbes* (Dec. 17, 1984), p. 149.
26. James Billington, *Fire in the Minds of Men: Origins of the Revolutionary Faith* (New York: Basic Books; London: Temple Smith, 1980), p. 76.

religious exaltation in identifying with the masses and articulating a social ideal that went beyond Parisian politics to suggest secular salvation."[27] They volunteered in the forces of revolution. They sold their souls for a mess of ideological pottage. And a lot of them lost their heads.

Dr. Vickers is not exactly a red curate. Furthermore, today's revolutionary (and even stodgy) humanists think they are in no need of support from would-be red curates. The acids of humanism have done their work, especially in academia. But Dr. Vickers apparently needs psychological consolation. He needs to know that his lifetime efforts in the academic slough of despond were not wasted. He claims to have found a treasure to share with the rest of us untutored Christians, who still believe in such outmoded economic principles as supply and demand, paying off our debts, the gold standard, competition, and responsibility — individual, familistic, and ecclesiastical. He wants us to relearn all this, for it is antediluvian, meaning pre-Keynesian, in perspective. We must "get with it," as he did when he was a young man. We, too, must adopt the new economics of 1936. We, too, must join gray-haired revolutionaries emeritus in their continual celebration of a revolution which is now half a century old.

So he wrote *Economics and Man*. He announced a revolution to tenured Christian scholars everywhere. Nobody came. Well, not quite nobody. A few faculty members at Westminster Theological Seminary showed up for a few of his lectures. In Australia, his book was quietly — but unsuccessfully — promoted at Reformed Theological College. Other than this, Dr. Vickers' recruitment program has been a failure.

After you finish this book, you will understand why nobody else came.

Conclusion

When Dr. Vickers explains Van Til's philosophy in his shorter book, *A Christian Approach to Economics and the Cultural Condition*, he

---

27. *Ibid.*, p. 72.

drifts into uncharacteristic clarity, but as soon as he brings up the subject of economics, he becomes muddled. (His longer book on Van Til, *Man in the Maelstrom of Modern Thought*, is muddled, perhaps because he was trying to be scholarly.) Keynes suffered from this same affliction: "clear when writing outside his field, muddled when he got serious." There is a reason for this. Both Keynes and Vickers shared the power of competent expression, but they both adopted the economics of confusion. Dr. Vickers' fate is that instead of remaining an amateur theologian and amateur philosopher, where he occasionally shows at least a minimal competence, he decided to write books in his chosen field of economics, in which he defends the arguments of a charlatan. John Maynard Keynes is a false giant who is surrounded by real pygmies. Dr. Vickers had a choice: to join full-time the tiny throng surrounding a real giant, Cornelius Van Til, or to join full-time the pygmies surrounding Keynes. Sadly for him, he chose the latter.

Dr. Vickers is at war with the specific teachings of the Bible regarding economics. He is unwilling to abandon his youthful enthusiasm at being a minor participant in an intellectual revolution — a revolution which has brought the West to the brink of economic disaster.

2

NEITHER CAPITALISM NOR SOCIALISM (MAYBE)

. . . we shall argue that a well-designed and well-articulated national policy on wages and prices is most decidedly necessary at this time. To argue to the contrary is to lean too far in the direction of a reactionary economic conservatism. [1]

"All those who want to identify themselves as reactionary economic conservatives, please stand up!" I love this sort of argument. It is so . . . so utterly Keynesian.

One of the problems we face today is that self-proclaimed Christian scholars have adopted philosophic relativism as their intellectual foundation. They have been compromised by today's climate of intellectual opinion. This great philosophic shift of the past 300 hundred years — from truth to relativism — has been well documented. Commencing with René Descartes, who hypothesized a radical dualism between mind and matter, between human understanding and mathematical precision,[2] modern man has backed himself into a corner where he is no longer able to ascertain what is true and is not true.[3] Immanuel Kant's dualism between the phenomenal realm of scientific truth and the noumenal realm of human ethics and freedom[4] was the culmination

---

1. Vickers, *Economics and Man*, pp. 179-80.

2. E. A. Burtt, *The Metaphysical Foundations of Modern Physical Science* (Garden City, New York: Doubleday Anchor, [1932] 1954), ch. IV.

3. William Barrett, *Irrational Man: A Study in Existential Philosophy* (Garden City, New York: Doubleday Anchor, [1958] 1962).

4. Richard Kroner, *Kant's Weltanschauung* (Chicago: University of Chicago Press, [1914] 1956).

of two millennia of philosophical debate. Today, modern man
vigorously denies that truth is anything more than a matter of
opinion, either cultural[5] or personal.[6] Even the rigor of Kant's
cause-and-effect phenomenal realm of scientific knowledge has
been undermined by certain aspects of modern (post-Heisenberg)
physics and by modern existentialism.

G. W. F. Hegel's unique nineteenth-century contribution to
this philosophical malaise is the idea that truth is obtained from
Kant's dualistic world by means of a process of synthesis. All ideas
or statements (thesis) have an alternative (antithesis). Truth is
arrived at by compromising these two opposing ideas (synthesis).
The result becomes a new thesis, which in turn is opposed by its
antithesis, and the truth of the matter is again arrived at by synthesis. This dialectical procedure goes on and on into the dim
recesses of the future, like the "good vs. evil" dualism of ancient
Manicheanism, for Hegel never admitted that somewhere, at
some time, one (or more) of those theses just might be true for all
men, for all times, in all places. Not even on the day of judgment.
There is no historical day of judgment in Hegel's system. This is
the essence of Hegel's system, and of all other humanist systems:
no final judgment.

Consistently Christian thinking denies such a position. Truth,
says the Christian, is not just a matter of opinion. There are
truths which are at present, were in the past, and will continue to
be in the future, true for all mankind. Such a statement depends
on the Biblical view of God and creation for its foundation. There
are three basic facts to consider. *First*, God has existed from all
eternity. There is no time when He did not exist. Truth, therefore,
is not relative, but rooted in the eternal being of God. *Second*, all

---

5. Karl Mannheim, *Ideology and Utopia: An Introduction to the Sociology of Knowledge* (New York: Harvest, [1936]).

6. Carl Becker, "Everyman His Own Historian," his presidential address to
the American Historical Association (1931), and his book by the same name
(Chicago: Quadrangle, [1935] 1966); Charles A. Beard, "Written History as an
Act of Faith," a 1933 address to the American Historical Association, reprinted in
Hans Meyerhoff (ed.), *The Philosophy of History in Our Time* (New York: Double-
day Anchor, 1959).

else that exists apart from God was created by Him. Truth therefore originates in God and not created reality. *Third*, the Creator has communicated Truth to His creation. God has spoken. A Christian theory of knowledge rests upon the doctrines of God, creation, and revelation.[7]

Denying these three things, modern man finds himself incapable of determining what is true or false, right or wrong, just or unjust. Nevertheless, his language is consistently couched in these terms. We cannot have capitalism, says the socialist, for it is socially unjust and inequitable. The same moral appeal is sometimes implicitly used by the capitalist when he argues against socialism, though more commonly, the economist defends capitalism by means of an appeal to economic efficiency (reduced waste) and the legitimate autonomy of the individual decision-maker. Over six decades ago, the German sociologist and historian Max Weber argued that this dualism between humanist social ethics and market efficiency is inescapable.[8] He has yet to be proven wrong. Hardly any economist has even attempted to prove him wrong. Economists just ignore him.

Dr. Vickers' "Synthesis"

In the realm of economics, the ideas of socialism and capitalism were once presented as the only alternatives available (thesis and synthesis). This certainly was Karl Marx's vision. He believed that capitalism contained the seeds of its own destruction, and the crisis in capitalism would inevitably lead to the proletarian revolution and the establishment of socialism. John Maynard Keynes challenged this view by arguing that enlightened State planning can overcome the contradictions of an economic order

---

7. Cornelius Van Til, *A Christian Theory of Knowledge* (Phillipsburg, New Jersey: Presbyterian & Reformed, 1969).

8. Max Weber, *Economy and Society* (New York: Bedminster Press, [1924] 1968), pp. 107-13, 583-89, 635-40. Cf. Gary North, "Max Weber: Rationalism, Irrationalism, and the Bureaucratic Cage," in North (ed.), *Foundations of Christian Scholarship: Essays in the Van Til Perspective* (Vallecito, California: Ross House, 1976).

based on enlightened personal self-interest. For this reason, Keynesian theory is rejected by Marxist scholars. But they recognize the importance of Keynes' contribution. Writes one Soviet economist: "The importance of Keynesian theory is due above all to the fact that it laid the foundations for macroeconomic theory, a new department of bourgeois political economy, without which state-monopoly regulation is now inconceivable."[9]

Is this just an example of extreme Communist scholarship?[10] Is it totally unjustified? Not if you believe Keynes. In a little-known document, Keynes admitted — indeed, bragged — that his economic theories work far better in a system of total State planning than under a free market. His followers were for decades completely unaware of this admission. They would have been even more embarrassed by its place of publication: the Preface to the German language edition of *The General Theory*, which was published in 1936 in Nazi Germany. Keynes frankly admitted:

> The theory of aggregate production, which is the point of the following book, nevertheless can be much easier adapted to the conditions of a totalitarian state [*eines totalen Staates*] than the theory of production and distribution of a given production put forth under conditions of free competition and a large degree of laissez-faire. This is one of the reasons that justifies the fact that I call my theory a *general* theory.[11]

You can easily understand why this juicy citation is never, ever referred to in any pro-Keynesian textbook, and rarely in narrow monographs on Keynes. It is conveniently ignored by those few scholars who are aware of its existence. The only economist I have read who even hinted at Keynes' role in promoting National Social-

---

9. Irina Osadchaya, *From Keynes to Neoclassical Synthesis: A Critical Analysis* (Moscow: Progress Publishers, 1974), pp. 7-8.

10. J. M. Letiche, "Soviet Views on Keynes: A Review Article Surveying the Literature," *Journal of Economic Literature*, IX (June 1971).

11. This was first translated by Dr. James J. Martin, and placed side-by-side with the original German, in the libertarian periodical, *Rampart Journal of Individualist Thought*, III (Spring 1967), pp. 39, 41. Martin later reprinted this in his book, *Revisionist Viewpoints* (Boulder, Colorado: Ralph Myles Press, 1971), pp. 203, 205. The citation now appears in the 1973 edition, in the *Collected Writings*, Vol. VII, p. xxvi.

ism is the late Wilhelm Röpke,[12] whose works were burned by the Nazis, and who was, more than any economist of his day, the one most concerned about Christian values. It will be interesting to see what, if anything, Dr. Vickers will do with this citation. Nothing, I would bet. He will hope we all forget. But we won't. A quote like this is unforgettable.

Drowning in "Deeper Springs"

Dr. Vickers, a disciple of Keynes, would have us believe in this third alternative (synthesis) in between free market capitalism and State socialism. But he does so because he is a Christian. First, he rejects the more common epistemological presupposition of free market economists, namely, that economics is a value-free science. This is argued by Milton Friedman and Keynes,[13] as well as by Ludwig von Mises.[14] Economics, says Dr. Vickers, is not a "value-free inquiry." Then he adopts a "mixed economy" concept which supposedly overcomes the needless dualism of socialism and capitalism. (He also adopts a "mixed English" form of linguistic communication.)

Economic inquiry is not exhausted, or even its limits properly defined, by arguments for the priority of individualism, socialism, *laissez-faire* capitalism, or collectivism. To allow inquiry to proceed or begin on levels corresponding to thoughtforms inherent in alternatives such as

---

12. "Indeed, it was his [Keynes'] fate — one in which, initially, he even appeared to find some visible satisfaction and which at any rate he did not explicitly disavow — to become the intellectual authority for economic policy in National Socialist Germany." Röpke, *Economics of the Free Society* (Chicago: Regnery, 1963), p. 221. This is the English translation of the 9th German edition (1961) of his 1936 book, *Die Lehre von der Wirtschaft*. The Gestapo seized the book, published in Austria, when Germany invaded Austria.

13. "Positive economics is in principle independent of any particular ethical position or normative judgments. As Keynes says, it deals with 'what is,' not with 'what ought to be.'" Friedman, "The Methodology of Positive Economics," in Friedman, *Essays in Positive Economics* (Chicago: University of Chicago Press, 1953), p. 4.

14. "It is true that economics is a theoretical science and as such abstains from any judgment of value." Mises, *Human Action: A Treatise on Economics* (3rd ed.; Chicago: Regnery, 1966), p. 10.

these is to betray the possibility of successful and meaningful results right at the beginning of the journey. It is to shunt the engine of economic discovery immediately onto tracks that exit from meaning and intelligibility, at least as far as the ultimate objectives of inquiry are concerned.[15]

When "meaning and intelligibility" are the issue, Dr. Vickers' style is a bit suspect. But I digress. Dr. Vickers wants to avoid "the tendency to equate the legitimate limits of economic objectives and behavior with the narrowly defined interests of atomistic, personal, individualistic satisfactions . . ." as well as the "deeper categories behind such pragmatic expressions as the capitalism-socialism debate. . . ."[16] After all, according to Dr. Vickers, if we think in the area of individualism, we are "in danger of being trapped in the fruitless morass of anarchies, exploitation, and social disharmonies."[17] There are much "deeper springs and motivations of human action" than are to be found in the "capitalism-socialism and collectivism-individualism dichotomies. . . ."[18]

In other words, *we should not think in traditional categories of economics.* The reason why we should not think in this manner is not stated, and unfortunately his writings do not clarify precisely what these "deeper springs" are, or what he perceives to be the "anarchies, exploitation and social disharmonies." Moreover, Dr. Vickers argues that the avoidance of these "deeper springs" also leads to the avoidance of "the logical and ethical demands of the notion of stewardship. . . ."[19]

Now this is an interesting method of argument on Dr. Vickers' part. Not one concrete economic theory or Scriptural reference is offered, yet Dr. Vickers is endeavoring to manipulate his readers' consciences in such a way that we feel guilty for having had such a "simplistic" view of economics: an *either-or choice* between capitalism and socialism.[20] In addition, "Economics is suddenly no longer

---

15. Vickers, *Economics and Man*, p. 3.
16. *Ibid.*, pp. 2, 3.
17. *Ibid.*, p. 2.
18. *Ibid.*, p. 3.
19. *Idem.*
20. For further examples of argument by guilt manipulation, see David

quite so sure of itself,"[21] the innuendo being that *all* economics is unsure of itself, a sweeping generalization and most difficult to prove. In contrast, Dr. Vickers seems absolutely sure of himself. He expresses no doubts concerning the authenticity of the theories he defends, despite the fact that *he has abandoned the epistemological neutrality of modern humanist economics without clearly substituting a specific, concrete, Biblical law-based alternative.* Yet in a single sentence, Dr. Vickers attempts to wipe out the past two hundred years of economic thinking, leaving the economically untrained reader with considerable doubt as to what should, or should not, be believed.

Conclusion

We must therefore ask: Is what Dr. Vickers says at this point true? Is there really an alternative to the "simple" ideas of capitalism and socialism? More importantly, are such generalizations given any support by the arguments Dr. Vickers offers in his book? Does he provide a Biblical blueprint which will enable us, as God-fearing people, to begin to reconstruct our economic world in terms of a Bible-sanctioned and God-required alternative to both socialism and capitalism? Or is Dr. Vickers simply "blowing smoke"? To answer these questions, an understanding of what Dr. Vickers presents as capitalism and socialism is necessary.

Chilton, *Productive Christians in an Age of Guilt-Manipulators* (3rd ed., Tyler, Texas: Institute for Christian Economics, 1985); cf. Chilton's essay "The Case of the Missing Blueprints" in *The Journal of Christian Reconstruction*, Vol. VIII, No. 1 (Summer 1981), (Chalcedon, P.O. Box 158, Vallecito, CA 95251), pp. 132-154.

21. Vickers, *op. cit.*, p. 4.

2

THE HARMONY OF INTERESTS

The real kernel of the significance of his [Keynes'] work lies on an essentially methodological level, in that he gave us a new way of looking at things, or, to use Schumpeter's felicitous phrase, a new "vision," which could never have been achieved as long as we wore the blinkers of the classical and neo-classical assumptions of automatic harmonies. [1]

Capitalism, *laissez-faire*, or the free market, is an anathema to Dr. Vickers. "Sin . . . is abroad in the world"[2] and any "theory of automatic economic harmonies"[3] cannot be expected to work. The fact that no economist of repute in history has ever argued in favor of automatic economic harmonies[4] is no doubt beside the point — deliberate nit-picking on the part of his critics. Dr. Vickers also contends that the "invisible hand" doctrine of Adam Smith implies "that the consistent pursuit of individual economic self-interest would lead *automatically*, via the interdependent market mechanism in the system, to the maximum benefit for society as a whole."[5] The fact that Smith did not teach such a doctrine, and that you would be hard-pressed to find any textbook on the his-

---

1. Vickers, *Economics and Man*, p. 212.
2. *Ibid.*, pp. 289, 355; cf. *A Christian Approach to Economics and the Cultural Condition*, p. 119.
3. *Ibid.*, p. 288.
4. The one exception noted in the textbooks is the mid-nineteenth-century French pamphleteer, Frederic Bastiat. Another possible exception was the nineteenth-century American economist, Henry C. Carey. Nobody has read Carey, except as a historical curiosity, for a hundred years.
5. *Ibid.*, p. 8, emphasis added; cf. p. 288.

39

tory of economic thought which says that he does, is also no doubt beside the point — deliberate nit-picking on the part of his critics.

This is the problem the serious reviewer has when he tries to take Dr. Vickers at his word. You think through what he has plainly written, and if you know anything at all about economics, or the history of economic thought, you realize that what he has written is such utter nonsense that it is inconceivable that he could have written it, except that he did. You reread it, just to make sure. Yes, he really wrote it. So you point out that what he has written is utterly wrong. And then you almost hear him saying, "Picky, picky, picky."

Dr. Vickers never sits quiet. He keeps compounding his errors. "These classical economic notions — the invisible hand and the *guarantee of automatic full utilization* of the resources of the nation and thus the maximization of economic welfare — quickly solidified into a firm orthodoxy."[6] As an analytic hypothesis, yes, this notion did become orthodox, but economists always knew that this was simply a hypothetical model, not a perfect description of reality. They were discussing what they have long called *equilibrium*, which is defined as the way the world of economic exchange would operate *if* all participants possessed perfect knowledge of the present and the future. Economists all know that such a world can never exist. So did the classical economists. Keynesians also use equilibrium models, as do all humanist economists, which Dr. Vickers knows very well. But Keynesian critics of free market economists have a tendency ("other things being equal") to chide classical economists for holding a position which none of them ever held — a bit of historical deception which makes the highly questionable "new economics" of Keynes less costly to sell to naive undergraduates.

It is not only the classical economists who, according to Dr. Vickers, believed that "the economic system would *automatically equilibrate* . . . at a position of maximum economic welfare."[7] He

---

6. *Ibid.*, pp. 10, 11, emphasis added.
7. *Ibid.*, p. 8, emphasis added; cf. pp. 136, 147, 195.

warns his readers that there are "schools of economic thought which tend to rely on the classical and neo-classical assumptions of underlying and *inevitable harmonies* in the economic system."[8] I wonder who he has in mind. The Austrian economists? The Chicago economists? Or even worse, the dreaded Christian Reconstructionist economists?

Here is a description of Dr. Vickers' perception of *laissez-faire*, or capitalism, and, more importantly, Adam Smith's "invisible hand" metaphor. We should note, in addition, that Dr. Vickers uses this conception of "automatic harmonies" to berate Gary North for his argument that the interest rate is the "equilibrating device" between savings and investment. "Here, at the beginning of an attempt to construct a Christian perspective on economic analysis and policy, a total capitulation is made to the classical notion that whatever part of the nation's income is saved will automatically flow into investment. . . . But to assume they will *necessarily* and *automatically* be re-employed in the manner suggested is to betray economic analysis before it gets under way, and before it has a chance even to ask the really meaningful questions of social and economic significance. Such a procedure is declaring a Christian economics bankrupt before its real mission can even begin."[9]

After all, he goes on, "*laissez-faire* could not be expected, from a Christian perspective, to produce the generalized beneficial results which might be hoped for from it. Considerations of greed, rapacity, selfishness, monopoly, and exploitation, as indeed the sheer difficulties of adjustment of complex economic mechanisms, might be expected to keep on getting in the way."[10]

There is one crucial problem with these comments of Dr. Vickers regarding the classical economists' defense of capitalism: *they are not an accurate interpretation of classical economic theory.* This leads him to another problem: *Dr. North has never relied on any such notions of automatic harmony either.* To prove this to ourselves, and to

---

8. *Ibid.*, p. 265, emphasis added; cf. pp. 195, 212, 350.
9. *Ibid.*, p. 27.
10. *Ibid.*, p. 9.

get a better understanding of the extent of the reliability of Dr. Vickers' rhetoric, we need to evaluate the historic accuracy of his accusations in greater detail.

"Automatic Harmony"

Consider Dr. Vickers' claim that Adam Smith and the classical economists taught an "automatic harmony" theory. The objection here is with the word "automatic," for this gives the connotation of being self-propelled or self-motivated, as if there is something inherent in a *laissez-faire* economy that acts in accordance with, and at the discretion of, its own volition. This, however, is not what Adam Smith, or those following him, meant by the metaphorical expression "invisible hand." The evidence for this is in Dr. Vickers' book, in the quotation he gives from Smith's *Wealth of Nations*. It is only necessary to look at the final sentence of that quotation to show Adam Smith had *no* concept of an "automatic" economic system. "By preferring the support of domestic to that of foreign industry, he [the individual] intends only his own security; and by directing that industry in such a manner as its produce may be of the greatest value, he intends only his own gain, and he is in this, as in many other cases, *led by an invisible hand* to promote an end which was no part of his intention."[11]

It is often suggested that *laissez-faire* implies that *all* actions that are motivated by self-interest promote the well-being of society as a whole. This charge cannot be sustained against Adam Smith, however. Elsewhere, in his book *The Theory of Moral Sentiments*,[12] Smith argues there are actions which could be harmful to society. An unbridled "virtue of selfishness" cannot be found in the writings of Adam Smith.

Dr. Vickers appears so preoccupied by the phrase "invisible hand" and his assertion that this means "automatic" or "inevitable

---

11. Adam Smith, *Wealth of Nations*, 1776 (New York: Modern Library, ed. Edwin Cannan, 1937), p. 423, quoted in *Economics and Man*, p. 10, emphasis added by Vickers.

12. Reprinted by Liberty Press, Indianapolis, Indiana.

harmonies" that he overlooks Smith's contention that industry is directed in such a manner that "its produce may be of the greatest value." In other words, Adam Smith is saying that it is the *profit motive* which influences and controls the free market. Contrary to Dr. Vickers' claim, this is not an "automatic" harmony theory but simply a statement which says if a person wants to make the maximum profit, he does so by serving the best interests of the consumers he intends to supply, and the better way of serving potential customers is to produce quality goods at as low a price as is profitable. In this manner "public interest" is promoted, as an attempt is made to obtain maximum use of resources.

To illustrate, a farmer who is able to increase his wheat yield from three to five tons an acre usually does so with the purpose of making "greatest value"—that is, greatest profit—from the use of his land. At the same time, he serves the public interest by producing more food, the additional supply of which has a tendency to reduce the price of wheat.

Smith was well aware that groups of producers might band together and attempt to promote their own interests against the public interest. He criticized "that exclusive corporation spirit which prevails in them. . . ."[13] Here is the man who wrote that "The government of an exclusive company of merchants is, perhaps, the worst of all governments for any country whatever."[14] This is the man who wrote some of the most famous lines in the history of economic thought regarding the evil intentions of merchants: "People of the same trade seldom meet together, even for merriment and diversion, but the conversation ends in a conspiracy against the public, or in some contrivance to raise prices."[15]

I am not saying that Dr. Vickers has never sat down and read Smith's *Wealth of Nations* cover to cover, as any professional classroom economist should do several times during his career. I am not saying that he has never read Smith's *Theory of Moral Senti-*

---

13. *Wealth of Nations*, p. 429.
14. *Ibid.*, p. 537.
15. *Ibid.*, p. 128.

ments. What I am saying is that he doesn't think that his readers have ever done so, and he therefore expected to be able to get away with academic murder at low or zero cost.

Now, what about Dr. North? Has Dr. North ever relied on the concept of automatic harmonies in the free market society? He devotes an entire chapter of his book, *The Dominion Covenant: Genesis* to this very problem, "The God-Designed Harmony of Interests." He says very clearly that *before man's fall into sin*, there was a universal harmony of economic (and all other) interests. Not so after the Fall. What the free market does, he argues, is to provide *economic incentives for men to cooperate voluntarily*. It does not automatically create this tendency. It simply puts economic penalties on fraudulent and violent behavior. He makes his views quite plain:

> It must be understood that the biblical doctrine of the harmony of interests is not the same as the one which has been used in the past by humanists in their defense of the free market. Actually, modern defenders of the market do not use such an argument, although socialists and Marxists sometimes attribute such an argument to them. A few economists of the nineteenth century, most notably the pamphleteer, Frederic Bastiat, argued along these lines, but not many economists have. It is the willingness of free market economists to recognize the innate *dis*harmony of interests that has led them to extol the benefits of the market as a system of coordination. [16]

Dr. North then devotes two pages to citations from Wilhelm Röpke, the free market economist. Röpke challenges the whole notion of an innate harmony of interests. Dr. North summarizes his position:

> Röpke concerned himself with the problems of society, not just with the more narrow sphere of economics. He was convinced that it is naive and misleading to base one's defense of the market on the hypothetical ability of the market to cleanse itself of all fraud, monopoly, and coercion. He did not believe that the market economy is, in his words, "a

---

16. Gary North, *The Dominion Covenant: Genesis* (Tyler, Texas: Institute for Christian Economics, 1982), p. 94.

self-dependent cosmos," or a truly "natural order."[17] Producers want the highest prices possible for their goods or services, while the buyers want the lowest prices. There is a disharmony of interests apart from the mediating influence of the competitive free market, he concluded. Beware of those seeking monopolistic power. But the easiest way to achieve monopoly, he knew, is to gain the assistance of the civil government. If you wish to release the underlying disharmony of interests, he said, all you need to do is unleash the monopolistic powers of the civil government. What he described as the enemy of the harmony of interests, the enemy of a market-produced, competition-produced harmony of interests, is precisely the statist system which has been constructed by those who ridicule the market's form of competition, who ridicule the idea of a competition-produced harmony of interests.[18]

While Dr. North wrote these words in a book published six years after *Economics and Man*, there was no indication in his earlier writings, especially in *An Introduction to Christian Economics*, that Dr. North ever held to a Bastiat-like version of the harmony of interests. Since no economist of the twentieth century has ever argued for the innate harmony of interests, why should Dr. Vickers have imagined that Dr. North did?

What North argues is that in order to reduce the disharmony of sellers vs. buyers, we need a broad, open free market in which *"sellers compete against sellers,"* and *"consumers compete against consumers."*[19] What he extols is competition within a framework of Biblical law. This seems to be what has most outraged Dr. Vickers — not that Dr. North is some sort of anarchistic defender of a harmonious zero-civil government society, but that he and Rev. Rushdoony are proponents of a social order in which the civil government enforces Old Testament legal sanctions. I assume that Dr. Vickers wrote *Economics and Man* with the intention of leading his readers to his conclusions. His concluding chapter is a denouncement of Rushdoony's *Institutes of Biblical Law*. He refers specifically to Rushdoony's position as "a defect on the level of

---

17. Wilhelm Röpke, *Civitas Humana* (London: Hodge, 1948), p. 49.
18. North, *The Dominion Covenant: Genesis*, p. 95.
19. *Ibid.*, p. 224.

teleology."[20] In short, Dr. Vickers recognized very clearly that North was not an advocate of the innate harmony of interests as the foundation of a free market social order. Had Dr. North believed in such a defense, he would never have adopted his views on the necessity of the civil government's enforcement of Biblical law. But if Dr. Vickers recognized this, why does he argue the opposite?

There are three possible answers to this question. First, Dr. Vickers chooses not to read carefully. In short, he is lazy. Second, Dr. Vickers tries to read carefully, but he is unable to do it. In short, Dr. Vickers is a mental incompetent. Third, Dr. Vickers self-consciously parodied Dr. North, just as he self-consciously parodied Adam Smith and the classical economists. In short, Dr. Vickers is: 1) a lazy scholar, 2) a mental incompetent, or 3) a knave.

I doubt that he is lazy; he has not only read lots of insufferably dull academic tomes, he has even gone to the trouble of writing several of them. The turgidity of his writing style does indicate mental incompetence, but his determined inability to state his opponents' position accurately, or even give a standard college textbook account of their beliefs, indicates his self-conscious distorting of rival viewpoints. What any C+ grade average upper division economics major knows is not true, Dr. Vickers tries to palm off as standard knowledge.

In short, the man cannot be trusted. Whether his weakness is primarily intellectual or moral, the reader should decide for himself after finishing this book and then by rereading (if it seems worth the effort) Dr. Vickers' two "Christian" economics books.

Conclusion

There was indeed a God-designed harmony of interests prior to the Fall. After the rebellion of man, the ground was cursed (Gen. 3:17-19), and other changes took place. The ethical goal of the institutional reconstruction of society still exists. We are to work to build a society in which the harmony of interests is *progres-*

---

20. Vickers, *Economics and Man*, p. 358.

sively restored. The death of Christ and His resurrection has made such an effort meaningful and possible.

One aspect of this restoration is the creation of civil law which respects the private property of all law-abiding people. The free market is society's most effective institutional means of putting a price tag on non-cooperation. It puts a premium on harmony and places economic restraints on those who violate social harmony. It cannot eliminate disharmony, but it enables all participants to bid for the cooperation of their neighbors. The defense of the free market must not be in terms of an innate harmony of interests in a fallen world; on the contrary, its defense rests on the theoretical accuracy and historical reality of the potential for economic growth and personal advancement of those who cooperate through voluntary transactions in a free market society.

The State is not to become a primary owner of goods and services. Combined taxes of all levels of civil government are to be kept under the level of the tithe, meaning under ten percent of income. The State is to be shrunk radically. In short, we are to seek deliverance from today's Egypt. Keynes is one of "Egypt's" major economists. (Marx is the other.) If Dr. Vickers were well-known and influential, he would be, too. But he would be employed as a taskmaster's agent, to calm the people in bondage. He would tell us that we are actually in the promised land, and that any talk of freedom from bondage is the heresy of those who would lead them into the wilderness to die. In the wilderness, there are no leeks, no onions, and no State welfare checks.

4

GOD'S CREATION AND CAPITALISM

*Men are constituted, in short, in such a way as to minimize the
expectation that, if left to itself, the economic society could function
with that natural harmony of interests which we have seen the classical
economists and their latter-day intellectual progeny to suppose. Personal freedoms, individual rights, the dignity of man, and the accordance of liberty to hopefully responsible self-interest, can all too easily
degenerate into an economic anarchy. The Christian proposition,
espoused on the sanction of clear scriptural prescription, that the state
has been "ordained by God" for the restraint, correction, and punish-
ment of evil, has as positive and pervasive an application in the economic sphere as in other more readily acknowledged realms.*[1]

We have already seen that Dr. Vickers' claim that the classical
economists, let alone Dr. North, relied on a concept of the innate
harmony of interests is a false claim. This misrepresentation also
undergirds his 1982 book on economics. Since he persists in cling-
ing to this misleading historic summary, it must be important for
his overall argument. It is an argument which cannot be sustained. He begins with a false premise. Now he wants us also to
believe that economic anarchy looms because the State — meaning
politicians and safely tenured bureaucrats — has a positive role to
play in economic planning, in order to avoid "an economic anarchy." This conclusion, he says, is in accord with Paul's letter to the
Romans, chapter 13, verse 1 and following.

---

1. Vickers, *Economics and Man*, p. 73.

Creation and Providence

To reply to Dr. Vickers, we need to know the *origin* of the capitalist system. First, the Christian economist can and must argue that the world is not based on chance. It was created by a God who is not the author of chaos but of order and harmony, and He controls whatsoever comes to pass. It is presently sustained by that God providentially.

Second, the Christian economist should be wise enough to say that economics is the study of sinful human beings and the actions they take to improve their well-being. *Homo sapiens* is made in the image of God, and is a thinking and intelligent being. His actions are *thoughtful* actions even though we admit that increased knowledge can influence the way man will act. His actions are *purposeful*, just as God's actions are. In principle, we can say that all human action is purposeful. Whether a particular action will achieve its aim, however, is another question. Whether it is morally good or morally evil is also another question.

Third, individual human actions fall within a higher, overall plan. They do not happen by chance, but fall within the counsel and providence of the Creator (Eph. 1:11). The capitalistic system has been defended in the past without reference to God and His eternal decrees, the reason being that *laissez-faire* economists have adopted a self-consciously secularized version of the doctrine of providence, with the impersonal market substituting for a personalistic social order.[2] This does not mean that free market defenders are necessarily wrong in all that they say, for Christian roots run deep in market theory. Some economists have understood how influential historically the Biblical arguments concerning providence were for the economists' concept of economic order.[3] What I am arguing, following Gary North's lead, is that *laissez-*

---

2. See R. J. Rushdoony, *The Roots of Inflation* (Vallecito, California: Ross House Books, 1982), p. 67 ff.

3. Jacob Viner, *The Role of Providence in the Social Order: An Essay in Intellectual History* (Philadelphia: American Philosophical Society, 1972). Sadly, Dr. Viner did not live to complete this introductory study.

faire theory is closer to Biblical truth than other economic systems are, for reasons which will be discussed throughout this book — reasons denied by Douglas Vickers.

Moreover, if all action is purposeful action, we can safely conclude that the essential difference between a *laissez-faire* economic system and any other economic system comes down to the way individual human actions are viewed. The essence of free market theory is that individuals should generally be left to themselves to determine and pursue their own goals. The market in principle honors Philippians 2:12: "Work out your own salvation with fear and trembling."

Is the Free Market Random or Disorderly?

This reliance on individual decision-making is far from saying that the market is chaotic, contrary to the Marxists and socialists. The market is orderly. What the socialists refuse to admit is that there is a *bottom-up, decentralized order* in economic affairs. It is the interaction of voluntarily choosing individuals which produces economic order, if they are operating under a system of private ownership and laws against violence and fraud.[4] The actions of individuals have consequences. There is nothing "automatic" about this, nor does it possess some magical quality. It is merely a recognition that people act a certain way under given circumstances; they act in their own best interests *as they perceive them*.

A *laissez-faire* system is not uncontrolled in the sense that Dr. Vickers implies when he states that if left to itself, the market will "gyrate uninhibitedly and randomly of its own accord."[5] Far from being uncontrolled, the market is governed by the *subjective* valuations of all buyers and sellers, as manifested in their actual decisions to buy and sell. (Remember, buying is always selling, and vice versa.) Individual subjective valuations, and the actions resulting from these valuations, control the free market economy.

---

4. F. A. Hayek, *The Constitution of Liberty* (Chicago: University of Chicago Press, 1960).

5. Vickers, *op. cit.*, p. 234.

This intellectual defense of this market process has been known to professional economists for over a century.[6]

Marx's Argument

To call the free market "economic anarchy," or to say that it is a "rampant and potentially anarchic individualism,"[7] is mere hyperbole on the part of Dr. Vickers. It was also hyperbolic on the part of Karl Marx, in *Das Kapital* (1867), when he argued that the "anarchy in the social division of labor" required an "authoritative plan" to bring coherence.[8] It was equally hyperbolic when Frederick Engels, the co-founder of Communism (Marx's associate), argued the same way in 1877: "The contradiction between socialised production and capitalistic appropriation now presents itself as *an antagonism between the organisation of production in the individual workshop and the anarchy of production in society generally.*"[9] Hyperbole is not economic analysis.

I am of course not arguing that Dr. Vickers is a "closet Marxist." What I am arguing is that there is a familiar theme in the writings of those who propose that the State's bureaucrats serve as overall planners for the market, whether socialists (State ownership of the means of production), fascists (private ownership with State control), or interventionists (State manipulation of the economy through taxation, spending, and monetary policy). They all come to the market with a built-in bias, which in turn is based on a view of God and His creation. They assume that "rationalism" is essentially a *top-down phenomenon*. They assume that anything which is not top-down rationalism is essentially irrational. It is this perspective, which F. A. Hayek has battled for over four dec-

---

6. Carl Menger, *Principles of Economics* (New York: New York University Press, [1871] 1981), pp. 114 ff.

7. Vickers, *op. cit.*, p. 125; cf. p. 190.

8. Marx, *Capital* (Modern Library edition, reprint of the 1906 edition), pp. 391-92.

9. Engels, *Socialism: Utopian and Scientific* (New York: International Publishers, 1935), p. 61. This was an extract from Engels' book, *Herr Eugen Dühring's Revolution in Science (Anti-Dühring)*, published in 1877.

ades,[10] which Dr. North has called the mythology of Darwinian central planning.[11]

Former U.S. Secretary of Defense Robert McNamara has expressed this viewpoint forthrightly: "Some critics today worry that our democratic, free societies are becoming overmanaged. I would argue that the opposite is true. As paradoxical as it may sound, the real threat to democracy comes not from overmanagement, but from undermanagement. To undermanage reality is not to keep it free. It is simply to let some force other than reason shape reality. That force may be unbridled emotion; it may be greed; it may be aggressiveness; it may be hatred; it may be ignorance; it may be inertia; it may be anything other than reason. But whatever it is, if it is not reason that rules man, then man falls short of his potential. Vital decision-making, particularly in policy matters, must remain at the top."[12] Perhaps the most eloquent critique of the results of McNamara's dedicated top-down rationalism is chapter 12 of David Halberstam's masterpiece on the Johnson Administration's handling of the Vietnam War, *The Best and the Brightest* (1972).

Also notice McNamara's concern with "greed." We shall be confronted with this theme again, when we examine Dr. Vickers' defense of Keynesian interventionism.

Interest Rates and Market Decisions

Dr. Vickers is concerned about the "anarchy" of the free market. He has not taken seriously the idea that there is another kind of rationalism, the rationalism of voluntary cooperation in a private property social order. He refuses to acknowledge *the free market's integration of decentralized individual economic plans* as the primary

---

10. Especially in his book, *The Counter-Revolution of Science* (Indianapolis, Indiana: Liberty Press, [1952] 1979).

11. Gary North, *The Dominion Covenant: Genesis* (Tyler, Texas: Institute for Christian Economics, 1982), Appendix A, "From Cosmic Purposelessness to Humanistic Sovereignty."

12. Robert McNamara, *The Essence of Security: Reflections in Office* (New York: Harper & Row, 1968), pp. 109-10.

institutional source of a society's productivity. We see this same "analytical myopia" (to borrow a phrase Dr. Vickers uses to describe his opponents[13]) when Dr. Vickers deals with Dr. North's comments on interest rates being the "equilibrating device" between savings and investments.[14]

We need to understand in advance how important the question of interest rates is. It is the central phenomenon in guiding men's decisions to save or spend. No other problem is more important to solve for the overall economy—the "macroeconomic problem"—than this one. Prof. Roger Garrison has pointed this out. "The market's ability to solve this more global coordination problem—conventionally conceived as the problem of coordinating savings decisions with investment decisions—has always been the central issue in macroeconomics."[15]

The Discount of Future Asset Value

Before launching into a discussion of interest rates, we need to ask ourselves a few basic questions? Are men omniscient? Are men immortal? Are men limited in time and space? Do men live in a world of scarcity, defined as a world in which they cannot get everything they want at zero price? Do men have to make decisions about what they want? Do they make trade-offs, decisions to take more of one scarce resource and less of another? Isn't it legitimate to describe economic decisions as the voluntary exchange of one set of historical circumstances for another? Finally, is this economic decision-making *purposeful?*

If we see man as limited, mortal, and constrained by time and scarcity, we then have to ask ourselves another question: *How do we evaluate the future?* Do we value a future asset as highly as we value the same asset right now? Obviously, we don't. In the example Dr. North is fond of using, if you were to win a brand-new,

---

13. Vickers, *Economics and Man*, p. 248; cf. pp. 76, 178, 190.
14. *Ibid.*, p. 27.
15. Roger Garrison, "A Subjectivist Theory of a Capital-using Economy," in Gerald P. O'Driscoll, Jr. and Mario Rizzo, *The Economics of Time and Ignorance* (London: Basil Blackwell, 1985), p. 170.

tax-free Rolls-Royce automobile, but you were given a choice of delivery date either today or five years from now, which delivery date would you choose? You would choose today. Why? *Because you discount the value of future goods and services.*

Another example he uses: If you decide to buy a farm which will produce a net return of one ounce of gold per year for a million years, will you pay a million ounces of gold for it today? Obviously not. Why not? Because you do not value that millionth ounce of future gold as highly as you value the millionth ounce of today's gold. Think about this. It is really a very simple concept. If you agree that the example is correct, then you should not fight the additional insight that you do not value the hundredth ounce of future gold as highly as you value today's hundredth ounce.

You now understand why *there must always be an interest rate.* The rate of interest is basic to life. Even in a risk-free world (which ours isn't ever going to be) and an inflation-free world (which it isn't today), there will still be a rate of interest. This "originary" rate is simply *the discount which we impute (apply mentally) to the value of future goods in contrast to those same goods in the present.* Put simpler, "a bird in hand is worth two in the bush, depending on how long it takes us to get to the bush." An ounce of gold today is worth more to us than an ounce of gold in the future.

What I am getting at is simple enough: we plan for the future. We make decisions about the future. Everyone does. How do we assess the profitability of giving up a scarce economic resource to-day in order to receive a return on the investment in the future? If I am future-oriented (as Christians should be), then I will give up today's asset (save it, meaning invest it) for a lower rate of return in the future than a present-oriented person would demand. Dr. North gives the example of Esau, who was so present-oriented that he sold his birthright for a mess of pottage.[16]

How can a society plan for the future? How do people make intelligent, efficient decisions concerning how much to give up and how much to consume now? People look at the prevailing rate

---

16. North, *The Dominion Covenant: Genesis,* pp. 182-83.

of interest on investments of varying time and risk, and they decide either to invest or spend on consumer goods and services. Either they choose *future goods* or *present goods*. There has to be some indicator which tells rational, purposeful people whether it is to their advantage to invest or spend. Dr. North says (following the "Austrian School" economists) that market interest rates guide people in their time-oriented economic decisions, and that these various rates are the product of men's shifting time-preferences in the market place. While each decision-maker faces *objective* market rates of interest, some *personal, subjective* rate of interest discounts the future value of assets in his decision-making, with or without a published rate of interest in some newspaper.

If the prevailing available return on his money is higher than his subjective rate of time-preference, he will invest the money, thereby foregoing the benefits of immediate consumption. The person with lower time-preference (a comparatively high valuation of the future) lends money to people with higher time preference (a comparatively low valuation of the future). Each person buys what he prefers. One person buys the present use of assets and gives up even more future assets, while the other sells present assets in order to receive even more future assets. These people get together as a result of their own profit-seeking search, and the "searchlight" they use to locate each other is the market rate of interest.

If this sounds simple enough, it is because it *is* simple. If Dr. Vickers' discussion sounds complex, it is because it is confused. This confusion was also basic to Keynes' discussions of the interest rate.

The Keynesian View(s) of Interest

To understand Dr. Vickers' deliberate misrepresentation of Dr. North's position, it is only necessary to refer to Dr. Vickers' quotation of Dr. North. "The *rate of interest* is supposed to act as an *equilibrating device*. . . ."[17] Now, when Dr. Vickers concludes that

---

17. North, *Introduction to Christian Economics*, p. 63, quoted in *Economics and Man*, p. 27, emphasis in original.

Dr. North is incorrect in assuming the interest rate for loans would act "*automatically*" and "*necessarily*," Dr. Vickers makes an error. Dr. North did *not* say the interest rate would "*necessarily* and *automatically*" bring a balance between savings and investments. What Dr. North *did* say is that the interest rate is "*supposed* to act" (emphasis added) as the equilibrating device. What Dr. North stresses throughout his economic writings is what all "Austrian School" economists stress: the key element in all economic actions is future-oriented, profit-seeking, uncertainty-bearing *entrepreneurship*. There is nothing automatic about entrepreneurship.[18]

Dr. Vickers' contention that Dr. North has presented a "bankrupt" economic theory is dependent upon his own *mis*statement of Dr. North's position. When Dr. Vickers later admits that the interest rate *is* the determining factor in savings and investment, we may begin to suspect even more his allegations against those he is arguing against. For, in suggesting economic policies from the Keynesian perspective, Dr. Vickers states that finance can be made "more difficult to obtain" by allowing "the interest rate to increase." An "increase in interest rates . . . may render unprofitable and no longer economically worthwhile certain investment projects which would otherwise have been undertaken."[19] In other words, the interest rate *does* influence savings and investment. This is what Keynes believed, too.[20]

How Dr. Vickers can reconcile this with his earlier assertion that "the level of national income" is the "equilibrating device"[21] is impossible to ascertain, for he does not seem aware that he has offered two *contradictory* theories regarding savings and investment and what determines the balance between them. Dr. Vickers has first of all argued that the *national income* is the equilibrating device

---

18. Israel M. Kirzner, *Competition and Entrepreneurship* (Chicago: University of Chicago Press, 1973); Kirzner, *Perception, Opportunity, and Profit* (Chicago: University of Chicago Press, 1979).

19. Vickers, *op. cit.*, p. 261.

20. Thomas Sowell, *Say's Law: An Historical Analysis* (Princeton, New Jersey: Princeton University Press, 1972), pp. 207-8.

21. Vickers, p. 29.

between savings and investment, and then later suggests that *interest rates* ought to be manipulated to make some projects unprofitable.

Which is it, "national income" or "interest rates"? He does not provide an explanation of exactly how a broad aggregate such as "national income" would equilibrate (adjust) investments and savings. What he refuses to accept is the assertion by Dr. North and economists such as Mises and Hayek that we must begin our economic analysis with the *decisions of acting individuals*. We must begin with a discussion of *purposeful human behavior*. Obviously, "national income" does not "decide" what to invest or where. "National income" does not go down to his friendly local bank and make a deposit. But it is quite clear how the interest rate adjusts *individuals'* decisions concerning spending, saving, and investing. If certain projects are expected to be unprofitable because the expected rate of profit will not be high enough to repay the investors or lenders, people will not invest in them or loan money to them. If the rate of interest (the so-called "rate of return on capital") is higher than the project is expected to produce, the rational individual will put his money elsewhere. This is the logical reason why Dr. Vickers sometimes uses the interest rate as an explanatory tool in economic analysis. Thus, Dr. Vickers is saying that interest rates *will* sometimes act as an equilibrating device between investment and savings.[22] Why not *all* the time?

If all this sounds muddled and confused, this is because Dr. Vickers is muddled and confused. He has adopted the analysis of

---

22. Interest rates affect savings in the same manner, for example, that the price of computers affects their purchase. People do not buy because of price. They buy a computer because they perceive that what they gain will be of greater benefit than what they hand over in the transaction. The price is the *result* of the exchange between buyer and seller. Similarly, the determining factor in what amount will be saved is really the *preference* people have between present and future consumption, between using an economic commodity now, or putting off its consumption until a future date. The interest rate is the *result* of the valuations which both buyers and sellers make of the time period involved. The interest rate allows subjective preferences (valuations) to be calculated in economic terms. See W. H. Hutt, *The Keynesian Episode*, pp. 235ff. On subjective valuation, see especially Ludwig von Mises, *Human Action: A Treatise on Economics* (3rd ed.; Chicago, Illinois: Regnery, 1966), ch. 11; on interest, see chapter 19.

Keynes' *General Theory*, which was *deliberately* muddled and confused. Dr. North's observation is insightful: Keynes in his early writings was clear and concise, yet the *General Theory* is obscure to a fault, as his followers admit. There has to be a reason. His guess: Keynes wanted to become obscure, the better to hide the anomalies and outright contradictions of the *General Theory*.[23]

Has Greed Destroyed the Case for Capitalism?

There is an additional accusation by Dr. Vickers that historical facts "belied the theory"[24] of the classical economists because "greed, rapacity, selfishness, monopoly, and exploitation,"[25] as well as the complexity of the economic system, kept getting in the way of the free market. Unfortunately, Dr. Vickers does not bother to say *whose* "greed, rapacity, selfishness . . . and exploitation" disturbed the system. He also does not explain *how* their "greed, rapacity, and selfishness" got in the way of the free market. It is *not* the fact that people are greedy (how defined?) or rapacious which is significant. What *is* important is how their *particular form* of greed or rapaciousness overcame the institutional restraints of private property, competition, and law enforcement against fraud and violence in *specific historical instances*.

Irrespective of this silence, his claim that "a pure and untrammelled state of economic *laissez-faire* has never existed or been able to exist"[26] means he has undermined his own contention that "facts" have disproven *laissez-faire* theory. Simply put, if *laissez-faire* never existed in history, then how did the "facts" overcome it?

Here we get to the old "bait and switch" technique which has been so important in the intellectual arsenal of capitalism's critics over the years. First, you tell people that what capitalism's defenders claimed for *pure theory* was also claimed by them for the historical manifestations of capitalism. Next, you tell them that

---

23. Gary North, *Moses and Pharaoh: Dominion Religion vs. Power Religion* (Tyler, Texas: Institute for Christian Economics, 1985), p. xviii, footnote 17.

24. Vickers, *op. cit.*, p. 8.

25. *Ibid.*, p. 9.

26. *Ibid.*, p. 10.

the unpleasant facts of the real world overcame the imperfect real world manifestation of the capitalist model. Then you conclude that this unpleasant sin-filled reality refutes the theory of capitalism. And, just to make the whole argument irrelevant, you top it off with the observation that capitalism has never really existed anyway, implying that it is just too utopian for any society to adopt it.

Well, not to put too fine a point to it, they are starving in Marxist Ethiopia, and they aren't in any capitalist society. Socialist ideologues might reply that this is "too crass" an argument. I am trying to compare apples and apples (actual societies). Unfair, they shout. What I should be comparing is apples and oranges — socialism's ideal theory vs. real world capitalism's sin-filled performance. That is what they always compare, and what is good enough for them had better be good enough for all of us.

Any classical economist would agree with Dr. Vickers that an unhampered free market has never existed, if only because the "greed, rapacity, selfishness . . . and exploitation" of government bureaucrats and special-interest groups (farmers, trade unionists, manufacturers, importers, Keynesian economists, etc.) have been *State-legislated obstructions* to the operations of competitive markets. The classical economists would say that the *lack* of a free market is precisely the problem.

Let us freely admit that people are greedy, rapacious, and just plain unpleasant. They are sinners in rebellion to God. Why should we expect sinners to be all sweetness and light with each other, people made in that hated God's image? The question is: *What kind of social order channels men's sinful motives into productive efforts that serve their neighbors?* It was the insight of Adam Smith in 1776 that the free market order is the most effective device to turn evil motives into productive efforts. We should begin with men's self-interest if we wish to get them to serve us. We should therefore start with the assumption of the depravity of man. Very early in *The Wealth of Nations*, Smith wrote his classic lines:

But man has almost constant occasion for the help of his brethren, and it is in vain for him to expect it from their benevolence only. He will be more likely to prevail if he can interest their self-love in his favor, and shew them that it is for their own advantage to do for him what he requires of them. Whoever offers to another a bargain of any kind, proposes to do this. Give me that which I want, and you shall have this which you want, is the meaning of any such offer; and it is in this manner that we obtain from one another the far greater part of those good offices which we stand in need of. It is not from the benevolence of the butcher, the brewer, or the baker, that we expect our dinner, but from their regard to their own interest. We address ourselves, not to their humanity but to their self-love, and never talk to them of our own necessities but of their advantages.[27]

Notice that Smith said that we do not expect help from our neighbors "from their benevolence *only*." Yes, it is true that they may occasionally lend a helping hand, but it is more often that they will help a lending hand. The borrower is servant to the lender, after all (Prov. 22:7).

Those who would criticize the classical economists for their inability to understand the social reality of greed and rapacity have very little understanding of the classical economists. Those who would criticize the market order for its inability to deal with greed and rapacity have only tyrannies to offer in their place. How well does socialism restrain greed? How well does Keynesian central planning eliminate greed? How well does the Gulag Archipelago restrain greed?

Isn't my best defense against a greedy seller my ability to locate an even more greedy seller? Never forget: *sellers compete against sellers*. Isn't the genius of the free market its system of open entry, meaning the ability of new potential sellers to enter the auction place and offer a better deal to consumers? Isn't this a more likely way to reduce the *effects* of greed than any bureaucratic scheme? Who is to guarantee that the bureaucrats will not seek their own interests, too, but without the restraining pressure of open entry and new competitors? Not Keynesian economists, certainly. Not Douglas Vickers, certainly.

---

27. Adam Smith, *The Wealth of Nations* (Modern Library, Cannan edition), p. 14.

Conclusion

The evidence so far indicates that Dr. Vickers does not really understand classical economic theory, or if he does, he does not think his readers will, which therefore allows him a great deal of "creative latitude" in describing classical economic theory. He has not offered any substitute explanation for how people will be able to decide between spending and investing, between now and then, apart from freely fluctuating interest rates. He has not explained why savings will not equal investments, and neither did his mentor, Professor (a term he despised) Keynes. He has not explained how aggregate statistical concepts such as "national income" somehow allocate capital — decisions that are made by acting individuals.

Dr. Vickers has adopted at least a mild version of the standard socialist refrain: "Capitalism is anarchistic, and it therefore needs a guiding hand." Dr. Vickers would substitute the literal *clenched fist of the government bureaucrat* for Adam Smith's analogy of the invisible hand of free market orderliness. He believes that top-down rational planning is necessary to compensate for the supposed blindness and greed of the market process.

The problem is that he has not offered a cogent substitute for the competitive market's system of self-interested service to neighbors. If we do not expect to appeal to men's self-interest in order to gain our objectives, are we not living in a fantasy world? The question is: "What system of rewards and constraints makes men's self-interest most productive for their neighbors?" That is the "question of questions" that was asked by the classical economists. They did not answer it well enough to satisfy a serious Christian economist, but certainly John Maynard Keynes, in all his terminology, equations, and obfuscations in the *General Theory*, did not answer it nearly so well as his classical and neo-classical predecessors did. The "Austrian School" economists answered it better than any of them. This is why Dr. Vickers never summarizes the arguments of the "Austrian School." He sees his job as winning a debate, not enlightening his readers, and a debater wins no points for bringing up his opponents' best arguments — arguments that he is intellectually incapable of answering . . . or perhaps even understanding.

5

MAN'S REBELLION AND SOCIALISM

. . . in the complexities of modern times responsibility for an over-sight of the economic health of the system must reside in the central government authorities acting on behalf of the people. . . .[1]

All economic systems revolve around some pivotal point. There is some particular theory or doctrine which becomes the central determining point for all additional theories and ideas. It is possible to say that *all* economic theories are determined by their attitude to property rights. There are only two possibilities: either God owns it, or someone else does. Either God delegates control over property to His subordinates, or these subordinates own it autonomously.

Then there is the secondary question: Is man's stewardship (or autonomous ownership) *private* or *public*, meaning individual or statist?[2] Either individuals have final say over property, or the State does. This does not mean that a number of individuals may not voluntarily cooperate to control property. In the sense we are talking about, this would still come under the heading of private ownership. Private ownership, in other words, is opposed to public or State ownership. Individual men are the ones who decide to

---

1. Vickers, *Economics and Man*, p. 205.
2. This is not to imply that all theories are determined *exclusively* by their idea on property rights. Other key doctrines could also be the determining factor for a generalized theory. A particular view of Scripture, and how to interpret Scripture, will also determine which direction the development of economy theory takes.

63

sell or not to sell a given piece of property; no State bureaucrat need be consulted.

Within these two broad headings — private vs. public ownership — all humanistic economic theories can be subsumed. Any economic theory can be tested by its commitment to ownership: where ownership ultimately resides. But once we have established in which category a particular theory lies, there still lies a central doctrine or theory which sets that particular theory apart from others. For example, one particular theory which sets the neo-classical Austrian School apart from other classical and neo-classical theories is its understanding of and attitude towards increasing the money supply (monetary inflation).[3]

Vague Definitions

When Dr. Vickers makes reference to the idea of capitalism, he does at least offer a definition of the term, albeit an inaccurate definition. But it is an entirely different matter when he discusses socialism, for he offers no definition at all. There is a good reason for this. If he can keep the readers of his books in a state of mind where they are never sure precisely what he is talking about, perhaps they will be more than willing to agree with his view that Keynesianism is Christian economics. The claim that he is advocating neither capitalism nor socialism, however, is *meaningless* until he defines *precisely* what he is talking about. Precision of language, however, is not one of his strong points.

Dr. Vickers has no intention of being clear. "There is no need to allow the argument to become enslaved to words or terminology at this early stage. It should be hoped that economic argument can avoid a needless degeneration into empty logomachy."[4] (Empty logomachy? What does he want, *filled* logomachy?) True, empty logomachy is not needed. But clarity and understanding

---

3. See Ludwig von Mises, *Theory of Money and Credit* (Irvington-on-Hudson, New York: Foundation for Economic Education, [1912] 1971). A reprint of this has been released by Liberty Press, Indianapolis, Indiana.

4. Vickers, *Economics and Man*, p. 49.

concerning what he and those he disagrees with are saying would go a long way towards assisting those searching for a Biblical economics. John Kenneth Galbraith said it best: "In the case of economics there are no important propositions that cannot, in fact, be stated in plain language."[5] Either Dr. Vickers refuses to assent to this principle, or chooses to ignore it. (One other possibility exists: perhaps he thinks that, unlike important propositions, unimportant propositions cannot be stated in plain language, and he regards his propositions as unimportant.)

In the light of Dr. Vickers' omission, it appears reasonable to adopt the dictionary definition of socialism to see, in spite of the lack of clarity on his part, if it is possible to come to an understanding of the Keynesian economic theories Dr. Vickers would like us to embrace.

The *Shorter Oxford English Dictionary* defines socialism as "a theory or policy of social organization which advocates the ownership and control of the means of production, capital, land, property, etc. by the community as a whole, and their administration or distribution in the interests of all." It is instructive to note that the same dictionary defines communism as "1. A theory of society according to which all property should be vested in the community and labor organized for the common benefit. 2. Any practice which carries out this theory." *There is no economic difference between communism and socialism.* Both advocate *State* control of property. Individuals are not allowed to have the final word over things in their possession. Individuals are to become servants to the community at large and serve some supposedly "higher" purpose.

Property Rights

The Christian must begin with one crucial premise: the final and absolute ownership of all things by God (Ps. 50:10). The question then is: To whom or to what agency or agencies has God delegated the responsibility of temporal control of any given asset at any particular point in history? Who has the *legal authority* to *rep-*

---

5. Cited by "Adam Smith," *New York Times* (Sept. 30, 1979).

resent God in the management of any given asset? Who is *God's appointed steward* of any given asset?

The Scriptures plainly teach the concept of *private* property rights or *private* ownership. The commandments against theft and covetousness (Ex. 20:15,17) teach explicitly that there are possessions that belong rightfully to other private citizens which we may not take, nor even desire, because they belong to someone else. The owner of at least some possessions has the right to exclude others from the use of his property, so long as he adheres to Biblical law with respect to the use of his property. It is this concept of having the *final earthly word* — to buy or sell, to keep or destroy — which delineates where ownership resides. If a State or community official can tell the individual, in the final analysis, what is to be done with something in the individual's possession, then temporal ownership resides in that official, not the possessor of the goods. The question then is: Who has *Biblically legitimate* temporal control over any given asset?

What does the secular economist mean by "property rights"? He means, first of all, the legal right (legal *immunity*) to *exclude others* from the use of the property. Second, it means the right to collect any income from the asset. Third, it means the right to sell or rent the property or its income stream.[6] In other words, the owner has the legal right to *dis*own an asset. If he does not have the right to disown it, he does not truly own it.[7] Thus, the whole idea of "common ownership" is fraught with difficulties, not just administrative difficulties (which are legendary in economic literature), but theoretical and legal difficulties.

The Biblical Concept of Ownership

Private property, however, is even more fundamental than mere control. It is rooted in the nature and character of the Triune

---

6. Steven Cheung, *The Myth of Social Cost* (San Francisco: Cato Institute, 1980), p. 34.

7. F. A. Harper, *Liberty: A Path to Its Recovery* (Irvington, New York: Foundation for Economic Education, 1949), p. 106.

God.[8] The premise of private ownership underlies the whole of Scripture and forms the basis for the Biblical notion of stewardship. God, the ultimate Owner of all things, gives to people as He chooses, and requires of them proper use of those possessions; what is proper being defined by Him in His Word. But if I, as an individual, must give way to an official in deciding how the goods in my possession may be used, how can I be held responsible for their use? Isn't the responsible agent that bureaucrat who is now making the decision in my place?

There are some, including Dr. Vickers it seems, who are not convinced that the command against theft is sufficient reason for Christians to hold to the idea of private ownership in the sense described above. If we adopt the view that the Bible does explain itself clearly, then we can turn to other passages to substantiate our claims. We can find two passages which illustrate ownership in the terms defined here.

Naboth and Ahab

The first of these is King Ahab who, spying Naboth's vineyard, approached him with the objective of buying it (I Kings 21:1-29). "Give me thy vineyard, that I may have it for a garden of herbs, because it is near unto my house: and I will give thee for it a better vineyard than it; or, if it seem good to thee, I will give

---

8. As Dr. F. N. Lee observes, "Scripture anchors private property in the Triune God Himself, before the foundation of the world! In Him, the propriety of private property is immediately apparent. For the Father, the Son, and the Spirit have Each, from all eternity past, always possessed some 'private property' which the Other Two of Them never have and never will possess. (Compare Mal. 3:6 with Rom. 11:29,36 and Jas. 1:17.) Only the Father possesses paternity (Heb. 1:5-8). Only the Son possesses filiation (John 1:14-18). And only the Spirit possesses procession (John 15:26). Paternity is the private property of the Father; filiation is the private property of the Son; and procession is the private property of the Spirit - alone! Each of the Three Persons' private property is intimately connected to His own individual personality quite distinguishable from that of Each of the Other Two Persons (Luke 3:21-22). As the great modern Reformed theologian William Geesink rightly remarks: 'Property rights root in eternity, and precede all man-made laws.'" Lee, *Christian Private Property Versus Socialistic Common Property* (unpublished essay, 1985).

thee the worth of it in money" (v. 2). It is of interest to note here that *there is no attempt by Ahab to get out of paying a reasonable price for the land*. His financial offer was more than fair, from a pure market perspective. Ahab simply wanted the land because it was near to his palace. Possibly he was lazy and did not want to travel so far. More to the point, his servants probably exhibited the signs of all bureaucrats and a keen eye needed to be kept on them in order that a fair day's work was put in tending the herbs. But it is Naboth's answer which attracts our attention. "The LORD forbid it me, that I should give the inheritance of my fathers unto thee" (v. 3). In other words, Naboth's unwillingness to sell his land was based on the fact that the Lord had forbidden it. His land was an inheritance to him and his descendants and Naboth could not disinherit them.

Some commentators might raise the question that this land, in Canaan, was the product of a special act of God in giving it to His chosen people, and that is true. But it is also true that the land obtainable today and all the other possessions we have are also the gift of God to us and to our descendants. For all possessions, including the Promised Land, are given *on condition* of covenantal obedience to God. *There is no such thing as unconditional inheritance in Scripture*, not now nor in God's past dealings with Israel. Neither is there any Biblical warrant for some other person — even the king — to assume the prerogatives of deciding when and how the land is to be distributed and used. In other words, Ahab had no *rightful* power or authority over Naboth's property unless Naboth *voluntarily* chose to give him such, which he did not.

The Parable of the Employer

The second Biblical illustration of the meaning of ownership is to be found in Matthew 20:1-16. Although it is true that the point of this parable our Lord is telling is not the meaning of ownership, what Jesus teaches at this point is dependent upon the view of ownership that we have defined here. Jesus is using a parable to teach His followers about *the absolute sovereignty of God* in distributing rewards for their earthly service. Sinful human beings cannot earn any rewards in the kingdom of heaven, for all acts are tainted with our sin nature. Perfection is the standard required by God, and no one manages to attain to that standard. What then is the basis for our future rewards? The basis is the same as that on which we obtain salvation: God's mercy. Since no person can claim that he will be saved because of what he has done in this life, therefore no one will be able to put his hand out for rewards on the basis of what he has done. All that comes to sinful man is by way of grace, God's unmerited favor. Our Lord's parable here is in response to Peter's question, "Behold, we have forsaken all, and followed thee; what shall we have therefore?" (Matt. 19:27). The answer comes back: rewards will be given according to God's determination, and when we complain that others receive more when they have done less for the kingdom, the reply will be, "Is it not lawful for me to do what I will with mine own?"

Although Jesus is here teaching about the kingdom of heaven, the point He is making *depends* upon a concept of covenantal property rights. He expected his listeners to grasp His point. We need to understand it, too, even if we are university economists. *The Lord Jesus Christ believes in the private ownership of property.* [9] We are to exercise *derivative* and *analogous* authority over the property which God has delegated to us.

There are other examples in Scripture which lend support to this concept of private ownership. The well-known and much-abused passage in Acts 5:1-11 about Ananias and Sapphira is further evidence that, as owners of their possession, they had a freedom to control the use of those things which they had. The point, however, has been made and substantiated for all those who are willing to take Scripture as the voice of authority on the matter. It is

---

9. Mises is incorrect when he says "all efforts to find support for the institution of private property generally, and for private ownership in the means of production in particular, in the teachings of Christ are quite vain." *Socialism* (London: Jonathan Cape, 1936), p. 418. (This book has been reprinted by Liberty Press, Indianapolis, Indiana.) See also Carl F. H. Henry, "Christian Perspective on Private Property," in Samuel L. Blumenfeld (ed.), *Property In A Humane Economy* (LaSalle, Illinois: Open Court Publishing Co., 1974), pp. 23-45.

no coincidence that in the past our forefathers condemned socialism, for they had Biblical warrant to do so. The *Thirty-Nine Articles*
of the Anglican Church (#38), and the *Belgic Confession's* (#36) con-
demn the Anabaptists and their attempts to establish community
of goods.[10]

Vickers on Private (Sort of) Property

Dr. Vickers acknowledges the concept of property rights. He
says, for example, that "the right of property carries with it, it is
clear, the right of disposal. . . ."[11] There is "in the parables of
Christ. . . an affirmation of the right of private property. . . ."[12]
But Dr. Vickers does not intend such property rights in the sense
of having final and exclusive control. Instead, he argues that exclusive ownership exists "*in the general case*. . . ."[13] According to
Dr. Vickers, this is an implication of the Reformation and its
understanding of "the individual person. . . ."[14] You would have
to conclude that his language is a bit vague. It would not be easy
for a social reformer to reconstruct society's economic institutions
by using Dr. Vickers' definition as his guideline.

Dr. Vickers' sole defense of his own view of property rights is
that apparently it was the same view which was put forward by
those during the period of the Reformation. This historical assertion, however, is a debatable point. Private property rights had
major support during the Reformation. According to Gottfried
Dietze,

the Reformation was probably the most revolutionary event in modern
church history. It challenged the most powerful church on the earth. It

---

10. In an age when the communist philosophy of ownership pervades the
Church, it is not surprising to find attempts to abolish previously accepted doctrines condemning socialism. Thus, the Reformed Churches which adhere to the
Belgic Confession are embarrassed by its condemnation of the Anabaptist movement to the extent that some have altered this article of faith.

11. Vickers, *op. cit.*, p. 113.

12. *Ibid.*, p. 126.

13. *Ibid.*, p. 292, emphasis in original.

14. *Idem.*

brought forth strong denunciations of the wealth of that church combined with exhortations that the clergy lead a more modest life. It seemed, by threatening an institution that owned great material wealth and by criticizing the use of that wealth, to question the institution of property. But it did not do so. Throughout the Reformation, private property continued to be considered an ethical value. In fact, the bases for its protection were expanded. Catholic thinkers had contented themselves with claiming that property was protected mainly by natural law. Protestant theologians also emphasized that property was sanctioned by the Scriptures. Not merely a broader justification was rendered, but also, the function of property to promote progress was stressed to a greater extent. With this emphasis, the Reformation stimulated the industry and energy of men, and had no small influence upon the rise of such powers as the Netherlands, England, Sweden, the United States and Germany.[15]

There is no reason to accept Dr. Vickers' assertion about the Reformation's supporting his view of property ownership. To be true, there was a movement which called for the commonality of goods, but the mainline Reformers saw the falsity of the idea and argued against it on Biblical grounds. Luther, for example, supported the idea of private ownership as against some form of public ownership, which in reality is what Dr. Vickers is advocating. If property rights only inhere "in the general case," then what happens to the exceptions? More importantly, *who* is to decide which are the general cases and which are the exceptions? Dietze continues:

Luther's support of private property was matched by John Calvin. . . . He realized that common ownership is utopian and denounced the Anabaptists' plan to abolish property and inequality. God the supreme legislator, by decreeing 'Thou shalt not steal,' ordained the protection of property. What each individual possesses has not fallen to him by chance, but by the distribution of the Sovereign Lord of all. . . . The state should see to it that every person may enjoy his property without molestation. The prince who squanders the property of his subjects is a tyrant.[16]

---

15. Gottfried Dietze, *In Defense of Property* (Baltimore, Maryland: The John Hopkins Press, 1971), p. 17.

16. *Ibid.*, p. 18.

One suspects that Dr. Vickers would not totally disagree with this. After all, he is not trying to be against private property as such "in the general case." It is only those instances which deny his economic ideas of "conservation, development, and equity" which must be brought under exterior control. But let us look at what Dr. Vickers advocates in the way of interference before we make our decision about his position.

Defining Away One's Problems

After making the effort in one part of his book to say he agrees with private ownership, Dr. Vickers now qualifies this by saying that "corrective and regulatory economic action is, from time to time and in specifiable circumstances, necessary on the part of the state. . . ."[17] Since there are "legitimate and necessary economic functions of the state,"[18] there should be "suitable compensatory economic policy action . . . taken"[19] by the "government authorities and their economic advisers" who must "be alert to the need for prompt and effective action. . . ."[20] After all, the State is a "God-ordained institution for the restraint of evil and the *right ordering of social affairs* . . . it is properly within the province of the economic responsibilities of the state to *regulate and control* the limits of uninhibited action of individuals in such a way that the economic health and stability of the system as a whole will be preserved."[21]

What Dr. Vickers is saying that "*oversight of the economic health of the system must reside in the central government authorities* acting on behalf of the people"[22] who must attempt a "skillful diagnosis"[23] of the economy so that "a sensible mixture of compensatory economic policies" may be applied.[24]

---

17. Vickers, p. 75.
18. *Idem.*
19. *Ibid.*, p. 185; cf. p. 186.
20. *Ibid.*, p. 188.
21. *Ibid.*, pp. 188, 191, emphasis added; cf. pp. 291, 343.
22. *Ibid.*, p. 205, emphasis added.
23. *Ibid.*, p. 206.
24. *Ibid.*, p. 207.

In other words, there are deep flaws in the free market, and God has given well-trained Keynesian economists the necessary insights to compensate for these weaknesses in the market. They will be able to use the coercive power of the State to bring full employment and economic justice into an otherwise unstable and unmerciful free market order. And this can be done without creating a monster of bureaucratic efficiency or a totalitarian State. How, he does not say. It just can be. Trust him.

Socialism?

Socialism? Initially, it sounds like it. But before Dr. Vickers may be accused of being a socialist, heed this disclaimer: "To object with a cry against an imagined socialism at this stage is quite beside the point."25 (Touchy, isn't he? Ready to warn us against calling him a socialist. No one has called him a socialist . . . yet. At this point I cannot resist citing Proverbs 28:1: "The wicked flee when no man pursueth.") This is not socialism he is calling for. Oh, no! It is just your imagination — and mine! — which *thinks* he wants socialism. No, he has just told us he is all in favor of personal property rights. After all, the authorities must have "adequately good reason" for usurping the rights and prerogatives of individuals. They must "satisfactorily meet the burden of proof" to show that reasons do exist for their interference.26 In fact, "*very good* and *rigorously necessary* reasons must be found to exist before the state can properly assume and perform those economic functions which can be shown to be well within the normal domain of individual responsibility."27

At this point it is probably worth recalling Dr. Vickers' verbal commitment to Reformed Christianity and the work of Cornelius Van Til. If Dr. Vickers were consistent at this point, he would remember Van Til's observations that "proof" is already contained within the presupposition with which thinking commences.

---

25. *Ibid.*, p. 191.
26. *Ibid.*, p. 295.
27. *Ibid.*, p. 293, emphasis added.

Therefore, if we begin with the premise that government regulation is needed, "proof" will always be forthcoming to justify the regulations. Alternately, if we begin with the premise there should be no government control, we will always "prove" that regulations are unnecessary. Where we need to begin is with the Bible. What does the Bible reveal *specifically and concretely* about the role of the State in economic affairs? That question, above all other questions, is the one Dr. Vickers avoids.

Dr. Vickers is committed to the idea that regulatory interference is necessary in the economy. It is indicative of Dr. Vickers' concept of proof that the only reason he gives for State regulations is the statement that "we live also in a fallen society, and our economics must therefore be the economics of a fallen society."[28] As a result of this fallen condition, "our modern economies . . . are inherently unstable."[29] There are, he says, "inherent instabilities in the mixed capitalist economic system. . . . [T]he mixed capitalist enterprise system with which we are familiar is inherently unstable."[30] As I read him, I seem to get the impression that he regards capitalist economies as inherently unstable. I hope no one will accuse me of exaggeration. In the light of all this, Dr. Vickers wants to "suggest that the time has come, such are now the accumulated pressures to economic disorder, for *new guidelines* to be laid down *for permissible private economic behavior* in certain instances. . . . [W]e do call for *new kinds of regulatory frameworks* within which individual economic activity can function. . . ."[31]

Why are capitalist economies inherently unstable? He does not say. Marx tried to say, but hardly anyone takes Marx's economic analysis seriously any longer.[32] More to the point, why are capitalist economies more unstable than socialist economies? He

---

28. *Ibid.*, p. 234.
29. *Ibid.*, p. 212.
30. *Ibid.*, pp. 213, 223.
31. *Ibid.*, p. 337, emphasis added.
32. Anyone who does owes it to himself to read Eugen Böhm-Bawerk's 1896 essay, "Unresolved Contradiction in the Marxian Economic System," in *The Shorter Classics of Böhm-Bawerk*, Vol. 1 (South Holland, Illinois: Libertarian Press, 1962). This essay has also been titled, *Karl Marx and the Close of His System*.

does not even raise the question. Most to the point, why are un-hampered free market economies more inherently unstable than Keynesian-guided economies? He does not demonstrate this any-where in his books. He merely *assumes* it.

Keynesian Assumptions

He is following in the footsteps of his more famous humanist peers. When it comes to explaining why recessions and depres-sions take place, they have no consistent explanations, either. As Garrison remarks, "In the typical treatment of macroeconomic phenomena, the variation in final output is attributed to the ex-tent to which resources, both capital and labor, are idle. This is the standard textbook rendition of Keynesian theory. The exist-ence of unemployed resources on an economy-wide basis is simply assumed."[33] Yet it is not simply that they assume that resources under capitalism are idle. It is that they do not offer a theoretical explanation for the *successful* use of *all the other* resources. The crucial question is: Why shouldn't *all* resources be idle? This was F. A. Hayek's question to Keynes half a century ago — a question which still remains unanswered in terms of Keynesian economic analy-sis. "The situation seems here to be that, before we can explain why people commit mistakes, we must first explain why they should ever be right."[34]

Keynesians assume that resources will be idle under unham-pered capitalism. They cannot explain precisely why. "Textbook Keynesianism may be able to show how variations in final output are related to variations in resource idleness, but it cannot explain why there should be resource idleness in the first place."[35] It is as if Dr. Vickers and his peers have never bothered to read W. H.

---

33. Roger Garrison, "A Subjectivist Theory of a Capital-using Economy," in Gerald P. O'Driscoll, Jr. and Mario Rizzo, *The Economics of Time and Uncertainty* (London: Basil Blackwell, 1985), p. 175.

34. F. A. Hayek, "Economics and Knowledge," *Economica*, IV (new series, 1937); reprinted in Hayek, *Individualism and Economic Order* (Chicago: University of Chicago Press, 1948; London: Routledge & Kegan Paul, 1949), p. 34.

35. Garrison, *op. cit.*, p. 175.

Hutt's book, *The Theory of Idle Resources* (1939).[36] Hutt argued brilliantly that there can be no such thing as an idle resource. Every scarce economic resource is owned by someone. Every resource is therefore the object of purposeful human action. People may keep resources off the market, but they have reasons for doing so. Keynes never replied to Hutt. He at least had an excuse: he was running Britain's monetary policy during World War II. His disciples have no excuse.

If the economic model used by the Keynesians does not tell us "where the market went wrong"—and the analytical bankruptcy of Keynes' supposed refutation of Say's Law indicates that he had no such model—then they are stuck with some other model, or even worse, no model at all. What we need is explanations, not assertions. If the market economy employs resources efficiently in the vast majority of cases (which Keynes never denied), then how does it accomplish this? What explanatory device can the Keynesians offer which shows that the free market is almost always successful in employing resources, yet not quite successful enough so as to allow us to dispense with the services of an ever-growing army of economic planners?

How Private Should Ownership Be?

Private ownership? It depends, after all, on how you define it. Dr. Vickers is happy to concede private ownership, *if* the individual's actions are subservient to those of some regulatory agency of the State. This is not the kind of ownership which the Bible talks about, when even the King may be refused his request.

Imagined socialism? Far from it. Dr. Vickers is advocating government economic planning. What is socialism if not this? His arguments are the same tired arguments that Marx and Engels used—the alleged anarchism of free market production and distribution—and his conclusions are similar: more government control over this supposed anarchy. Nevertheless, he prefers to call his system "Christian economics." Why? Does his reluctance to

---

36. Second edition: Indianapolis, Indiana: Liberty Press, 1979.

place the more familiar name on his system stem from his concern that if his Christian readers really begin to perceive where he and his system are headed, that they will refuse to follow? Does he suspect that Christians are innately conservative and hostile to socialism because they read their Bibles, and the Bible utterly rejects anything that even hints of socialist planning?

He has a difficult selling job. He has to sell the benefits of the power State to people who recognize its origins: the pits of hell. He hides its origin by calling for mild planning, or partial planning. But in principle where does such control lead? To bureaucratic failure. And with each failure comes the cry for more controls, better planning. "It didn't work before, but it will work this time! Trust me!" What does he recommend as his Christian policies? Only these: ". . . industrial arbitration and grievance procedures . . . unemployment insurance . . . national education policies . . . [and] provisions to motivate and facilitate the economic and geographic migration of workers. . . ."[37] There should be redistribution of incomes through progressive taxation and inheritance taxes, monetary and fiscal policies to insure a "satisfactory rate and direction of growth," as well as "a certain amount of welfare expenditure," tariff and quota restrictions, and a "well-designed and well-articulated national policy on wages and prices is most decidedly necessary at this time."[38]

If this is not socialism, then there is only one other alternative. It must be *fascism* (called "National Socialism" in Nazi Germany). If we are supposed to call his recommended system the private ownership of the means of production, then it is private ownership with the *control* over what is done with those assets lodged in the State. This, historically, is what polite economists call "the corporate State," but which historians who understand Nazi Germany and fascist Italy are willing to call fascism.

To summarize, Dr. Vickers suggested policies are: 1) government-regulated money to manipulate the business cycle, 2) gov-

---

37. Vickers, *Economics and Man*, pp. 342-43; cf. p. 153.
38. *Ibid.*, pp. 319, 340, 150, 294, 298-310, 317, 228, 229, 180.

ernment-planned fiscal manipulation to control the business cycle,
3) government-specified income and price controls, 4) government-
fixed exchange rates (foreign currency prices), 5) tariffs, 6) manpower control, and 7) industrial structure regulation.[39] Shades of
Karl Marx! If such a comparison is regarded by over-sensitive
readers as an exaggeration, then consider a few of the ten steps
that Marx proposed for the establishment of a communist State in
The Communist Manifesto: a graduated ("progressive") income tax;
abolition of inheritance rights; centralized credit in the hands of
the state; population redistribution; and free education for all
children in public schools.[40] We might well inquire just where Dr.
Vickers differs in economic principle from these Marxian proposals. The answer is: he does not![41] He would argue only about the
details and the *degree* of government control — and, of course, he
would reject the *label*. (If he thinks Marx was wrong in principle,
let him speak out in the name of God and His word against a central bank, against public education, against the progressive [grad-
uated] income tax, against all inheritance taxes, and so forth. If
the shoe doesn't fit, don't wear it. Take it off. Publicly.)

The Corporate State

This is not to say that Dr. Vickers is uniquely a socialist in the
midst of a nation of true-blue capitalists. The doctrines of socialism have taken over the thinking of most voters and their elected
representatives, despite their free market rhetoric. Norman
Thomas, the perennial Socialist Party candidate for President of
the United States (1932-48), complained after his vote total fell by
50% in the 1936 campaign that the Democratic Party had stolen

---

39. *Ibid.*, pp. 296-297.
40. Karl Marx and Frederick Engels, "Manifesto of the Communist Party"
(1848), in Marx and Engels, *Selected Works*, 3 vols. (Moscow: Progress Publishers,
1969), I, pp. 126-27.
41. The connection between Keynes and Marx has been well documented by
Paul Mattick in his book *Marx and Keynes* (Boston, Massachusetts: Extending
Horizons Books, 1969). It should be of no surprise to find the link also exists between Vickers and Marx.

his party's 1932 platform.[42] Since that time, the Republican Party has stolen most of the platform provisions of the Democratic Party of 1936. So has every other political party in the Western world that hasn't adopted something even more socialistic. The fact that a lot of self-proclaimed defenders of free enterprise, including businessmen, refuse to recognize what they have become in the name of "the mixed economy" should not keep us from seeing what kind of economy that Dr. Vickers is really recommending in principle. The modern Keynesian "mixed economy" is the piece-meal road to socialism.[43]

The failure of economic planning is obvious today. It may not have been obvious to Dr. Vickers when he received his doctorate so long ago, but today the whole world knows. Central economic planning has produced slow economic growth, unemployment, and price inflation wherever it has been tried.[44] The theoretical case against socialist planning was made by Mises in 1920, and by Hayek in the 1940's.[45] The case has been strengthened repeatedly since then.[46] Don Lavoie's book asks the appropriate question: *National Economic Planning: What Is Left?*[47] The answer is clear: from a theoretical standpoint, nothing is left.

A wage and price control policy itself is sufficient for the creation of a socialist State. It was by means of price controls that the Nazis ran Germany.[48] It was also how the Allied Powers kept Ger-

---

42. William Manchester, *The Glory and the Dream: A Narrative History of America, 1932-1972* (Boston: Little, Brown, 1973), p. 207.

43. Ludwig von Mises, "The Middle of the Road Policy Leads to Socialism," in Mises, *Planning for Freedom* (South Holland, Illinois: Libertarian Press, [1952] 1980), ch. 2. The company is now located in Spring Mills, Pennsylvania.

44. *The Politics of Planning: A Review and Critique of Centralized Economic Planning* (San Francisco: Institute for Contemporary Studies, 1976).

45. Ludwig von Mises, "Economic Calculation in the Socialist Commonwealth" (1920), in F. A. Hayek (ed.), *Collectivist Economic Planning* (London: Routledge and Kegan Paul, [1935]), ch. III; Mises, *Socialism, op. cit.*; Hayek, *Individualism and Economic Order, op. cit.*, chaps. 7-9.

46. T. J. B. Hoff, *Economic Calculation in the Socialist Society* (London: Hodge, 1949). A reprint has been released by Liberty Press, Indianapolis, Indiana.

47. Cambridge, Massachusetts: Ballinger, 1985.

48. Hans Sennholz, "The Second German Inflation and Destruction of the Mark (1933-1948)," *The Journal of Christian Reconstruction*, VII (Summer 1980).

many near starvation, 1945-48.[49] If all prices and wages are regulated by the central authorities, *effective* control of the total economy (except the "black" or underground market, which is simply the free market still in operation) has passed into their hands. Using price regulation (wages being the price for labor), the State is able to decide what will be produced, bought, and sold; it can cause profits and losses, wealth or pauperism, thereby determining who will be producers and who will be workers; and it may actually determine where people will live and how long they remain there.[50] The wage control Dr. Vickers envisages is explicit. Workers "might even be taxed to the full extent of the amount by which their wage increases . . . exceed nationally established norms."[51] That, dear reader, is socialism with a vengeance! And if it isn't, then it is fascism. It is the economic system described by lawyer Charlotte Twight in her book, *America's Emerging Fascist Economy* (1975).[52] It is certainly not "imagined capitalism."

Even his call for managed exchange rates by "the monetary authorities [who] have reason to believe that too wide a fluctuation in the exchange rate" has occurred must be seen as a crucial move towards the totalitarianism of a socialist State.[53] In the words of F. A. Hayek, "Nothing would at first seem to effect private life less than a state control of the dealings in foreign exchange, and most people will regard its introduction with complete indifference. Yet the experience of most Continental countries has taught thoughtful people to regard this step as the decisive advance on the path to totalitarianism and the suppression of individual liberty. It is, in fact, the complete delivery of the individual to the tyranny of the state, the final suppression of all means of escape —not merely for the rich but for everybody. Once the individual

---

49. Nicholas Balabkins, *Germany Under Direct Controls: Economic Aspects of Industrial Disarmament, 1945-1948* (New Brunswick, New Jersey: Rutgers University Press, 1964).

50. See Sudha R. Shenoy (ed.), *Wage-Price Control: Myth and Reality* (St. Leonards, New South Wales: The Centre for Independent Studies, 1978).

51. Vickers, *Economics and Man*, p. 340.

52. New Rochelle, New York: Arlington House.

53. Vickers, *Economics and Man*, p. 233.

is no longer free to travel, no longer free to buy foreign books or journals, once all the means of foreign contact can be restricted to those of whom official opinion approves or for whom it is regarded as necessary, the effective control of opinion is much greater than that ever exercised by any of the absolutist governments of the seventeenth and eighteenth centuries."[54]

Conclusion

The policies suggested by Dr. Vickers are simply socialism in disguise — and not very well-disguised at that. But they are socialism in fact. Dr. Vickers does not admit that the Keynesian policies he offers are socialistic; instead, he tries to argue they are Christian. He does not prove his case that he is not an implicit socialist. He fails to see that regulations *must* usurp private ownership. As Rushdoony has noted, "Property can be alienated by expropriation, injury, *restrictive legislation*, and a variety of other means."[55] Dr. Vickers' claim that the "new guidelines" and "new kinds of regulatory frameworks" are not a call "for the specific control and direction of any person's economic activity" is deceptive, to say the least, if he implies these regulations can exist and, at the same time, maintain private property rights in the sense we have argued here.[56] By definition, *regulations must specifically control the individual at some point; otherwise they are not regulatory.*

Dr. Vickers will never be content until the supposed causes of disharmony are removed. He believes that government economic planning and regulations can remove many of these causes of disharmony. His policies move inexorably towards complete control by the authorities. We call such a system *socialism.* To give it any other name is self-deception.[57] Socialism is not a system of planned harmonies; it is a system of planned chaos.[58] To masquerade

---

54. Friedrich A. Hayek, *The Road To Serfdom* (Chicago: University of Chicago Press, [1944] 1976), p. 92, n. 2.
55. Rushdoony, *Institutes*, p. 497, emphasis added.
56. Vickers, *Economics and Man*, p. 337.
57. Mises, *Socialism*, p. 253.
58. Mises, *Planned Chaos* (1949); reprinted in *Socialism*, Epilogue.

socialism as "Christian economics" is an attempt to deceive every-one. Especially oneself.

6

ANTINOMIANISM AND AUTONOMY

*The Christian thinker, while he can in no sense devalue the impor-
tance of the individual and personal experience of the salvation which
God has set forth for His people in Christ, nevertheless is aware that it
is in the midst of the world that God has redeemed and established His
church. This world is the world over which God reigns as Creator and
King, and the Christian necessarily sees it as part of his God-given
task to understand, and where possible to influence, societal structures
so that they are brought into closer conformity with the scripturally
articulated preceptive will of God. It is not that it is proper to speak of
the fact or possibility of a Christian society. For society is fallen,
apostate, inherently and structurally pagan.* [1]

Here is the heart and soul of Dr. Vickers' world-and-life view.
He believes that Christ is a King, but that Christ's kingship will
never be manifested in time and on earth. Jesus regenerates men,
but regenerate men never have sufficient numbers or sufficient influence to reconstruct the world's pagan institutions along Biblical
lines. Therefore, since God's people will not be able to do this, Dr.
Vickers implicitly argues throughout his book, *God no longer has
given us a law structure by which we might reconstruct this world, and, even
more important psychologically for Dr. Vickers, a law structure which God
holds us responsible to promote.*

In order for us to establish that what Dr. Vickers is calling for
is a disguised version of socialism or communism, it has been nec-

---

1. Vickers, *Economics and Man*, pp. 44-45.

essary to determine what the Scriptural teaching is concerning property rights. The Biblical basis for private ownership was argued in terms of the Ten Commandments. At least two of those commandments established the right of private property, although private property is assumed by the other eight.[2]

Restrained by *Whose* Law?

It is indicative of Dr. Vickers' position that he does not give any consideration to Biblical law and the commandments of God. On the one hand, he declares that "as to the sanctity and the continuity of the moral law there can be no argument at all."[3] Nevertheless, in attempting to disagree with the Christian Reconstructionist position that there is an abiding validity in the detailed laws given to Israel unless Scripture itself modifies or sets them aside, Dr. Vickers draws the conclusion that as "we live in a fallen society,"[4] and that since "the economics with which we have to deal is necessarily the economics of a fallen society,"[5] it would be "a grave mistake . . . to imagine that economic legislation, at the conceptual or pragmatic level, is or can be legislation for a theocracy, in the sense, for example, in which God's people in the Old Testament economy constituted a theocracy."[6]

The preposterous yet inescapable implication in this line of reasoning is that *we* live in a fallen society but Israel did not; hence, we must not adopt Israel's legal code. Yet Dr. Vickers contradicts this when he correctly observes that "the scriptural address to the world is always an address to the world as sinful."[7] *Always?* This implies that Israel was sinful after all. Dr. Vickers unfortunately makes no attempt to reconcile the contradiction in his thinking at this point, or at any other point, for that matter. In

---

2. Gary North, *The Sinai Strategy: Economics and the Ten Commandments* (Tyler, Texas: Institute for Christian Economics, 1986).
3. Vickers, *Economics and Man*, p. 313.
4. *Ibid.*, p. 47; cf. p. 362.
5. *Ibid.*, p. 355; cf. p. 289.
6. *Ibid.*, p. 47.
7. *Ibid.*, p. 119.

his economic expositions, self-contradiction is a way of intellectual life.

Unshackling the State

Although it is true that what he *says* is contradictory regarding the validity of God's law, in reality Dr. Vickers is *against* the requirements of the moral law of God. We have seen this already in his willingness to forgo a Biblical definition (or even a free market economist's definition) of private property rights. There are two further illustrations of this.

The *first* is his call for progressive taxation. Dr. Vickers initially draws attention to the idea that Biblical taxation consisted of a poll tax, or head tax, which was an amount equally payable by all males twenty years of age and over.[8] He also observes that tithing was a *proportional* tax.[9] Yet, for the sake of what he calls "Christian desiderata of equity and justice," Dr. Vickers is prepared to argue that there ought to be "some kind of progressiveness in the taxation scales. . . . If, of course, we were legislating for an ideal society, or, again, for a theocratic order of an earlier kind, then a strictly proportional tax, such as the tithe, would probably be all that would be required."[10] In other words, Biblical law is irrelevant to a fallen society. We must ask ourselves: "Why?"

The *second* example is to be found in his contentions against North and Rushdoony over the Biblical requirements for "hard" money, money by weight and fineness of precious metals, specifically gold and silver. It would appear an appropriate method in disputing with someone, especially when that person substantiates his argument from Biblical texts, first, to set forth *accurately* his arguments and the verses used as support, second, show how

---

8. *Ibid.*, p. 314. This tax was collected only during a census, and a census was conducted only immediately prior to war. It was really a payment to God, not the State, for each fighting-age man was to give half a shekel as "a ransom for his soul unto the Lord" (Exodus 30:12-13). The money was to prevent a plague from God. See James B. Jordan, "The Mosaic Head Tax and State Financing," *Biblical Economics Today*, IV (June/July 1981).

9. *Idem.*

10. *Ibid.*, p. 319.

these verses have been misinterpreted, and third, to follow this with an alternative interpretation. Remember that Dr. Vickers' purpose in writing is "to contribute to a correction" of the North-Rushdoony perspective, which is the reason for the manner in which he has developed his argument.[11] With this as background, consider Dr. Vickers' treatment of Biblical texts, since he disagrees with North and Rushdoony.

Ignoring the Bible's Plain Teaching

A careful reading of *Economics and Man* reveals Dr. Vickers' unwillingness to take seriously the Old Testament. He apparently regards it, in the words of Dr. North, as "the word of God (emeritus)." It is a sort of discarded first draft. We do not have to take it seriously as a blueprint. When it says that something specific is evil, then we must begin our study of analogous evil in general, but only on the assumption that the generalized evil which we will derive from the specific example somehow will release the specific practice from the category of "evil." Thus, we can go right on doing what the Old Testament says is evil, but we can reassure ourselves that we are nevertheless honoring the principle concerning evil in general. In short, "Thank God for general implications of specific evil practices; they enable us to ignore the specifics." There is more than a faint echo here of the words which God spoke through the prophet Hosea: "Though I wrote for him ten thousand precepts of My law, they are regarded as a strange thing."[12]

Metallic Money

The Bible is very clear concerning the evils of debasing the monetary unit. Douglas Vickers is equally clear in his rejection of any such obvious interpretation of the text, though his arguments are not all that clear.

---

11. *Ibid.*, p. 241.
12. Hosea 8:12, New American Standard Bible.

How the faithful city has become a harlot, she who was full of justice! Righteousness once lodged in her, but now murderers. Your silver has become dross, your drink diluted with water. Your rulers are rebels and companions of thieves; everyone loves a bribe and chases after rewards. They do not defend the orphans, nor does the widow's plea come before them.[13]

Dr. North argues that Isaiah's criticism of mixing dross metals (base, cheap metals) with silver was a criticism of counterfeiting. Discussing the North-Rushdoony exposition of Isaiah 1:22, Dr. Vickers regrets what he perceives to be their error in arguing for a metallic monetary system from this verse. *First*, Dr. Vickers gives the *impression* that his interpretation of this verse is the same as Dr. North's,[14] but this is not the case. Dr. North has cogently argued that Isaiah 1:22 lists *specific* sins of Israel, thereby pointing to the underlying spiritual state of the people.[15] In context, there is no valid *exegetical* reason to assert, as does Dr. Vickers, that verse 22 should not be taken literally. There is a valid debating reason, however: the text points to the immorality of monetary debasement, which means the immorality of unbacked paper or credit money, which Dr. Vickers promotes. Therefore, ignore the text.

Dr. Vickers, in contrast to Dr. North, sees these verses only as an *analogy* of their spiritual condition. These two interpretations are *not* the same thing. Dr. North's interpretation implies an essential unity between the actions of the people and their spiritual state, whereas Dr. Vickers, by holding that their actions are only an analogy, makes the spiritual life of the people and their actions two distinct entities. Dr. Vickers' appeal to other passages of Scripture to illustrate this "analogical reasoning"[16] does not necessarily prove his case. Ultimately, it is the *context* of a particular verse which must govern its interpretation. Therefore it is possible to agree with Dr. Vickers that in Jeremiah 6:28,30, for exam-

---

13. Isaiah 1:21-23, New American Standard Bible.
14. *Ibid.*, p. 244.
15. North, *op. cit.*, p. 4.
16. Ezk. 22:18-19; Ps. 119:119; Jer. 6:28,30; Lam. 4:1-2.

ple, the Israelites are referred to as "brass and iron" and "repro-
bate silver," because the context clearly warrants this. But the
same is not the case in Isaiah 1:22, where Isaiah is clearly naming
specific sins. What Dr. Vickers is desperate to avoid is the obvious
conclusion: specific sins imply a violation of *specific laws*. This in
turn implies that men are required to obey these specific laws.
This is anathema to Dr. Vickers. Why? Because Dr. Vickers rejects Biblical law.

Second, irrespective of the differences in interpretation of this
verse, Dr. Vickers makes an incorrect conclusion that Isaiah 1:22
is the basis for the North-Rushdoony argument for *money by
weight*. "But the grave economic error that North and Rushdoony
have made, and the misdirection of scriptural economic thought
of which they accordingly become guilty at this point, lies in their
transition from the proper terms of the analogy to the supposition,
a magnificent *non sequitur,* that because money in Isaiah's time was
frequently in the form of metallic ingots changing hands by
weight, money should therefore always and only be of this
form."[17] Dr. Vickers is absolutely correct when he says such a conclusion would be "a magnificent *non sequitur*." But it is a conclusion
North and Rushdoony never made!

The Biblical basis for a "hard" money system is to be found in
what Gary North calls the "law of honest weights and measures."[18]
That law is found in Leviticus 19:35-36. I will have more to say on
this passage when I discuss the meaning of inflation; meanwhile,
it is sufficient at this point to note that the Scriptures speak of
money as *weight*.[19] In so doing, God is declaring what the legal
basis of money shall be: a commodity which possesses precisely
the weight and fineness that are announced on an ingot or coin or
other shape. This immediately takes the decision out of the domain of man. Neither the State nor private citizens have the right

---

17. Vickers, *Economics and Man*, p. 245.
18. North, p. 6.
19. Rushdoony, *Institutes*, pp. 468-473; cf. Rushdoony, "Hard Money and
Society in the Bible," in Hans F. Sennholz (ed.), *Gold is Money* (Westport, Conn.:
Greenwood Press, 1975), pp. 157-175.

to declare dross the economic equivalent of precious metal. But Dr. Vickers gives no consideration to this passage of Scripture. It is as if this verse does not exist in his thinking. But since he perceives an error on the part of some Christians for using the verse to argue for a gold or silver monetary unit, he has an obligation to point out the correct interpretation of the verse to highlight the error.

The argument for a "hard" monetary system is *not* based on Isaiah 1:22 as such. Isaiah 1:22 is simply a *case-law application* of the general prohibition against false weights and measures. Isaiah declared a specific application of this law of weights and measures by pointing out that the *secret* debasment of *any* economic asset is a sin. Passing off diluted silver as the real thing is something for which they will be judged, declared the prophet. His challenge included the practice of monetary debasement, but it did not apply exclusively to such a practice. Water-diluted wine was equally sinful.

Here is another fine example of how Dr. Vickers leads the trusting reader away from the facts, so that Dr. Vickers may substantiate his own opinion. We have already noted that he has misstated the classical idea of "the invisible hand," and how he has argued against a non-existent version of the harmony of interests. We see at this point he has again used the same device — misstatement — in his disagreement with those who want to re-establish "hard" money in society. The device of misstating the position of those with whom he disagrees allows Dr. Vickers to present what appears, on the surface, to be a scholarly and Christian presentation of Biblical economic theory. In reality, it is a debate tactic which he uses, perhaps unintentionally, to avoid the real arguments, and it also enables him to ignore completely the requirements of Biblical law.

If Dr. Vickers is genuinely interested in "equity," and if he has a sincere desire to promote justice in economics, then he will stand on the solid foundation of Scripture[20] and declare that the use of false balances is *oppression*.[21] Instead of the words of modern

---

20. Matt. 7:24.
21. Hosea 12:7.

academia, "In my opinion . . .", we could have the words, "Thus saith the Lord." Dr. Vickers has foolishly traded the Word of God for the autonomous word of man. Such a trade is unprofitable in the long (especially eternal) run.

Deficit Financing by the State

Does Dr. Vickers really believe that "the canons of justice and equity"[22] can be obtained from human reasoning? Apparently so, and this can be seen clearly in his argument for deficit financing. Again, he offers no discussion of the appropriate Biblical verses against debt.[23] The only argument he advances is that "it makes no necessary economic sense" to begin with an "*a priori* notion that budgets should necessarily be balanced. . . ." In fact, he claims, "it would be economically criminal. . . . such an action would be culpable in the highest degree."[24] In other words, "economic sense" takes precedence over Biblical principles!

Here we see illustrated the fundamental difference between the reconstructionists and all of their critics, both secular and theistic. The reconstructionists define "sense" in terms of what the Bible reveals. If the Bible tells us specifically that such and such is true — the six-day creation, for example — then we must accept this truth as our operating presupposition. We must then criticize all conclusions that are not consistent with this presuppositional starting point. This is the essence of Van Til's methodology. And this is why we must conclude that although Dr. Vickers may think he is a follower of Van Til, and he may choose to defend himself by occasional appeals to Van Til's name, in fact his methodology is radically opposed to everything Van Til ever wrote.

How Dare We Disagree?

Notice his attempt to motivate the reader by guilt manipulation. How dare we disagree with Dr. Vickers? To do so would make us "economically criminal" and that would be the last thing

---

22. Vickers, *ibid.*, p. 319.
23. Rom. 13:8, Deut. 15:6; compare Prov. 22:7 with I Cor. 7:23.
24. *Ibid.*, pp. 331, 332.

we would want, right? Such an argument is designed to make the reader feel reprehensible for having the audacity to suggest such a thing as a balanced budget. The Psalms say that "The wicked borroweth, and payeth not again" (Ps. 37:21), but Dr. Vickers pays no attention. He simply argues for wickedness in the name of Christian ethics.

Once we put Dr. Vickers' accusation in its rightful place, and ask "What saith Scripture?" we find a different answer from the one he is offering. Even if we take at face value his supposition that economics from a Christian perspective must be based on the three ideals of conservation, development, and equity, we find no substantiation of his Keynesian policy conclusions from Scripture. It is as if the Bible contained no *specific* teachings on disciplining and restricting the State. See, for example, his claim that civil government's policies and individual freedom are "subject to the preservation of the on-going development which the economic aspect of the creation mandate requires, and subject to the preservation of equity in the distribution of economic benefits."[25] The difficulty with this comment is that the Bible does not give a rate of economic development which is required by the creation mandate, nor does it provide any indication of what an equitable distribution of economic benefits would be, at least not in the sense that Dr. Vickers means it. The whole of Scripture implies economic blessing is a gift which God bestows upon the just (and often the unjust) in accordance with His Divine purposes. Attempts to enforce policies based on the ideas of economists, bureaucrats, politicians, and dictators are therefore an attempt to usurp God's functions. It is an endeavor "to be as God."

Legislating Keynesian Immorality

It seems as if the reality of the situation is that Dr. Vickers really would like the Old Testament left out of the controversy. Incredibly, he comes up with that old sinner's slogan, "morality cannot be legislated."[26] So what can be legislated, *immorality?* Where

---

25. *Ibid.*, pp. 334-335.
26. *Ibid.*, p. 219.

is he getting this principle from, Van Til's apologetics or a 1962 Hugh Heffner "Playboy Philosophy" column? Is he a Ph.D. in economics or a sophomore student in business with a C– grade point average? It is beyond belief! Here is a scholar who proclaims his adherence to the Bible and to Van Til, and yet he tells us that morality cannot be legislated. What then can be legislated? Of course! Neutral law. You know: the thing Van Til has spent his entire career arguing against.

Dr. North has said it well: "You cannot legislate anything *except* morality." A law says that you must do something, or that you must not do something. The law *excludes*. It does so on the basis of a moral vision. It does so on the basis of right vs. wrong. It is never a question of legislating or not legislating morality. It is inescapably a question of *which* morality. It is a question of *whose* morality.

Dr. Vickers likes Keynes' morality. No, not his homosexuality. He wants to legislate Keynes' *economic* morality, which we all know had nothing to do with his personal sexual tastes. (We all know this because it is a bit embarrassing as a Christian economist to find oneself aligned too closely with a pervert.) He argues that progressive taxation is justified in order to "institutionalize and make compulsory in a fallen society what there is every reason to anticipate would, in an ideal society, be done voluntarily. . . ."[27] This indicates clearly that legislation *does* have a moral basis. And with that idea we agree, for *all* legislation declares one action to be the right one, and others to be wrong. The purpose of legislation, therefore, is to impose someone's moral code on everyone else. The question we face is: *Whose* moral code do we want to be legislated? For the Christian there can only be one answer, for only God can declare what is right and wrong. He alone is the arbiter of what is moral.

Given the Biblical view of the law of God, it is surprising that Dr. Vickers would have us disregard it in favor of some "higher" set of economic principles. The law of God is called "perfect" and

---

27. *Ibid.*, p. 319.

"pure." Because God's laws are "righteous" and "true" they are to be desired more than gold, and in keeping them, we are informed, there is great reward (Ps. 19:7-11). The whole of Psalm 119, the longest chapter in the Bible, is devoted to declaring the glory of the law and statutes of God. Yet Dr. Vickers wants us to bypass these specifics in favor of economic principles originating in the mind of sinful man. That is the essence of humanism, making man the arbiter of what is right and wrong (Gen. 3:5).

Ah, Dr. Vickers would say. What the reconstructionists are arguing for is theocracy. But we don't want a theocracy, do we? Why, that idea was tried for centuries and led to tyranny every time. ("Even in ancient Israel?" I would ask. All of a sudden, I hear arguments that sound suspiciously like situation ethics. "Well, back then God wanted men to obey Him and honor Him publicly, in every sphere of life, including civil government. Today, however. . . .") No, what we need is democracy, the rule of the demos, the People, not theocracy, the rule of God. "Vox populi, Vox Dei"?[28] Well, no, not that exactly, but, but. . . .

Dr. Vickers rejects the reconstructionists' vision of economics because he sees what sort of foundation such a view of economics — or anything else — necessarily rests upon. The reconstructionists have drawn the line: *God's laws or man's laws.* Dr. Vickers does not want to step over that line in front of all his hell-bound Ph.D. peers. So he prefers to think that God no longer requires His faithful servants to draw such a line. He prefers to imagine that the reconstructionists are heretical, or at least seriously misinformed. He wrote *Economics and Man* to prove this. We therefore need to look a little more closely at Dr. Vickers' arguments against a theocracy, for therein, we believe, lies his central reason for ignoring the Scriptures as a source of details for economic policy and practice.

The Meaning of Theocracy

A "sign of the times" is the increased involvement by Christians in areas they formerly despised. Although the Christian

---

28. "Voice of the people, voice of God."

school movement is possibly the best example of this, there is also increased activity in the areas of politics, law, economics, and many other disciplines. In each case, there is some attempt to come to grips with the idea that the Scriptures, as God's revealed Word, contain principles which can be applied in these areas to give guidance on how we should live and act.

If there is a word that can quickly divide those who are calling for increased Christian involvement in society, that word is "theocracy." Dr. Vickers, for example, goes to great lengths to disparage the idea of a theocratic civil government. "It is a grave mistake . . . to imagine that economic legislation, at the conceptual or pragmatic level, is or can be legislation for a theocracy, in the sense, for example, in which God's people in the Old Testament economy constituted a theocracy."[29] Dr. Vickers is so obsessed with the idea that we must not, under any circumstances, imagine that we can have a theocratic civil government, that he reinforces this point several times in *Economics and Man*. After all, there is the "fact that sin is in the world, and that the economics with which we have to deal is necessarily the economics of a fallen society."[30]

It is a theme which he returns to in *A Christian Approach to Economics and the Cultural Condition*. Dr. Vickers recognizes that the Israelites, having been brought out of Egypt, "were given full, explicit, and adequate legislative guidance for the organization and administration of the economic affairs consonant with the theocracy that was thereby established. But we no longer live in that sense in a theocracy. At the initial point of our inquiry we must acknowledge that we live in a fallen world. Sin is abroad in the world and in the hearts of men. And that fact is determinative of the forms and structures and practical potential of the economic arrangements we see around us. . . . All our social, cultural, and economic prescriptions, explanations, and diagnoses must accordingly be those which are consonant with the fallenness of that society."[31]

---

29. *Ibid.*, p. 47.
30. *Ibid*, p. 355; cf. pp. 48, 74, 289, 319.
31. Vickers, *A Christian Approach to Economics and the Cultural Condition*, pp. 5, 180; cf. pp. 90, 126, 130, 154.

Let's get this straight. The Hebrews were given the law of God when they fled from Egypt. They were told to enforce these laws as a condition of their remaining safe in the Promised Land. But we are not bound by these laws because we live in a sinful world. Now it does not take a Ph.D. in logic to come up with the next question: "In what kind of world did the Hebrews live?" This is so obvious that it makes me wonder whether there may be a relationship between the hatred of God's law and the ability to think straight. This, by the way, is precisely what Van Til has argued for years: that the hatred of God *does* inhibit the covenant-breaker from thinking straight.

Dr. Vickers is not content with arguing against the idea of a God-governed civil government which enforces God's law instead of Satan's law (for there are only two choices, after all). He goes so far as to call any attempted application of the laws of Israel to modern society a grave mistake. "A social philosophy which insists on the contemporary normative status of the economic institutional arrangements of theocratic Israel is gravely in danger of overlooking two things: first, the fact that the prior economic question in modern times is more sharply related to the problems of economic stability, progress, and welfare in an economic structure of things which is naturally propense to disequilibrium; and second, that we have consistently to do not with the economics of a theocratic nation-state, but with the economics of an obviously fallen society."[32]

Autonomy: Self-Proclaimed and Legislated

We are still left with the question as to why there is such disapproval of the idea of a theocracy. There is nothing magic about the word "theocracy," after all. It means, literally, *rule by God*. The Greek word *theos*, God, is combined with *kratos*, meaning rule or sovereignty. A theocracy, therefore, is nothing more than the civil government's recognition that God rules, not man. It does not mean *ecclesiocracy*, the rule of the institutional church. It means

---

32. Vickers, *Economics and Man*, p. 362.

theonomy, the rule of God's law. This includes civil law, but is not limited to civil law. It includes every area of life — in short, in every area where God is sovereign.

Anyone who denies that God's law should rule over civil government implicitly is denying the sovereignty of God. This shocks traditional Calvinist predestinarians, who swear allegiance to the doctrine of God's sovereignty but who also cling to some version of natural law. Dr. Vickers is one such traditional Calvinist. This is why traditional Calvinists who don't like where Dr. Vickers is taking them had better rethink their own presuppositions regarding the law of God.

Dr. Vickers' arguments fall into the category of nonsense. To assert that we cannot have the laws of Israel today because *we* live in a fallen society, is to declare that Israel was not a fallen society. Nothing could be further from the truth: to the contrary, it was precisely because of sin that the law of God was given in the first place. Man, in his rebellion, becomes his own God, determining for himself what is right or wrong, good or evil (Gen. 3:5). But then God appears and declares that He is the one who rightfully determines what is right or wrong. Here, by the way, is the list: don't have other gods; no idols; don't misuse My name; honor parents, wives and neighbors, and so forth (Ex. 20:1-17).

There is one way to explain why Christians deny that men need a theocracy, meaning the rule of God's law in every sphere of life: they still cling to the *humanist Greek idea* that after all is said and done, we human beings, though we are sinful, are capable of making our own way in life without consulting or enforcing God's law. Yes, we do need some Biblical principles to guide us, but these principles are fortunately so vague as to leave *us* with the necessity of determining what is right or wrong. In short, *fallen man is autonomous*. Fallen man is sovereign. His law-order testifies to this sovereignty — a law-order which we Christians must promote in the name of democratic pluralism.

This is precisely what fallen men have been saying since Adam and Eve ate the forbidden fruit. The anti-theocrats have always joined hands with the pagan God-haters and covenantbreakers, and they have declared together: "We want to live under *any* law but Old Testament law." In short, the anti-theocrats are inescapably antinomians — anti-God's law — and therefore they have become implicitly the defenders of the idea of autonomous man.

Freedom Under God

Does a theocracy lack checks and balances, as some critics have argued? Nothing could be further from the truth. There are clearly defined and delineated roles for the State, for the priesthood, for the tribe of Levi, and for the family. For example, taxes are limited (Ex.30:11-16), people are told to be charitable to their neighbors who are not as fortunate as they (Deut. 14:22-29), debts are for a limited period only (Deut. 15:1-6), and the list goes on.

Rushdoony has pointed out that "Few things are more commonly misunderstood than the nature and meaning of theocracy. It is commonly assumed to be a dictatorial rule by self-appointed men who claim to rule for God. In reality, theocracy in Biblical law is the closest thing to radical libertarianism that can be had."[33] A theocracy does not mean totalitarian rule by some human person or institution. Neither does it lack checks and balances. It is the fact that the Scriptures lay down *limited* functions for *all* earthly institutions which provides the necessary checks and balances in a fallen world. For example, it is because the Scripture forbids even the civil authorities taking property which belongs to someone (I Kings 21:3,20; cf. Ex. 20:15) that a person may find refuge and security in possessing the property in the first place. Understandably, *socialism-promoting anti-theocrats within the church are repelled by this very limitation of State power.* They hate Biblical law because they love the State.

A theocratic civil government is one which acknowledges the God of Scripture as the source of all legitimate power and authority. Writes Rushdoony: "There are thus a variety of spheres of

---

33. *The Meaning of Theocracy*, Chalcedon Position Paper No. 15, available from Chalcedon, P.O. Box 158, Vallecito, CA 95251.

government under God. These spheres are limited, interdependent, and under God's sovereign government and law-word. They cannot legitimately exceed their sphere."[34] From the human perspective, there are several institutions, each with equal authority, the functions of which are carefully set forth in Scripture.

Highest Law

A theocracy, therefore, is simply a nation which acknowledges a higher law than what the State can legislate or than what autonomous men can conceive of—specifically, the law of God. This is not some vague natural law concept of the law of God, a law supposedly equally understood by fallen men everywhere. It refers instead to the revealed law of God, Old and New Testaments.[35] Romans 13 speaks of civil magistrates *everywhere* being servants (Greek: *diakonos*) of the Living God. As servants, they are not free to make their own rules and regulations. They are required to acknowledge the law of their Maker. But if *all* men everywhere are to be obedient to the law of God, then all nations are in essence theocracies. "*If* a 'Theocracy' is a nation under *obligation* to enforce God's law, then Scripture teaches . . . that *all* nations are 'Theocracies.' "[36]

To argue against a theocracy is to argue against having the law of God as our rule and guide. It is, in other words, denying the God whom we say we worship. It is also contradictory on the part of those who on the one hand say they want Scripture applied to every area of life, and who then insist that "we don't want any kind of a theocracy." This is muddled reasoning.

What we need to learn is that although ideas in general are talked about, those who deny the idea of a theocracy do not want to be too specific about what the Bible teaches. On the one hand, it is simple to say we should apply the Scriptures to every area of

---

34. *Idem.*

35. Greg L. Bahnsen, *By This Standard: The Authority of God's Law Today* (Tyler, Texas: Institute for Christian Economics, 1985).

36. Greg L. Bahnsen, *Theonomy in Christian Ethics* (2nd ed.; Phillipsburg, New Jersey: Presbyterian & Reformed, 1984), p. 431, emphasis in original.

life and thought, but then we need to ask some *specific* questions. Should a 30-year mortgage be taken in order to get a home? Should pieces of paper with pictures of politicians on them serve as currency? What should be done with a murderer? Should a thief be jailed or made to repay what he has stolen? What is a "just" rate of taxation? Ten percent, or something like the fifty percent levels currently applicable in the Western democracies? What should the civil magistrate do with homosexuals? (Read their economics books? Make them advisors to the British Treasury?) Who is to decide these things? As Christians we say God determines them; but if this is true, let us be *specific* about the answers.

By What Standard?

The difficulty many Christians have in providing specific Biblical answers arises because Christians want to deny the validity of large portions of the Bible. Too many have bought the lie that the laws of Israel were only given for Old Testament Israel. They believe these laws were not given to the gentile nations, either then or now. But if this is the case, what did Jonah preach to Nineveh? Could he have asked the Ninevites to turn to obedience to Jehovah unless His law was the standard by which they should live? If God's law was given to Nineveh, then the laws of Israel *were* intended for those outside that special nation.

God, through the prophet Amos, condemned the nations surrounding Israel for their sin. Because sin is simply disobedience to the law of God (I John 3:4), it is reasonable to conclude that God intended nations outside Israel to keep His law.

Is it possible to preach a message of repentance without *first* detailing the law of God? "This is the standard from which you have departed; you should turn back to it." That is what repentance is all about. Is it any wonder that we hear little today about the need for repentance? The talk now is about "accepting Christ" or "make a decision for Jesus." But wherein lies the call for repentance, for turning away from that which *is* evil unto that which *is* righteous, the law of God?

Having denied God's "royal law" (James 2:8) in favor of humanistic law, modern Christianity has abandoned its basis of appeal to the lost. It can no longer show a fallen world how far short of God's perfect standards it has fallen, and therefore can no longer explain the need of a Savior (cf. Gal. 3:24). If man is not so bad, he might be able to pull himself into heaven by his own bootstraps after all.

To deny the idea of theocracy is thus to deny the law of God, and to deny the law of God is to undermine every essential tenet of the Christian faith. In short, we must say: No law, no God. No law, no sin. No sin, no Savior. No Saviour, no justification. No justification, no sanctification and adoption as sons and heirs of the Living God. No law, no justice and righteousness, for it is the law of God which defines what is just and righteous. No law, no eschatological fulfillment, for there is no need to make all things new. The centrality of the Biblical message is thus theocracy, the rule of God, as manifested on earth as it is in heaven: "Thy will be done." Or, in the words of Dr. Bahnsen, "Theonomy is pitted against autonomy; no man can take stand in between, for no man can serve two masters (Matt. 6:24). . . . We do not attempt to be as God, determining good and evil; rather, we gladly take our place beneath the sovereign Lordship of the Triune God. His word, not our autonomous reasoning, is our law. Theonomy is the *exclusive* normative principle, the only standard, of Christian ethics. It is all or nothing, ethic or non-ethic, obedience or sin."[37]

Conclusion

It is instructive to note that those who deny the validity of the idea of theocracy are usually silent on the *specifics* of living the Christian life. A growing number of Christians have been vocal in denouncing abortion, and rightly so. But to be a little more specific, if the Bible condemns abortion because it is murder, does it also tell the civil magistrate how he should treat such murderers? Or are the civil authorities free to determine for themselves how

---

37. *Ibid.*, p. 306, emphasis in original.

they will treat those who practice abortion?

A similar difficulty appears for Dr. Vickers. Having denied the idea of a theocracy in order to deny the specifics of Old Testament law, it should not surprise us that little use is made of the Scriptures to provide explicit guidelines on how our economics should be developed. We have observed earlier that Keynes was hostile to Biblical Christianity, and it comes as no surprise to find that he was not informed at any point by the light of Holy Writ. But to find a professing Christian paying lip service to the intellectual ravings of an economic, philosophic, and moral philistine is somewhat disconcerting, to say the least.

7

ECONOMIC LAW

But the scriptural principles do not imply that an inherited societal structure is necessarily, at any given time, to be regarded as being in full accordance with the preceptive law of God. To argue that they did would overlook entirely the pervasive operation in the world of the cankerous principle of sin, and the need for society continually to be returned to a closer conformity to the patterns of rectitude and integrity and righteousness that God has prescribed. [1]

In discussing Dr. Vickers' view of economic law, we must give initial attention to his view of Biblical law. He says that he is a Christian. He says that he is arguing Biblically. I argue that he is arguing humanistically, from start to finish, and that this implicit humanism is visible in his view of law, both Biblical and economic. He contrasts himself with Dr. North and Rev. Rushdoony throughout his book. He wrote his book to refute them. They believe in Biblical law and economic law. He believes in neither. This is the "bottom line" in understanding why Vickers' system makes no sense, either Biblically or economically.

You should pay close attention to his line of argumentation. First, no "inherited societal structure" is "in *full* accordance with the perceptive law of God." Obviously not. We live in a world of sin. No human institution since the Fall has been perfect. Is this any reason to argue that God's law doesn't apply? Shouldn't we argue instead that this is why God's law *must* be applied to institu-

---

1. *Economics and Man*, pp. 130-31.

103

tions? As we shall see shortly, *this line of argumentation becomes a smoke screen for lawlessness*. It places Dr. Vickers in the camp of the radical Anabaptists, who also have argued for four centuries that because of the sinfulness of human civil government and even church government, they are morally required to retreat from the responsibilities of applying God's revealed laws in society.

Second, he concludes that we therefore need to promote "patterns [ah, what a gloriously unspecific word — I. H.] of rectitude and integrity and righteousness." *Patterns*. Not the specific laws of God as found in the Old and New Testament, but *patterns*. It is all so vague. It is all so convenient. It is all so *lawless*. Dr. Vickers wrote this book to convince Christians that specific Old Testament laws are forever abolished; this is the message of the final chapter of *Economics and Man*. Dr. Vickers is a self-conscious *antinomian* with respect to God's specific, revealed, concrete laws.

Third, the specific, revealed laws of God will never be able to operate in society, and furthermore, they *should* not:

> In the third place, we mention again by way of summary a point which has already been made in earlier chapters. We do so briefly and without further argument at this time because the point does have critically important significance for the precise economic problems with which we have been concerned. This is the fact that we have found Rushdoony's argument consistently to commit the mistake of arguing from the sanctity and perpetuity of the moral law to the sanctity and perpetuity of certain of the institutional forms in which the pragmatic implementation of that law first came to expression. We have seen, for example, that this defect, which we saw in some respects to be associated with the economic arguments of Gary North, was instanced in Rushdoony's plea for metallic money and his view of the "immorality" and "theft" attached to "unbacked paper money," and to some of his propositions regarding scripturally admissable forms of taxation. A social philosophy which insists on the contemporary normative status of the economic institutional arrangements of theocratic Israel is gravely in danger of overlooking two things: first, the fact that the prior economic question in modern times is more sharply related to the problems of economic stability, progress, and welfare in an economic structure of things which is naturally propense to disequilibrium; and second, that we have consistently to do not with the

economics of a theocratic nation-state, but with the economics of an obviously fallen society.[2]

His logic, obviously, is preposterous. His contrast between the economics of ancient Israel and today's economics is nothing short of stupid. Anything this stupid is the work of a man who is desperate to avoid the clear teaching of the Bible regarding law. Question: Wasn't economic life in Old Testament Israel equally concerned with "the problems of economic stability, progress, and welfare"?

Furthermore, what is uniquely "modern" about a "structure of things which is naturally propense to disequilibrium"? Wasn't life in ancient Israel equally "propense to disequilibrium" from a Keynesian viewpoint, or equally propense toward equilibrium from a traditional free market viewpoint? Can you imagine Dr. Vickers standing in front of a conference of economists — Keynesians or any other school — and arguing that modern economics only applies to the historical world after the cross of Christ, and also outside of Israel prior to the cross, but that a different kind of economics applied in Israel from Moses to the resurrection? Reformed theologians such as Dr. Vickers' friend Meredith G. Kline have taught implicitly such a dualistic concept of law,[3] but Meredith Kline has never tried to be an economist.

Finally, wasn't "the economics of a fallen society" operative in Israel, *before* the death and resurrection of Christ? In fact, wasn't Israel even *more* sinful prior to Christ's resurrection? Didn't Christ's resurrection definitively *deliver* the whole world from the killing effects of sin? Aren't Christians working out *progressively* Christ's definitive victory over sin at the resurrection?

---

2. *Ibid.*, pp. 361-62.

3. Meredith G. Kline, *The Structure of Biblical Authority* (2nd ed.; Grand Rapids, Michigan, 1975), Pt. II, ch. 3: "The Intrusion and the Decalogue." Kline's position is implicitly a form of dispensationalism, but with the period of Moses to Christ as the "great parenthesis," rather than the Church Age. For an analysis of Kline's antinomianism, see Greg L. Bahnsen, "M. G. Kline on Theonomic Politics: An Evaluation of His Reply," *The Journal of Christian Reconstruction*, VI (Winter 1979-80); Bahnsen, Appendix 4 in *Theonomy in Christian Ethics* (2nd ed.; Phillipsburg, New Jersey: Presbyterian & Reformed, 1984).

What Dr. Vickers assumes throughout his book is implicitly heretical, namely, that *the post-resurrection world of Christianity is incomparably more fallen than the pre-Resurrection world of ancient Israel.* In other words, the revealed laws of God, as well as the laws of economics, no longer apply to the Christian world in the same strict sense as they applied in ancient Israel, because *today's world is uniquely fallen.* It is a fantastic line of argumentation, and he returns to it throughout the book.[4] Why? *Because antinomian scholars are in revolt against the law of God, and they will seriously consider even this line of reasoning, despite its obvious heresy, in order to escape their own responsibility to preach, obey, and convince the civil government to enforce Biblical law.*

This same willingness to accept heresy is true of pietism in general, and of the older fundamentalism in particular, whose theologians have had to reply on similarly flawed arguments to justify their own inaction and lack of dominion responsibility. But Reformed theologians usually distinguish themselves from fundamentalists, proclaiming their commitment to a broader historical and more well-rounded faith in Christ. They delude themselves.

What is important at this point is that the reader recognize Dr. Vickers' use of a three-step argument. First, this world is imperfect. Second, the laws of God therefore do not apply. Third, the laws of God will never rule society. What you need to recognize is this: *he also uses this same three-step argument to deny the existence of economic law.*

Imperfect Law Isn't Law

The key words in the following argument are "automatic equilibration":

We have argued at some length that the exigencies of sin in the fallen society with which we are concerned imply that there is no reason to be confident that, if left to itself, the economic system will automatically equilibrate at a high level of income, production, employment, and economic welfare. Our position implies, in other words, that we have no

---

4. Vickers, pp. 48, 73, 130-31, 357-62.

reason to be confident in the effective operation of the "invisible hand" of Adam Smith and the efficacy of the assumptions of automatic harmony on the basis of which the classical and neo-classical schools of economic thought proceeded. As we have seen, a more perceptive reading of economic history shows that a system of uninhibited *laissez faire* has never existed and cannot properly be expected to exist. The proper definition of the economic functions of the God-ordained institution of the state will therefore figure prominently in our analysis.[5]

I hate to bring it up again, but classical economics did not rest on the assumption of any "automatic harmony." No textbook account of the history of economic thought argues that classical economists (except the pamphleteer Bastiat) ever used such arguments. What classical economists did argue is that the competitive market pressures that are produced by the quest for profit serve as limiting devices. This free market competition places pressures on businessmen to serve the needs of customers. (If this argument isn't the essence of Adam Smith's *Wealth of Nations*, what is?) Not only is there no "automatic equilibration," the very *lack* of "automatic equilibration" in the market is what offers the hope of profit and the threat of loss to businessmen. If it were automatic, there would be no entrepreneurship, no seeking out of profit opportunities.[6]

The classical economists certainly argued that there is a *tendency* for prices to become equal, and for the rate of return on investments to become equal, and for wage rates to become equal *for the same goods, services and risks*. They argued — you won't believe this! — that if I can market a product for an ounce of silver per unit, and I try to sell it for five ounces, while you can also market it for one ounce, you will have an incentive to take away some of the sales I would generate. You will probably attempt this by selling units for something under five ounces a piece. *This is the essence of the classical economists' argument.* It was Keynes' "revolution" (following Parson Malthus, Chalmers, and a few other lesser-known *"temporary* general glut" economists) to *deny* that the market stead-

---

5. *Ibid.*, p. 195.
6. Israel Kirzner, *Competition and Entrepreneurship* (Chicago: University of Chicago Press, 1973).

ily clears itself of unsold consumer goods, unsold capital goods, and unemployed workers by means of this competitive pricing process. Dr. Vickers continues to argue as Keynes did: *inaccurately.*

This process of competitive pricing and *seeking out* profit opportunities is not "automatic." On the contrary, the very existence of profit and loss opportunities, argue the Austrian School economists, indicates that the market does not *automatically* do anything. It takes profit-seeking entrepreneurs to accomplish the so-called equilibration, which at most is a *tendency toward* equilibrium — a mental construct which can never manifest itself in history.[7] Dr. Vickers knows about the Austrian School economists. He wrote his book to refute Dr. North, and Dr. North follows the Austrians in their explanation of market pricing and entrepreneurship. But not a word of this line of reasoning can be found in *Economics and Man.*

Dr. Vickers returns to a similar line of reasoning (if it can be called that) which he used to dismiss Biblical law. Point one, he says that there is no such thing as automatic equilibrium, just as there is no such thing as sin-free societies today. Then he follows his previous line of reasoning. Point two, since there is no perfection — which everyone knows and no one has ever challenged, least of all Old Testament prophets or Adam Smith — he then concludes that there can never be a free market society which is capable of matching what State intervention can bring in terms of conservation, equity, and growth.

> Conservation, development, and equity, we have said, together exhaust the economic problem. . . . For to envisage the existence of a more or less centralized economic policy-making body which has legitimate functions to perform is to acknowledge that, as we recognized in our critique of historical classical and neo-classical economic thought, we have no confidence that if left to itself a complex economic system will automatically equilibrate at a condition of high employment, generalized prosperity, and maximum economic welfare. It will therefore be

---

7. It is not just the Austrian School economists who use such arguments. The classic formulation is found in University of Chicago economist Frank H. Knight's 1921 masterpiece, *Risk, Uncertainty and Profit.*

necessary to consider, at least in outline, what might be understood as the legitimate economic functions of the state.[8]

No Appeal to Principle

Let us review. Dr. Vickers has argued that because this world is sin-filled, the specific provisions of God's law, as revealed at least in the Old Testament, no longer apply. This means that we cannot legitimately appeal to the fixed law of God in order to reduce the power of the State, e.g., taxation above the 10% level or its imposition of fiat paper (or electronic) money. The State's law is sovereign over God's law, or "God's law (emeritus)."

Dr. Vickers similarly argues that because there is no "automatic equilibrium" in a real-world economy, it is therefore illegitimate to appeal to fixed free market principles in criticism of the State.

In short, *it is illegitimate to appeal to fixed principles in criticism of the State.* This, by the way, was also the opinion of Keynes. He hated principles, especially in sexual affairs — and I do mean *affairs* — but also in economics. Here is what he wrote in 1930 concerning economic principles:

All the same I am afraid of 'principle.' Ever since 1918 we, alone amongst the nations of the world, have been the slaves of 'sound' general principles regardless of particular circumstances. We have behaved as though the intermediate 'short periods' of the economist between our [one?] position of equilibrium and another were short, whereas they can be long enough — and have been before now — to encompass the decline and downfall of nations. Nearly all our difficulties have been traceable to an unaltering service to the principles of 'sound finance' which all our neighbours have neglected. . . . Wasn't it Lord Melbourne who said that 'No statesman ever does anything really foolish except on principle'?[9]

In Dr. Vickers' scheme, *all roads lead to the State.* There are only two roads for societies, once they have abandoned the fixed guidelines of Biblical law: into statist tyranny, or into lawless anarchy

---

8. Vickers, *Economics and Man*, p. 147.

9. Cited by D. E. Moggridge, *The Return to Gold, 1925: The Formation of Economic Policy and its Critics* (Cambridge: At the University Press, 1969), p. 90.

(from whence people flee back to tyranny). This is what both Rev. Rushdoony and Dr. North have argued for twenty years, and Dr. Vickers' book is a large grab-bag of footnotes proving their point.

At this point, we can begin to analyze the arguments Dr. Vickers uses in denying the existence of economic law. These constitute "point three."

Definitions

One difficulty encountered in analyzing Dr. Vickers' work is similar to that found in Keynes' *General Theory*. Anyone who has tried to read either book will know that both are singularly lacking in a logical arrangement of ideas. In addition, because there is a deficiency in definitions of terminology used, it is a mistake to imagine that words are used in their historic sense or in their usual meaning. Ideas introduced in an earlier part of Dr. Vickers' book are dropped for a while and returned to later on as if they had been explained. But nowhere does Dr. Vickers really *define* the terminology he is using. This means that it is very difficult to ascertain at times precisely what Dr. Vickers is talking about. In fact, it is almost impossible to come to grips with some of Dr. Vickers' views. Somehow we have to make our way through the intricate maze of ideas and weed out the various strands of his thought to determine what he means. In order to challenge his theories, there is the consistent need to discuss preliminary matters that have a direct bearing on the ideas propounded.

Economic Law

For example, a typical high school knowledge of economics, or even some ideas gleaned from the financial pages of a local newspaper or financial journal, would provide the thought that there are such things as economic laws, especially the laws of supply and demand. A common understanding of these laws would be that they are somewhat like scientific laws, in that they are a regular occurrence in the world, and come what may, the laws of supply and demand remain unchanged.

Dr. Vickers would like to challenge that belief. But "there does not exist a 'law' of economics in the same sense" as, to use Dr. Vickers' example, the "law of gravity."[10] True, the law of gravity is an unchangeable factor in scientific investigation, and any scientist wanting to send rockets to the moon, for instance, must take this law into consideration. Laws such as this allow the scientist to make the necessary calculations for such a venture, and the reason for this is relatively simple. If there were no laws in the sense indicated, this physical world would operate by pure chance, and if this universe is pure chance, the possibility of scientific investigation is, in principle, impossible. The physical sciences are dependent upon the fact that when scientists make an investigation, or conduct an experiment, there are certain "givens" which they can count on, things that will not change. Take as an example the attempts to place men on the moon. Certain calculations are necessary, based on the fact of certain "laws," one of those laws being in this case the law of gravity.

The idea of "laws" is inherently Christian in origin. It is no coincidence that the rise of scientific investigation has taken place in those countries heavily influenced by the Protestant Reformation.[11] Orthodox Christianity teaches that God controls whatsoever comes to pass according to the counsel of His own will (Eph. 1:11). It does not involve any violation of Scripture to make the deduction that we creatures may observe certain occurrences in God's universe and conclude that they will appear with some regularity. Observation then becomes the basis for determining the outlines of these regularities, and those things which do recur are called "laws." We do not hold them on the same level as the "laws" of Scripture, for that is the unchangeable Word of God. But on the creaturely level, we may rightly say that a regular occurrence is a "law" in that sense. What we must do, however, is consider that because these "laws" originate in the observations of finite human

---

10. Vickers, *Economics and Man*, p. 91.

11. For many citations to the scholarly literature, see the essays by E. L. Hebden Taylor and Charles Dykes in *The Journal of Christian Reconstruction*, VI (Summer 1979).

beings they *may* be wrong to some degree, and further observation might bring new evidence to light which could cause us to modify or abandon that "law."

Dr. Vickers, however, wants us to believe that there are no such laws as this in economics. There are, he says, only "statistical regularities."[12] Now, if Dr. Vickers means by this that we can never be absolutely sure that any "law" discovered by autonomous man will operate in the future, he may have a point, for man's knowledge, unless grounded in Scripture, cannot be guaranteed to be 100 percent correct. But this is not what he is getting at. He is also correct in arguing that we cannot discover a "one to one fit" between fixed law and the external realm. But this is also true for chemists, biologists, and every other scientific investigator. He may mean that men, being responsible agents before God, do not act in a predictable fashion. This, too, is quite true. This is what Mises and the Austrian economists have argued from the beginning.

So just what is Dr. Vickers trying to prove? He is trying to prove that the actions of men in a free market — an economy which is protected by law from violence and fraud — are not really predictable, *compared to a bureaucrat-dominated planned economy.* He is trying to prove that men who compete in a minimum-State free market environment do not usually produce goods and services that benefit their neighbors.

Free market economists have from the beginning appealed to economic law, by which they, too, mean statistical regularities, but they also implicitly mean "law" in a broader sense: *morally valid legal and institutional arrangements that promote freedom and therefore the benefit of men in society.* Only by denying the existence of regularities that are produced by acting *individuals* in a free market environment, can Dr. Vickers get us to accept those Keynesian theories he propounds — theories of human action that allow the State to step in and determine the true boundaries of the "latest" regularities, without reference to the law of God.

---

12. Vickers, p. 93.

Giffen's Irrelevant Theoretical Paradox

A closer look at Dr. Vickers' "proof" for the denial of the laws of supply and demand, what he calls an *exception* to the laws, is required in order to determine if he does in fact substantiate his allegation. Imagine, he says, a poor community which has a relatively low level of annual real income per capita, and which is forced to subsist mainly on potatoes, or some other easily obtainable food. The law of supply and demand tells us that if the price of potatoes drops, other things remaining equal, more potatoes will be demanded. Not necessarily, says Dr. Vickers. If the potato price drops, people would have more disposable income available to spend, and they may therefore purchase substitutes for potatoes. *Fewer* potatoes will then be demanded. With potatoes selling for less, there has been, Dr. Vickers accurately concludes, an increase in the *real* income of the people. But, adds Dr. Vickers, this purchase of "potato substitutes" may cause a diminishing of the demand for potatoes.

If such were the case it would have been shown that the fall in potato prices has led to a reduction rather than an increase in the quantity of potatoes demanded. In such an event the economist's normal law of demand would have been shown not to hold in that case at all. . . . But other possible exceptions to the normal law of demand could be examined. A reduction in the price of margarine, for example, may lead to an increase in the consumption of butter and to an actual reduction in the consumption of margarine.[13]

This statement is amazing. Dr. Vickers is saying that the way to run a clearance sale *may* be to raise prices instead of lowering them. (I can visualize the banner across the front of the store: "Selling Everything Fast — Prices Now Doubled!") We should note that he is not trying to deny completely the fact that lowering the price is the best way to attract potential buyers, but he is seriously suggesting there may be instances where price reductions might lead consumers to purchase other goods of a similar nature.

---

13. *Ibid.*, p. 92.

He is playing intellectual games at the expense of the reader's understanding of economics. Yes, *in theory*, such a thing is possible. In the literature, this is called the Giffen Paradox. It has been around for over a century. For instance, a consumer good may be very important in a poor family's "basket of goods." It is not a highly valued consumer good, but it is all this poverty-stricken family can afford. The price is lowered, so the family has extra money to spend. It is just enough extra money to enable them to reduce their purchases of this "Giffen good," and buy more of a good that they really wanted all along, but could not afford.

Let the reader be forewarned: during the last century of economic analysis, no economist has yet presented a *single example* of a real-life situation in which Giffen's Paradox has been demonstrated. Yes, when it is discussed at all, potatoes are usually offered as an example of "the type of Giffen good that might exist, *if* we could find one in real life." But no economist has ever offered any clear-cut example from economic history of potatoes being treated this way. The Giffen Paradox has always been an example of an intellectual peculiarity of economic reasoning. *But it has no impact in the real world.* Furthermore, it is such an obscurity in the history of economic logic that almost no textbook in the history of economic doctrines, thought, or analysis will even list it in the index. Yet Dr. Vickers is seriously offering it to buttress his case against the *real-world* operations of free market capitalism. His readers — the vast majority of whom Dr. Vickers knows will not have been formally trained in economics — are presented with an oddity of economic theory, as if it were a reality in economic practice. This should indicate Dr. Vickers' approach to economics: all theory (mostly inaccurate), no reality. All argument (mostly confused), no facts. His examples throughout the book are entirely hypothetical. *He makes them up as he goes along.* Quite frankly, so did Keynes. In short, *Douglas Vickers cannot be trusted.*

Unemployment

Dr. Vickers applies this same fallacious reasoning to the unemployment situation, and contends that a wage reduction may not necessarily cause an increase in employment.

For if action is taken to cause workers' incomes to be lowered, their expenditures must also be lower, and it must therefore be recognized that the assumption of a continuation of general expenditure levels is not compatible with the assumption of a generalized reduction of wage rates in the manner proposed. It therefore follows that rather than a generalized reduction in the price of labor inducing an increase in the demand for labor, precisely the opposite effect may follow.[14]

(Aren't you happy that you never had to major in economics? Aren't you glad nobody ever taught you to write this incoherently?)

I contend that Dr. Vickers simply makes up these examples. He *fakes* them. What does he mean, "if action is taken to cause workers' incomes to be lowered"? What sort of actions? By whom? With what results? If he means a single plant or firm, then workers will stay on the job only if they believe that this is the best deal available to them. If it really is the best deal, *then the employer had been overpaying them earlier.* Why not stop paying more for something if you get the opportunity? Workers certainly stop paying extra when they go shopping. That is what "sales" and "bargains" are all about, contrary to Dr. Vickers' "Giffen good" world.

But what if the workers see better opportunities, now that their wages have been lowered? They will quit. The employer will be given a lesson in market competition. His competitors will be given an opportunity to buy a resource from him: laborers.

General Wage Reductions

What is Dr. Vickers talking about? (I find that I ask this question to myself on almost every page of *Economics and Man*.) Is he talking about a *general* reduction of wages? How could such a general reduction in wages be accomplished? By an employers' cartel of virtually every employer in the country? Ridiculous! Imagine the cartel costs of holding that scheme together (let alone the astronomical costs of pulling the cartel together in the first place). You can see every employer joining, promising to hold wages down, and secretly thinking to himself: "All right, you idiots, go

---

14. *Ibid.*, p. 93.

ahead and drop the wages of your workers. Meanwhile, I will
offer your best workers secret cash pay-offs for quitting your firm
and coming to work for me." (Look, if Dr. Vickers is going to
argue throughout his book about the sinful greed of employers, at
least allow me to give an analysis based on sinful greed.) That cartel would last about a month. Maybe. Possibly less.

What about these general wage reductions? How general is
"general"? Every wage-earning worker in society? We have
already seen that a general wage reduction of this sort cannot be
sustained, and therefore is unlikely to be attempted, unless labor's
productivity has fallen, or unless the demand for labor's output
has fallen (e.g., in a tiny nation which exports only one or two
items, and which is also highly dependent on income from foreign
sales). He never tells us *how* general wages could be depressed by
businessmen. Wages can be depressed by governments, of course,
but then we are not talking any longer about free market capitalism. We are talking instead about *Dr. Vickers' recommended alternative*
to free market capitalism, the State-planned economy.

Local Wage Reductions

If he means that the wages of a few workers, or workers in a
region, or workers in a failing industry, can have their wages lowered, he is correct. Their wages drop because market demand for
labor's output has dropped. It is *consumers* who drop labor's wages;
employers are only the *middlemen* in the transaction between workers and consumers. Laborers, like retail sellers, understand a rule
of economics which Dr. Vickers constantly is at pains to ignore or
deny: "If you can't sell it, drop its price!" This law—yes, *law*—
applies to labor, too.

What Dr. Vickers is suggesting here is that a *specific* wage reduction may not necessarily be accompanied by a reduction in
prices generally, which we must admit is a theoretical, and often
practical, possibility. Maybe the firm which employs them is close
to bankruptcy. Maybe it needs a commitment from workers to
lower their demands for a while, so that the firm can get enough
profit to pay the bankers who are figuratively banging at the door.

Workers may be willing to do this temporarily in order to save their jobs, if the employer and his accountant can prove the case of imminent collapse. This in no way disproves economic law.

Local wage reductions that are not accompanied by price reductions in the goods and services produced by laborers who have their wages cut will usually result in lower sales and lower profits. The average reader may not understand this aspect of free market capitalism, but it is true. It is normally a mistake for businessmen to lower the wages of his workers unless there has been a drop in labor's productivity or a drop in the demand for labor's output. By reducing labor's wages, except as a last-ditch effort to save a firm or industry from bankruptcy, businessmen create a situation in which the more productive employees will begin to seek better opportunities. Businessmen wind up with the less productive workers. In short, *you get what you pay for.* If a businessman pays his workers as if they were low-productivity people, he will eventually wind up with a work force filled with low-productivity people.

Historically, capitalism has produced conditions in which high wages, low prices, and high profits accompany each other. This is what innovation is all about. This is why Henry Ford could revolutionize the automobile industry — and also the face of the West — when he raised workers' wages to an astounding five dollars a day, put them on a mass production line, and dropped the price of the "tin Lizzie" (Model T) to where the average Joe could afford to buy one. He became a billionaire. In short, *high wages, low prices, and high profits.*

Treating Workers as Idiots

Dr. Vickers argues that a lowering of wages may not increase the demand for labor.[15] Baloney. He is treating labor as if it were potatoes, and potatoes as if they were Giffen goods. Labor and potatoes are not Giffen goods (or services). (Nothing ever discovered has ever acted as a Giffen good or service.)

Let us consider a situation in which lower wages will not lead

---

15. *Ibid.*, pp. 269-270.

to an increase in labor services purchased. A firm is about to go bankrupt. The *quantity of labor demanded* is about to drop. Therefore, by lowering their wage demands, *the workers keep their jobs.* The quantity of labor actually demanded increases *from what it would have been had they not agreed to the wage cut.* Dr. Vickers may be able to provide statistical evidence that a drop in wages in some firm did not result in more workers being hired, but the statistics conceal the economic truth: had they not consented to reduced wages, *they would have been fired.* It is once again the case of what Bastiat called over a century ago *the fallacy of the thing unseen.*

We must begin with a reasonable presupposition: *laborers are not idiots.* This may not seem like a very remarkable insight, but Keynesian economic theory treats them as if they were idiots. The whole Keynesian "solution" to the great depression was to lower the *real* wages of workers by inflating the money supply, thereby forcing workers *unknowingly* to accept reduced income (higher prices, but fixed wages), instead of asking them, industry by industry, to take pay cuts in order to save their firms and their own jobs. Keynes thought that workers would not lower their *money* wages, but that they could be fooled into accepting lower *real* wages. Keynes even admitted that this was the nature of his little game: "Having regard to the large groups of incomes which are comparatively inflexible in terms of money, it can only be an unjust person who would prefer a flexible wage policy to a flexible monetary policy. . . ."[16] Cheat the workers, fool the workers — and anyone who isn't willing to go along with this nation-wide experiment in monetary debasement and deliberate subterfuge is an "unjust person." Spare me the moral lectures, Keynes; you are not well known for your moral vision. Not in Christian circles, anyway.

Conclusion

Dr. Vickers' conclusion that wage reductions might not result in an increase in the quantity of labor demanded is correct *only* if all other factors — including price levels — drop in the same direc-

---

16. Keynes, *The General Theory*, p. 268.

tion as wages. But if they do drop, then *real* wages have remained the same. In such a situation, what Dr. Vickers is arguing—a drop in *money* wages—is therefore irrelevant. But, then again, so is 90 percent of *Economics and Man*.

Dr. Vickers' argument that *lower* wage rates will cause *more* unemployment is not simply irrelevant; it is preposterous. It would be the equivalent of the "going out of business clearance sale" mentioned above. Imagine the employer's response to a trade union official who announces: "So you're going to fire us, are you? All right, we demand *double* our previous salaries. Now what are you going to do?" I will tell you what the employer will do, unless the civil government threatens him with immoral violence: he will fire them, *assuming that there are equally competent (or rapidly trainable) workers who stand ready to replace them at a lower wage.* And if there aren't, and the employer knows it, then his threat to cut their wages was simply a bluff. The workers should call his bluff.

Vickers: "But *State* Laws *Are* Laws"

One final comment is appropriate on his attempted denial of economic law: *Dr. Vickers does not really believe his own argument!* He *knows* economic laws do exist. In other contexts, he speaks of the "law of *absolute* advantage" and the "law of *comparative* advantage."[17] When discussing exchange rates, he concludes, without hesitancy, that "the price of any particular currency in terms of other currencies will depend on the volume of the demand for, and the supply of it. . . ."[18]

Question: How can Dr. Vickers conclude that these prices are dependent upon economic laws when he says the laws do not always operate? Furthermore, if they function in these instances, how does he know this, and can he be sure they always do? Answers to these questions are not to be found in either *Economics and Man* or *A Christian Approach to Economics and the Cultural Condition*, but on the evidence available, the only conclusion is that Dr.

---

17. *Economics and Man*, p. 227, emphasis in original.
18. *Ibid.*, p. 230; cf. p. 231.

Vickers *knows* the laws of economics are always found to function (other things being equal).[19] There can, then, be only one reason Dr. Vickers is prepared to present such a contradictory argument, and that is because *economic laws mitigate against the Keynesian system.*

Take Dr. Vickers' example on wage rates. He does not want wages lowered because that might lead to increased unemployment. (He cannot show why, however.) In other words, according to the Keynesians, *the only time economic laws don't exist is when they prove that Keynesian theories are wrong in theory and practice.*

The problem with Dr. Vickers' rejection of economic law is analogous to the Keynesians' failure to discuss why it is that the free market works most of the time. The main problem for the Keynesians is not to explain why the free market sometimes fails to clear itself of goods and services (i.e., allows unemployment); the problem is to explain by means of Keynesian theory why the free market should ever work at all. As Prof. Roger Garrison says, "we must know how things could go right before we can ask what might possibly go wrong."[20] The problem that Dr. Vickers needs to deal with is why there should be any statistical regularities at all. He also needs to answer this question: By what pattern of regularities will government planners govern the economy?

The denial of economic law is a necessary part of any socialist's armor. If there are no certain laws, such as the laws of supply and demand, chaos must reign in the free market. To remove this chaos, the Keynesians argue, let us have State regulation. In short, *the only reliable law is State legislation.* This is the essence of Dr. Vickers' arguments against capitalism and *laissez-faire.* (It is also the essence of modern Darwinism,[21] of which the

---

19. Vickers does not use the word "always." By "always" I do not mean in the sense of immutable, but rather that so far as man's experience extends the laws have been substantiated by "statistical regularity." Presumably they will occur in the future because of past regularity.

20. Roger Garrison, "A Subjectivist Theory of a Capital-using Economy," in Gerald P. O'Driscoll, Jr. and Mario Rizzo, *The Economics of Time and Uncertainty* (London: Basil Blackwell, 1985), p. 171.

21. Gary North, *The Dominion Covenant: Genesis,* Appendix A: "From Cosmic Purposelessness to Humanistic Sovereignty."

Keynesian system is a subset.) Recall his descriptive phrase concerning the free market, that market forces "gyrate uninhibitedly and randomly of [their] own accord."[22] Dr. Vickers wants us to believe that State regulation of the economy is necessary because of the market's apparent chaotic nature, and that his demands for conservation, development, and equity can only be met by regulation of the economy from the *top down*. But what makes the "statistical regularities" of State planning so predictable and scientific? What institutional controls need to be implemented to make politicians and bureaucrats trustworthy? Dr. Vickers never even raises the question.

Despite his assurances to the contrary, Dr. Vickers does not want the kind of society in which individuals are free to pursue their own goals. Why not? There can be only one reason: he believes *his* goals should be the goals of everyone in society! Keynesians want to impose *their* view onto everyone else. If they could prove that God's law supports them, we should listen, but this case, above all, is what Keynes would never have attempted to argue. He was self-consciously in revolt against God and God's law. This man-manipulating goal is the goal of all socialists, and Dr. Vickers, as we have seen,[23] is a socialist, if not of the first order (government ownership), then at least the second order (government control). Socialists are so convinced, for example, that it is somehow "immoral" for some to be wealthy while others are in poverty, that they insist that private wealth must be redistributed by various means, and the taxing system is the method Dr. Vickers would use.[24]

Tyrants through all ages have always thought their ideas superior to those of the common person. Plan as they will, however, the socialists cannot get past one undeniable fact, and that is that people *are* human beings who will act according to the way they think, irrespective of the rules which may be imposed upon them. They are inveterate "seekers after loopholes." They may conform for a time if sufficient force is used, but in the long run

22. Vickers, *Economics and Man*, pp. 234.
23. Chapter 5, above.
24. Vickers, *Economics and Man*, pp. 319, 340.

individuals always do what they perceive to be the correct action.

Dr. Vickers obviously likes "progressive" (graduated) income taxes. But at what level will he set, for example, the highest scale? Sixty percent, as we have in Australia? Perhaps he is a little more modest and would only want forty percent. The difficulty he will have, though, is that it is very well to tell someone he must pay a tax of sixty cents on the dollar, but if that person thinks this is too high, he is about to do everything possible to get out of paying it. It is no coincidence that tax avoidance and outright evasion abound wherever tax levels are on the increase.

Conclusion

It is never a question of laws vs. no laws. It is always a question of *whose* laws. It is always a question of *which* laws. It is always a question of whose ox gets gored. It is, in short, just what Lenin said it is: "*Who, whom?*" In a world created and maintained by God, it is this series of choices:

God's law or chaos
God's law or tyranny
God's law or God's wrath [25]

Dr. Vickers has no more proven his thesis that economic laws do not always exist than he has proven that the earth is flat, or that Keynes "refuted" Say's Law. It is just that in the latter case, he has not tried to prove it. But his attempts would meet with the same result. [26]

Again and again, when confronting Christian antinomians, we should ask them this question: *By what standard?* When they argue that God's revealed laws no longer apply, we must ask: *By what standard?* Who repealed them? On what basis? When they assure us that there is a better way to achieve social peace than by

---

25. Gary North, *The Sinai Strategy: Economics and the Ten Commandments* (Tyler, Texas: Institute for Christian Economics, 1986), p. 6.

26. See Eugen von Böhm-Bawerk, "Control or Economic Law," in *Shorter Classics* (South Holland, Illinois: Libertarian Press, 1962), I, ch. 3.

means of God's revealed law, we must ask: *By what other standard?* The fact of the matter is: *they do not like God's law.* They are embarrassed by God's law. They prefer to think that God changed His mind — about economics, politics, and morality. Especially morality. Keynes unquestionably had good reasons for hoping that God had changed his mind. He had good reasons for hoping that there is no God, and no day of judgment. He implicitly concluded: "No law — no God; no God — no day of judgment." It is understandable why the whole concept of fixed economic law, ordained by God, or fixed economic principles, ordained by God, would have been repugnant to him. Fixed laws reminded him too much of God.

What is Dr. Vickers' excuse? What is his reason for hoping that God has changed His mind and therefore changed His social laws? Is his reason primarily intellectual? Or moral?

What is Dr. Vickers' reason for thinking that God has not provided men with economic law? Is his reason primarily intellectual? Or moral?

And should we be surprised that both Keynes and Dr. Vickers wind up on the road to the central planning State?

8

FISCAL POLICY: DISGUISED COUNTERFEITING

But while monetary restraint can be quite effective in dampening excessively active economic conditions, it is doubtful that an easing of the monetary situation can be as effective in stimulating the economy out of a recession. . . . It is in such an economic situation that a heavier contribution from fiscal policy may be necessary, with the government taking action, via its budget policies in ways we shall consider in the next section, to boost the expenditure streams in the economy and thereby production and employment. [1]

Dr. Vickers' statement of the Keynesian position is characteristic of what Prof. Axel Leijonhufvud (no, I can't pronounce it either) identifies as the "revolutionary orthodoxy" branch of Keynesianism. He contrasts it with the "neoclassical synthesis" branch. "The orthodoxy tends to slight monetary in favor of fiscal stabilization." This is Dr. Vickers' position. Back in 1967, nine years before *Economics and Man* was published, Prof. Leijonhufvud commented: "As described, the orthodoxy is hardly a very reputable position at the present time. Its influence in the currently most fashionable fields has been steadily diminishing, but it seems to have found a refuge in business cycle theory — and, of course, in the teaching of undergraduate macroeconomics." [2]

Consider the implications of what he was saying. First, the school of Keynesian interpretation to which Dr. Vickers belongs

---

1. *Economics and Man*, pp. 305-6.
2. Axel Leijonhufvud, "Keynes and the Keynesians: A Suggested Interpretation," *American Economic Review*, LVII (May 1967), p. 401.

was by 1967 already out of fashion, not taken very seriously by the economics profession, and basically a thing of the past. Second, its members had been banned by their peers to the Siberia of the profession: teaching undergraduates and writing textbooks. Time plays cruel tricks on once-young intellectual revolutionaries. It turns them into fuddy-duddies. The methodological expropriators are expropriated.

Who is Axel Leijonhufvud? He is the author of the major reinterpretation of Keynes in this generation, which appeared a year after his essay.[3] Furthermore, the essay appeared in the *American Economic Review*, the most prestigious of all the professional economics journals in the United States, and therefore in the world, given the influence of U.S. economists. Leijonhufvud was announcing the demise of the previously reigning branch of Keynesianism, and he was doing so in the confidence that the bulk of the profession understood that he was correct. Those who refused to recognize it were precisely the aging holdouts whose opinions no longer counted.

What is ironic about the post-Keynesian revolution which buried the older Keynesians is that the older men continue to write as if they were still on the cutting edge of revolution, rather than under the cutting edge. They are rather like those aging neoclassical scholars in the late 1930's and early 1940's who expected "this Keynesian nonsense" to go away after the War. The major non-Keynesian scholars did recognize the challenge of *The General Theory* and tried to challenge it. They understood that a methodological earthquake was underway. It was the classroom teacher on the fringes of the profession who never quite knew what had hit him. So it is today. Dr. Vickers, as late as 1982, was still writing as if he were in the army of the innovators, in hot pursuit of the neoclassical Philistines:

> The outlines of this discontent are clear on only a minimal inspection. An earlier and comfortable orthodoxy has been shattered, and new

---

3. *On Keynesian Economics and the Economics of Keynes: A Study in Monetary Theory* (New York: Oxford University Press, 1968).

ways of looking at the world are being sought to repair the logical inadequacies and the empirical irrelevancies of economic science. Assumptions that the economic world was continually in some kind of describable equilibrium; that automatic harmonies existed and propelled the economy continually to positions of maximum benefit and welfare; that simplistic analyses that abstracted from the dynamics of real historic time could adequately explain observable states of economic affairs . . . these comfortable simplicities, these damaging illusions we might say, have been fairly completely shattered, and new paradigms of economic argument have emerged. The assumptions of equilibrium, of the presence in the economic system of so-called "risks" that could be assumed away by the application of a calculus of probability based on postulates of randomness and chance, of the safety in analysis of ignoring genuine time, have had to give way to newer perspectives. An earlier crust of orthodoxy has crumbled.[4]

What is astonishing about these words is that it is virtually at each of these points that the post-Keynesian economics revolution *against the older Keynesian orthodoxy* has been aimed: at Keynes' static model, at his ignoring of real time, at his model's de-emphasis of entrepreneurship. Even more astonishing, it is precisely on these points that the Austrian School economists have always concentrated their attack against Keynes, along with the static neoclassical equilibrium economics tradition *of which Keynes was clearly a part.*[5] Yet Dr. Vickers imagines that it is he and his retired Keynesian colleagues who are in the front lines of the offensive attack against stodgy conservatism. In the midst of a 20-year methodological rout of his army, retired Sergeant Vickers imagines that he is cheering on his old unit in a final charge against a nearly defeated enemy. If he weren't so arrogant in his confidence, he would be a pathetic figure.

The Flow of Money

Dr. Vickers leaves us in no doubt as to where he believes the heart of the Keynesian system lies. The "kernel" of the Keynesian system, says Dr. Vickers, is this: "The total level of the production

---

4. Vickers, *A Christian Approach to Economics and the Cultural Condition*, pp. 22-23.

5. Gerald P. O'Driscoll, Jr. and Mario J. Rizzo, *The Economics of Time and Uncertainty* (London: Basil Blackwell, 1985).

and output of goods and services in the economy, and thus the level of employment which producers and employers were able to offer, was dependent upon the total level of the flow of monetary expenditure or demand."[6] In a nutshell, *expenditure generates income.* "One individual's expenditure becomes, or generates, another individual's income."[7] This person's income, when spent, creates income for a second person, and so on. Thus, the total monetary demand is the amount of money flowing throughout the economy at any given time. So far, so good. Nothing too revolutionary here. Yet.

The deduction made by Dr. Vickers from this is that whenever a person refrains from spending his money, this causes a decrease in monetary demand and results in the loss of income to someone else. In turn, this results in reduced purchases, so businesses are forced to scale down their operations or close up shop altogether.

Let us be precise, that is, let us avoid Dr. Vickers' verbiage. "If he doesn't spend *his* money, I don't get *my* money." Alternatively, "If I don't spend my money, he doesn't get his money." Oh, yes, I forgot to specify that this is a *two-person model.* I want to be precise. I want to be scientific. I want to sound like a classroom economist.

In this form, the whole idea is a truism. This insight, plus a subway token, will get you a ride on the subway. But there is a hidden agenda lurking in the shadows. What the Keynesians really mean is that if I hoard my goods (represented by money), then nobody else will get access to them. Then we all stop trading with each other. The division of labor collapses, per capita productivity collapses, and therefore per capita wealth collapses. But wait, you say. To collapse the system completely, everyone has to hoard all his goods forever. Why would we all do such a stupid thing? Then you show absolute economic genius. You next ask: "If we all were to start hoarding, and as a result we all started to suffer a drop in our incomes, and therefore a drop in our wealth, wouldn't we drop our prices? And if everyone started dropping

---

6. Vickers, *Economics and Man*, p. 13.
7. *Idem.*

prices, wouldn't we start trading with each other again because of all the bargains coming on the market?" Now, smarty pants, you have just questioned your way out of a Ph.D. in economics from the University of Almost Everywhere. Or at least you would have, had you attended prior to the mid-1960's, when Dr. Vickers' crowd controlled the system.

The Refusal to Trade

Why won't I spend my money to buy what you want to sell? Here are the only reasons I can think of:

1. I don't know what you're selling.
2. You don't have what I'm buying.
3. Your price is too high.
4. Your price is acceptable to me, but I think you will take less later on.
5. The government has made it illegal (or expensive) to trade.

If you want to sell it to me, and my problem is ignorance, you will *advertise* what you have and the price you want (or are at least willing to accept). This costs you more money to make the sale, but you decide it is worth it. Your expenditure reduces my ignorance or lack of motivation, whichever is greater. (Salesmanship.)

If you do not have what I want to buy, you may be able to *get me to buy it anyway*, if you *lower the price* enough, or if you can convince me that there is someone else who will sell me what I want if I can offer him what you are trying to sell to me. (We are now at a three-person model, just for the record.)

If your price is too high, you can *lower the price*, or you can convince me that I really want it enough to buy it at the high price. (Salesmanship.)

If I think you will lower the price later on, you can either lower it now, or you can *sit and wait*. Maybe you *will* take a lower price later on. Maybe you won't. Time will tell. (But you probably won't wait forever to sell, will you? Something is better than nothing.)

If the government has made it illegal or too expensive to trade, we can both get together and *vote out the government*. Then we can trade. Or we can ignore the government, increase our risks of action, and trade anyway.

The Great Depression

What gave the Keynesian revolution its market in 1936 was the fact that for over six years, people all over the Western world had not been trading very much with each other. All the unpleasant results of a collapsing division of labor were manifesting themselves. People's incomes and their net wealth dropped. Why had this happened? More important to the average politician, what could be done about it? Actually, the average politician had already decided what should be done: spend government money. Keynes came along in 1936 to provide the academic justification for what they were already doing. (It took a world war to get the spending up, and the price controls on, sufficient to placate the voters.) Mises is correct:

The policies he advocated were precisely those which almost all governments, including the British, had already adopted many years before his "General Theory" was published. Keynes was not an innovator and champion of new methods of managing economic affairs. His contribution consisted rather in providing an apparent justification for the policies which were popular with those in power in spite of the fact that all economists viewed them as disastrous. His achievement was a rationalization of the policies already practiced.[8]

What had happened was that governments had done too much for the people . . . earlier. They had inflated their currencies from 1914 onward. They had suspended the gold standard when the First World War began. They had agreed to an inflationary version of the international gold standard, called the "gold exchange standard," at the Genoa Conference of 1922. Britain went back on the gold standard in 1925, but at an artificially high exchange rate for the pound, pretending that the pound was what

---

8. Ludwig von Mises, "Lord Keynes and Say's Law" (1950), in *Planning for Freedom* (South Holland, Illinois: Libertarian Press, [1952] 1980), p. 69.

it had been worth before the inflation of the War. The British government, through the efforts of the head of the Bank of England, Montague Norman, then pressured the U.S. Federal Reserve System to inflate the dollar, in order to keep foreign currencies (and gold) from flowing out of the Bank of England into the United States. In 1929, the Federal Reserve System tightened money, meaning that they stopped inflating, which led to a rapid rise in short-term interest rates, thereby creating a recession. (Remember, recessions are created by prior inflations.)[9] In 1930, the U.S. government passed the infamous Smoot-Hawley tariff, thereby reducing imports and simultaneously crippling U.S. foreign trade. This crippled Europe's ability to earn dollars by selling to the U.S. market, which reduced Europe's ability to repay loans to the U.S. The rest, as they say, was history.[10]

The Keynesian Solution

Keynes, a great defender of British tariffs after 1930, obviously didn't see things this way, that is, in terms of market economics. He had a different solution. Instead of investigating the lack of trade, output, and income in terms of restraints 1-5, and then thinking about how to solve the problem(s), Keynes added a sixth reason to explain why I refuse to buy your goods.

6. I need more money.

It is true, of course. If I had enough money, I would buy your goods, *assuming you would still sell me something I want at this moment's price.* If I had enough money, we could then overcome the impediments of any of the five. Yes, even if the government has made trading illegal. If necessary, I could bribe a bureaucrat. We could hide what we are doing. Anyway, if I just had more money, all my

---

9. Ludwig von Mises, *Human Action: A Treatise on Economics* (3rd ed.; Chicago: Regnery, 1966), ch. 20.

10. A readable account of all this is found in Paul Johnson, *Modern Times: The World from the Twenties to the Eighties* (New York: Harper & Row, 1983), ch. 7. He bases his narrative on the brilliant Austrian School analysis of Murray Rothbard, *America's Great Depression* (Princeton, New Jersey: Van Nostrand, 1963).

hesitation would go, *if I really want what you want to sell*. And if you
don't have what I want, I can get someone else to sell me what I
want, if I had more money, and then he can buy what you're selling. All I need is more money. But where am I going to get more
money? How am I going to get more money?

Keynes' answer? *Get it from the government*. This is called "fiscal
policy."

But where will the government get it? From taxes. Response:
then those who get taxed can't spend it. Aggregate spending
doesn't change. All right, you have a point. The government will
have to borrow it. Response: then those who loan the government
the money can't spend it. Aggregate spending doesn't change. All
right, the government has a third option. *It can print more money.*
This is called monetary policy.

No, you are saying to yourself. It can't be. Not that. That has
been tried over and over again since the dawn of the division of
labor economy based on money. That is just the same old government confidence game. That is the same old *government-approved
counterfeiting scheme*. That is the old-time religion of inflation.
Keynes must have offered something more constructive than this.
Surely there is some super-sophisticated answer buried in all that
verbiage, some magic formula hidden in all those equations.
Surely. Because if there isn't, and if economists and politicians
were to accept his answer, we would find ourselves in the age of
inflation.

And that, my friend, is exactly where we find ourselves.

The Age of Inflation (and Unemployment, Too)

We speak of the Keynesian revolution. So do the Keynesians.
We are assured that all pre-Keynesian economics is dead. The
winners in the competition for the minds of men are the Keynesians. We have the proof. Keynesian policies have produced universal prosperity. We are all trading with each other again. The
depression is over. It has been over for almost half a century.
There is one man who did it all: John Maynard Keynes. We are
now ready, announced Walter Heller in 1966, for the *New Frontiers*

in Political Economy.

Well, we were *not* ready. We were not ready for two decades of worldwide price inflation. Price inflation is where Keynesianism must lead, warned Mises and the other pre-Keynesian economists in the late 1930's. Price inflation is the Keynesian solution, Hayek argued for five decades. Swallow the Keynesian solution, and it will turn out to be a poisonous solution, they warned. Then the whole Western world swallowed it.

To Get People Buying Again

"The trouble is," says the disgruntled potential buyer to the seller who has just raised his selling price, "you cheated. Yes, you did. I was willing to buy. I didn't buy for a while, but then I got the newly printed money, and I decided to buy. But you changed the rules. *You raised your price.* You saw I had that new money, and then you got some, too, and you got greedy. You went and broke the rules."

What rule is this? Keynes' rule, on which he based his entire "revolution," namely, that *the sellers of goods, especially labor goods, are never supposed to catch on to the confidence game that the government is running.* If the sellers ever catch on *as sellers*, the Keynesian miracle collapses. They are allowed to catch on as buyers of goods (increased aggregate *demand*), but never as sellers. If they catch on as sellers, they will raise prices, thereby reducing aggregate demand for goods. In short, the Keynesian revolution is based on the preposterous assumption that each economic actor has two separate brains: a *buyer's brain* and a *seller's brain*, and these two brains are not supposed to understand each other. Unfortunately, they do understand. As soon as the seller's brain catches up with the buyer's brain, the seller raises prices, and trade impediments 1-5 appear again. The inflation-fueled boom turns into yet another recession. Unemployment rises.

Unemployment is up, all over the world. Why? If the Keynesian miracle is so miraculous, why are so many people unemployed? Because they are asking too much money in wages. Because trade union restrictions keep them out of the labor force.

Because other government restrictions against trade exist: wage floors, price floors, tariffs, etc. In short, *because of all those economic factors that Keynes categorically refused to consider as causes of unemployment.*[11]

We were told that if we inflated the currency, we could hold down unemployment. "Better six percent inflation than six percent unemployment," was the motto of the 1960's. So the United States got double-digit price inflation in the late 1970's, and over six percent unemployment. Remember, this was under the reign of President Carter and his Keynesian advisors.

What happened was simple: the public finally caught on to the game. They saw that people had more money to offer, so person by person, they asked for more money in return. *They refused to sell at yesterday's prices.* That spoiled the Keynesian miracle.

No, you're saying to yourself again. It can't be. That's all there was to it? You mean to say that when sellers finally started asking for more money, the same problem occurred again? People stopped trading again? You mean we are back to reasons 1-5?

Yes, that is exactly where we are. Except for one minor detail: *debt.* A trillion dollars in debt is owed to Western commercial banks, and as much as half of this cannot be collected. It will take more fiat money to repay this debt — repay it *nominally.* Add to this debt the trillions of dollars, pounds, "whatevers" that are owed by governments to their people in the form of economic promises — promises that are impossible to fulfill. Add trillions more in private debt internal to each nation. We have changed people's psychology. Keynesian economists told them: "Buy now, pay later." They took the economists at their word. Now, should we adopt monetary policies that do not spew ever-more quantities of money into the system in order to enable debtors to repay *existing* debt, the whole system collapses. We get another deflationary depression.

And then 1936 will look pretty good in retrospect.

---

11. Summarizing Keynes: "It is not necessary, moreover, to rely on 'monopolies,' labor unions, minimum wage laws, or other institutional restraints on the utility maximizing behavior of individual transactors in order to explain finite price velocities. Keynes, in contrast to many New Economists, was adamantly opposed to theories which 'blamed' depressions on such obstacles to price adjustments." Leijonhufvud, *American Economic Review* (May 1967), p. 403.

Fiscal Policy: "Inflation With Deception"

I have argued that the Keynesian kernel is simply to create money. That was not quite fair. We must give Keynes his due. He wanted to create money, all right, but he wanted to do it in a way which would confuse people. Also, he wanted to do it in a way which would increase the power of the State. It was not that he approved of private counterfeiting. No, what he wanted was *public* counterfeiting.

If the Treasury were to fill up old bottles with banknotes, bury them at suitable depths in unused coal mines which are then filled up to the surface with town rubbish, and leave it to private enterprise on well-tried principles of *laissez-faire* to dig the notes up again (the right to do so being obtained, of course, by tendering for leases of the note-holding territory), there need be no more unemployment and, with the help of the repercussions, the real income of the community, and its capital wealth also, would probably become a good deal greater than it actually is. It would, indeed, be more sensible to build houses and the like; but if there are political and practical difficulties in the way of this, the above would be better than nothing.[12]

Keynes was being clever, of course. But this is what brought the Keynesian revolution. It was not his equations but his charm and cleverness that persuaded his academic disciples. What his followers dare not admit, and what is inescapably true in retrospect, is that his clever analogies were the very heart and soul of the Keynesian revolution. The equations were window-dressing, or better put, the hard shells; the kernels of untruth were hidden inside. In promoting the theories of *The General Theory*, Keynes was a salesman far more than an economist.[13]

---

12. John Maynard Keynes, *The General Theory of Employment, Interest, and Money* (New York: Harcourt, Brace and World, 1936), p. 129.

13. Prof. Leland Yeager has commented: "Keynes made many contributions besides what became known as Keynesianism. But his main contribution, as I now see it, was an effective selling job for concern with the problems of employment and effective demand. . . . It is a sad commentary on the American economics profession that the wiles of salesmanship, instead of or in addition to sober analysis, should have been necessary to gain due attention to the problem

Useless Work

The first notable feature of Keynes' vivid analogy is the uselessness of the work. The Treasury could spend the money into circulation by paying for public housing projects. That was what he really preferred: government-built houses. But digging up filled-in holes was satisfactory.

The point to bear in mind is that when working men dig up coal, it is because they believe they will meet a consumer's demand for coal. It is not the activity, but rather the *consumer need fulfilled*, which is crucial in a free market arrangement. Digging up bottles filled with paper money is useless expenditure. Instead, dig for coal. But if the mine has played out, and it costs too much to dig it, then stop digging. You can just hand out the counterfeit money But *stop digging*. You are wasting time and money in digging. Yes, you get some coal, but it costs too much.

True, the government could construct houses. But this is no different from digging up coal which is too expensive to extract in terms of what it will bring on the free market. Do not build houses that would not otherwise sell. Do what the coal miners had to do: stop building. You can just hand out the counterfeit money But *stop building*. You are wasting time and money in building. Yes, you get some houses, but they cost too much.

Professionally Managed Counterfeiting

The second notable feature of his clever analogy is that the Treasury must print the notes. Why not private counterfeiters? He did not say. I think he might have replied: "People want to trust the government. They don't want to be arrested for dealing in counterfeit notes." So why not rewrite the law and allow private counterfeiting? "Because the government policy-makers must guide the overall creation of money, in order not to allow mass in-

---

of effective demand. Keynes, probably to his credit, saw and provided what was needed — enthusiastic polemics, sardonic passages, bits of esoteric and even shocking doctrine." Yeager, "The Keynesian Diversion," *Western Economic Journal*, XI (June 1973), p. 150.

flation." You mean that mass inflation is a possibility? "Yes, of course." And this is bad? "Yes, of course." What we need, you are saying, is "managed" inflation. "That's it, exactly!" (The public asks: "Oh, wise economist, how can you manage inflation?" The reply: "Don't worry; I'll manage.") What we need, in other words, is *professional counterfeiting*. This means *counterfeiting managed by Keynes-trained economists*.

Keynes believed that when you and I (buyers and sellers) refuse to make an exchange, we are hurting each other. We just can't seem to help it. Somehow, we just cannot sort out the problem and come to terms. What we need is an incentive to trade. We need the State to come in and provide the needed incentive. This incentive is *more money* for the buyer (seller of money), and *more illusion* for the seller (seller of goods and services).

If the problem is the shortage of money, why not allow private counterfeiting? Is it a form of theft? Then so is official counterfeiting. Will private counterfeiting debase the value of the currency and investments presently held by the public? Then so will official counterfeiting. Will private counterfeiting destroy the people's faith in the existing currency unit? Then so will official counterfeiting. Will private counterfeiters lack the self-restraint needed to steal from the public slowly, and to debase the people's holdings of money-denominated assets? Then we are arguing about *time*, not principle.

In short, if it is wrong and self-defeating for private counterfeiters, it is equally wrong and self-defeating for official counterfeiters. Yet the official counterfeiting still goes on. It is called progressive monetary policy. Keynes and Milton Friedman and the supply-side economists and the Social Credit cranks all agree: a little inflation of the money supply is necessary. But why? What is the difference who does it? The answer is clear: *the State can do it in a managed fashion, and if the bad results can be delayed until after the next election, the politicians will continue to print the money.* In short, the issue is time. Private counterfeiters get greedy. They will compete against each other. They will destroy the game too soon. Counterfeiting eventually will destroy the economy, but slow counterfeit-

ing—managed money—does not alert the victims until years
later. That, in essence, is the kernel of truth in the overall shell of
economic depravity. The public learns slowly. The public trusts
the experts, and the public learns slowly. *Official counterfeiting be-
trays the public's trust . . . slowly.*

This is the heart of the Keynesian revolution. This is why
Keynesians favor fiscal policy—taxing and spending and running
large deficits—rather than monetary policy, that is, outright inflation. The public can be fooled a lot longer if the central planners
disguise the theft of counterfeiting through government spending.
The government needs to spend the money to buy "something
productive," or build "something productive." If the government
just handed out the fiat money on street corners, the public would
figure out that the government's solution to depression is simply
the old con job of mass inflation. Prices would go to infinity, and
the game would start over. But in the meantime, everyone would
have been ruined, first by mass inflation, and then by the resulting depression. Keynes had learned the lesson of the German inflation of 1919-23. Fiscal policy was his answer: *concealed* long-term
mass inflation. In short, hide the reality as long as possible.

The Need for Government Pyramids

Does this mean that public works projects are nothing more
than modern-day pyramids? Are they really just smoke screens
for the engine of inflation? Are they really not much better than
digging holes in the ground, and piling up dirt somewhere else? Is
this the kernel of untruth in Keynesian fiscal policy? Yes, and
Keynes said so himself:

> In so far as millionaires find their satisfaction in building mighty
> mansions to contain their bodies when alive and pyramids to shelter
> them after death, or, repenting of their sins, erect cathedrals and endow
> monasteries or foreign missions, the day when abundance of capital will
> interfere with abundance of output may be postponed. "To dig holes in
> the ground," paid for out of savings, will increase, not only employment,
> but the real national dividend of useful goods and services.[14]

---

14. *Ibid.*, p. 220.

Of course, he really didn't believe in such a system of pyramid-building and hole-digging. Why not? *Because it was private.* So he added this qualification: "It is not reasonable, however, that a sensible community should be content to remain dependent on such fortuitous and often wasteful mitigations when once we understand the influences upon which effective demand depends." Effective demand therefore means *government* pyramids and holes.

Oh, yes, he was clever. So clever that he sold this nonsense to two generations of economists, who in turn made good incomes selling the justification for pyramids and holes to the politicians who, in the tradition of Pharaoh, had long since adopted the practical conclusions anyway.

DUNAGIN'S PEOPLE   By Dunagin

12-27

"My plan would stimulate the economy while holding down inflation . . . urge the people to bite the bullet, tighten their belts, and spend more money."

Any Christian economist who adopts such nonsense becomes the paid agent of the taskmasters of Egypt. Yes, I mean Dr. Vickers.

Where Does the Money Come From?

What if the economy is in a recession? According to Keynes and Dr. Vickers, this happens because the economy is in an equilibrium position in which resources are unused. (As Hayek said half a century ago, the problem is not so much explaining how resources are unused at any point in time, but rather how it is that they are properly used at any point in time.) The Keynesians love their free market equilibrium concept, but only so long as it is an *equilibrium with unemployment*. This is the only kind of free market equilibrium that "revolutionary orthodoxy" Keynesians are willing to discuss. Such an equilibrium—and Keynes never did explain how it could exist for very long, given the profit-seeking activities of entrepreneurs—calls forth the State to get things moving and fully employed.

Does Dr. Vickers really believe all this? Indeed he does: "Let us therefore, in order to focus clearly and soley on the point at issue, suppose that before the increase in investment expenditures occurred the economy was in a position of macroeconomic equilibrium in the sense in which that has already been defined, but that at that equilibrium position a certain amount of unemployed resources of manpower and equipment existed. This, then, implies that any increases in expenditures that occur can be expected to stimulate a higher level of production and call forth the higher required level of output, without exerting any upward pressures on the general level of prices."[15]

Here we are in depressionary equilibrium. On the one hand, he rejects the idea of an entrepreneur-driven *tendency* toward full-employment in a free market: "For this reason the system cannot be left, and Christian economic consciences cannot lightly agree to leave it, to gyrate uninhibitedly and randomly of its own accord."[16]

---

15. *Economics and Man*, p. 202.
16. *Ibid.*, p. 234.

You see, there are no stabilizing forces in an unhampered free market economy. (We are back to the Marx-Engels line of reasoning: anarchy of private production.) But on the other hand, we can have an equilibrium of unemployed resources in a free market, an equilibrium which is so stable that government economists know just what to do to make things better again. In other words, the free market *gyrates randomly*, which is clearly unacceptable, yet it also *stabilizes for years* at levels of high unemployment, which is equally unacceptable. Somehow, I get the impression that Dr. Vickers is determined to find the free market unacceptable.

We are told that an investment will "stimulate a higher level of production." Fine. Then why doesn't some profit-seeking entrepreneur make the required investment? *This question is one which Keynes and Dr. Vickers never want to answer.* For some reason, the entrepreneur won't invest. (Maybe it has something to do with profit.) So guess who will invest? Right! The government bureaucrat — you know, "Mr. Innovation." He will spend a hundred dollars on something or other. It really doesn't matter what. Pyramids, you know. Holes in the ground.

"The $100 increase in investment expenditure will obviously cause an immediate increase of $100 in GNP." Yes, it will. That is how the statisticians define one component of the Gross National Product: an increase in government spending, *on anything*. The statistician never asks whether the expenditure is productive. All GNP statistics *assume* that it is. Pyramids, you know. Holes in the ground. It's all GNP to the statisticians. "Abstracting now from all the other factors we have considered as affecting the relation between GNP and disposable income, let us suppose, again to focus on the single most important point at issue, that disposable income increases also by $100. Now this will generate an increase in consumption expenditures, the magnitude of the induced effect depending on the size of what we have just defined as the marginal propensity to consume."[17] Presto: *an increase in disposable income*. The economy gets rolling again.

---

17. *Ibid.*, p. 202.

I rub my eyes in disbelief. This is the "Keynesian solution"? You can see the problem as well as I can. *Where did the bureaucrat get the $100?* From the taxpayer? Then in doing so, he reduced disposable income in the first place. From borrowing? Then he reduced the disposable income in the first place. From the printing press (or bank)? Then this is the same old con game that coin clippers and counterfeiters have played since the dawn of money. There is no third alternative, and Dr. Vickers knows it. He describes the alternatives in detail.[18]

That's it, folks. That's all there is. Take away the graphs, charts, equations, and incoherent gobbledygook, and this is the famous bottom line. Spend yourself rich with counterfeit money. No, not quite: the *government* will spend the rest of us rich with its counterfeit money (minus 30% for handling).

Why Won't People Trade?

We have covered all five reasons. Let us review them once more.

1. I don't know what you're selling.
2. You don't have what I'm buying.
3. Your price is too high.
4. Your price is acceptable to me, but I think you will take less later on.
5. The government has made it illegal (or expensive) to trade.

How do we solve these problems? We allow the participants to solve them. We allow *each other* to solve them. We do not ask the State to coercively solve them. We ask few services from the State. The State guarantees the enforcement of voluntary contracts. The State does not tamper with the monetary unit. The State prohibits fraud and violence. The State keeps taxes below the tithe of 10 percent. That is just about it — a few roads, perhaps, but that is just about it.

What happens then? We make a deal.

---

18. *Ibid.*, pp. 316-334.

1. You advertise. I shop.
2. You locate what I want to buy and sell me the information on where to buy it.
3. You lower your price.
4. You wait to see if I offer more. I wait to see if you drop your price.
5. The government repeals all legislation which restricts trade.

If we cannot agree, then we go talk to someone else. If conditions change, we change. If we want to trade, we keep bargaining. We retain our freedom to bargain. This is what economists call *price flexibility*. Keynes did not believe that it works. He could never show theoretically why it doesn't work. It seems obvious to anyone that it can work. If it doesn't, then people will not trade until conditions get tougher. Eventually, they will trade. The price of not trading is too high. We do not need moral appeals to trade, such as the one Dr. Vickers has written.[19] We just need the freedom to trade without interference from politicians and bureaucrats.

The Keynesian logic about the breakdown of trade and the collapse of income is correct, but *only* under one specific condition: namely, where an *unchanging* price structure exists. It is true that a withholding of spending or consumption (i.e., a decline in monetary demand) will cause the predicted nasty results. There are, however, two possible solutions. On the one hand, the expenditure stream could be boosted in some manner, or, on the other hand, price reductions could occur which would bring supply and demand, measured in dollars and cents, closer to a *market-clearing price*, where all sellers and all buyers could make their exchanges and go home satisfied. The first solution, that of boosting monetary demand — monetary inflation — is the Keynesian answer to the problem. The latter, that of allowing prices to fluctuate, is the *laissez-faire* solution. For some unstated reason, Dr. Vickers — like Keynes — never mentions the effect price reductions would have on the economy.

The secret of Keynes' theory of "equilibrium with unemploy-

---

19. *Ibid.*, p. 122.

ment" is this: he did not want to see trade union members have to suffer *monetary* pay cuts. Instead, by creating money and lowering its value — that is, by allowing prices to rise in a world of stable money wages (!!!) — the government lowers the real income of workers. Thus, the invisible hand of the market takes over because of the *invisible tax* of price inflation. Keynes wrote: "Having regard to the large groups of incomes which are comparatively inflexible in terms of money, it can only be an unjust person who would prefer a flexible wage policy to a flexible money policy, unless he can point to advantages from the former which are not obtainable from the latter."[20]

But we *can* point to such advantages. The major one is that without monetary inflation, there will not be a repetition of the boom-bust cycle.[21] Another one is that the public's trust is not violated by official counterfeiters. Another is that people and governments are not tempted to amass huge debts on the assumption that the government will print the money to enable them to pay off their debts with cheaper money. Another is that governments will not be tempted to impose price and wage controls, which disrupt production. Another is that relative prices of economic resources will not be distorted by injections of fiat money into the system.

Perhaps the greatest irony of all is that Keynes' policies have led to the accumulation of debt on a massive scale by governments, corporations, and families. Yet it is debt, perhaps above all, that keeps sellers and wage-earners from lowering prices during a recession.

Conclusion

The kernels of untruth in the Keynesian system are numerous. Here are several:

1. Prices are downwardly inflexible.
2. The incentive to trade does not regularly overcome downward price inflexibility.

---

20. Keynes, *General Theory*, p. 268.
21. Mises, *Human Action*, ch. 20.

3. There can be free market "equilibrium" with unemployment (because of downward price inflexibility).
4. The government can "break the trade barrier" by taxing and spending policies.
5. The government can pay for this through monetary inflation without price inflation.
6. The government's bureaucrats are wiser investors for the public's good than profit-seeking entrepreneurs who are risking their own money.
7. Pyramids are as good as anything else to spend money on, if only governments build them.
8. The trick is to lower real wages through price inflation without letting the victims catch on.
9. The victims will not catch on, and they will not raise their wage or price demands.

Dr. Vickers calls this system Christian. I don't. I call it Egyptian to the core. Dr. Vickers would deliver God's people back into bondage. He is a defender of the power religion.[22]

---

22. Gary North, *Moses and Pharoah: Dominion Religion vs. Power Religion* (Tyler, Texas: Institute for Christian Economics, 1985), Introduction.

9

SAY'S LAW

Say's Law simply did not hold in fact. Supply did not create its own demand at all conceivable levels of employment. The aggregative economic system could and did stagnate at a permanently depressed level of employment and activity. It was the achievement of Keynes's General Theory *to demonstrate that the economy could, and in observable instances did, settle at what we have characterized as equilibrium income levels at which not all of the available work force was employed. What Keynes demonstrated, in other words, was the possibility of what henceforth had to be recognized as an underemployment equilibrium condition.* [1]

We now come to a somewhat rarified economic debate. It is really very important in understanding both the Keynesian system and Dr. Vickers' baptized version. I wish it weren't so important, for Dr. Vickers' presentation, like Keynes' presentation, does not lend itself to enjoyable reading. Yet Dr. Vickers and the Keynesian economists agree that Keynes' refutation of Say's Law was at the very heart of his revolution. It was the decade of unemployment and depression of the 1930's which softened the resistance to Keynes' revolution. The long-term unemployment, to use Thomas Kuhn's analysis,[2] was *the* anomaly to which the older classical economics (but not "Austrian" economic theory) no

---

1. Vickers, *Economics and Man*, p. 35.
2. Thomas Kuhn, *The Structure of Scientific Revolutions* (2nd ed.; Chicago: University of Chicago Press, 1970).

longer seemed to apply.[3]

I will say from the outset that Dr. Vickers gives no indication that he has ever read Thomas Sowell's standard account, *Say's Law: An Historical Analysis* (1972),[4] and this glaring omission from his books makes suspect everything he says about Say's Law and its implications. Given the inaccuracies of his discussions of Say and the implications of classical economic theory, it is clear that he desperately needs to read Sowell, as well as understand him.

Why Are There Gluts?

Answer: *Because sellers are asking prices that are too high.* (I'll bet you knew that already.) Because neither Dr. Vickers nor Keynes would accept this obvious answer, I feel obliged to devote time, energy, and pages to a discussion of Keynes and Say's Law. You may feel the same pressure, just for the sake of discovering one more case where Dr. Vickers is not playing fair.

Jean Baptiste Say, a French economist of the mid-nineteenth century, was the originator of "Say's Law." That law, in its Keynesian *mis*statement, says that "supply creates its own demand."[5] According to Dr. Vickers, it was Keynes who "exposed the fallacies of the classical school,"[6] one of those fallacies being Say's Law, the idea of "the impossibility of general overproduction."[7] The theorem, says Dr. Vickers, "that there could not be overproduction and that there could not be underemployment because there could not be a generalized deficiency of monetary demand for goods, rested on the *transparently fallacious proposition* . . . that the money values, or money incomes, earned from producing goods would automatically be spent. . . ."[8]

---

3. The economics profession, both pre-Keynes and post-Keynes, chose to ignore the Austrian view. Systematic selective ignorance on the part of both the guild masters and the revolutionaries is basic to any scientific revolution.

4. Thomas Sowell, *Say's Law: An Historical Analysis* (Princeton, New Jersey: Princeton University Press, 1972).

5. "From the time of Say and Ricardo the classical economists have taught that supply creates its own demand. . . ." Keynes, *General Theory*, p. 18.

6. Vickers, p. 12.

7. *Ibid.*, p. 11; cf. p. 35.

8. *Ibid.*, p. 12, emphasis added; cf. p. 35.

Why is Dr. Vickers so interested in this bit of "ancient history"? Because Keynes' supposed refutation of Say was the very heart of his supposed refutation of classical economics. If supply creates its own demand, then why did the great depression of the 1930's go on for a decade? Why couldn't the supply brought to market be sold?

The answer, of course, is that the prices asked by sellers were too high. But why did prices stay so high? Why don't sellers eventually offer lower prices? Why was Say's Law "nullified" during the Great Depression? *Because government policy favored price floors, meaning cartel prices.* The State punished sellers who adopted policies of "cut-throat competition." This explanation of the first four years of the depression in the United States was what led Keynesian economists to dispatch Murray Rothbard into professional "outer darkness."[9] Twenty years later, Rothbard's economics-based explanation was resurrected by popular (and eloquent) historian Paul Johnson, in *Modern Times* (1983). The explanation offered by Milton Friedman in that same year, 1963, was that prices were too high as a result of Federal Reserve (central bank) monetary policy, 1929-33[10] — a more acceptable theory to academic economists who generally favor monetary inflation.

What Say had argued is that *if prices are allowed to move upward or downward*, supply creates its own demand. More to the point, supply *is* demand. Put bluntly, if you have nothing to offer in exchange, you do not become a part of "aggregate demand." Or, in words that Dr. Vickers would regard as stylistically vulgar, "If you ain't got it to start with, you can't buy nothing with it."

Keynes' Strategy

It was this explanation of how markets work both in theory and in practice which Keynes had to refute in order to make way

9. Murray N. Rothbard, *America's Great Depression* (Princeton, New Jersey: Van Nostrand, 1963).

10. Milton Friedman and Anna J. Schwartz, *A Monetary History of the United States* (Princeton, New Jersey: Princeton University Press, for the National Bureau of Economic Research, 1963).

for the acceptance of his *General Theory*. Only if he could show that
the disastrous performance of the world's markets in the 1930's
was the result of faulty economic practice, which in turn was
based on faulty free market economic theory, could he expect
economists to accept his revolutionary prescription. As Hazlitt
and other critics have pointed out, his "revolution" was a return to
mercantilism, which Adam Smith had buried. Like Dracula rising from the grave, Keynes' mercantilism could be stopped only
by that legendary stake through the heart. Say's Law was that
stake. Keynes had to remove it from the hands of the market's defenders. He had to convince the profession that free market competition does not produce market-clearing forces. He had to convince them that the market can and has produced an *equilibrium of
unemployed resources* — in contrast to classical economics' *theory* of
equilibrium pricing, in which all resources will be fully employed
at some price. He did so by ignoring tariffs, cartels, and other
government-created impediments to *price competition*. He did so
also by misstating Say's Law and then refuting his newly produced straw man.

The fact that Keynes did not properly understand Say's Law
has been ably exposed by Henry Hazlitt and Ludwig von Mises.[11]
More recently, it has been exposed by Thomas Sowell — and by
"more recently," I mean several years *before* Dr. Vickers wrote *Economics and Man*.[12] Say's law *never* suggested that incomes would
automatically be spent. Again, we have an example of how Dr.
Vickers displays a tendency to misstate the position of those with
whom he disagrees. He builds a straw man to draw the readers'
attention from the real facts of the case. In this sense, he is very
much like his mentor. Sowell has pointed out: "The 'classical'
economist described in Keynes' *General Theory* was a straw man."[13]

---

11. Henry Hazlitt, *The Failure of the "New Economics"* (Princeton, New Jersey:
Van Nostrand, 1959), pp. 32-43. Ludwig von Mises, *Planning For Freedom* (South
Holland, Illinois: Libertarian Press, [1952] 1980), pp. 64-71. Vickers' contention
that Hazlitt's analysis of Keynes is "shallow" (p. 36) is meaningless without supporting evidence.
12. Thomas Sowell, *Say's Law: An Historic Analysis*, ch. 8.
13. *Ibid.*, p. 211.

Keynes never bothered to be honest enough in his scholarship to quote Say accurately, and it is somewhat surprising to find that a Christian economist wants to follow the same intellectually shoddy route. Of course, Dr. Vickers may have a legitimate excuse: he may never have read J. B. Say, just as he seems never to have read Thomas Sowell's book on Says Law.

"Goods for Goods"

Say's Law merely stated that a *general* overproduction of all commodities is impossible because, in economic terms, goods always exchange against goods, money being merely an inter-mediary acting as a common denominator showing the exchange ratio which exists between, for example, cars and bicycles, shirts and trousers, or potatoes and rice. In the words of Say, "you will have bought, and every body must buy, the objects of want or desire, each with the value of his respective products transformed into money for the moment only."[14] Money is a medium of ex-change, a commodity which facilitates the exchange of goods and services. But Say's Law depends upon exchange ratios (prices) be-tween goods and services being in perfect balance—that is, in equilibrium—a qualification Dr. Vickers (and Keynes) conven-iently chooses to ignore.

Dr. Vickers writes: "The logic of this argument implied that if supply created its own demand at any given or specified level of production and employment, supply would similarly create its own demand at all conceivable levels of employment. There could not therefore exist any obstacles to the full employment of the total work force available and willing to work."[15] Here we find the great Keynesian misstatement of Say's Law. (Apparently Dr. Vickers has made little effort to check primary sources which Keynes quoted. Had he done so, he would have discovered that

---

14. Jean Baptiste Say, "Of The Demand Or Market For Products," in Henry Hazlitt (ed.), *The Critics of Keynesian Economics* (New Rochelle, New York: Arling-ton House, [1960] 1977), p. 13.

15. Vickers, *A Christian Approach to Economics and the Cultural Condition*, pp. 59-60.

when Keynes quoted J. S. Mill's version of Say's Law, he conveniently omitted this important qualification.) When prices are no longer in equilibrium the result is a *relative* overproduction of *some* goods (the ones out of balance), but the market can be cleared of any surplus by a readjustment of the particular prices to reflect the changes in people's subjective valuations of those items. *Legally* flexible prices, *both upward and downward*, provide the necessary legal framework to allow profit-seeking, future-oriented entrepreneurs to seek out those buying and selling prices that will clear the market of a relative overproduction of goods by restoring the balance between the supply of such goods and the demand for them.

Note also the discrepancy which exists between Dr. Vickers' version of Say's Law and the actual words of Say. Nowhere does Say give any indication that "money values, or money incomes, earned from producing goods would automatically be spent." Here is another fine example of Dr. Vickers' inability to accurately represent those with whom he disagrees.

Downwardly Flexible Prices

A flexible price mechanism, however, is something Dr. Vickers chooses to omit from the discussion. "Say's Law did not hold in fact," he asserts, and cites the twenty-five percent unemployment rate in the United States during the depression years as proof. What Dr. Vickers neglects to discuss, however, is whether downwardly inflexible wage rates—legally inflexible, because of government interference—were a cause of this unemployment. Given the situation of the 1930's, and the unwillingness of many government-protected trade union members to take a reduction in wages, unemployment would have been predicted by any of the classical economists.

Dr. Vickers, by endeavoring to "refute" Say's Law, has to adopt that form of argument which he categorically disallows: the "fallacy of composition" argument. Since there can be a temporary overproduction of *some* goods because of erroneous prior forecasting by specific producers, Dr. Vickers draws the conclusion there can be a *general* and *continuing* overproduction, implying the general misforecasting by most producers. But is this not making the

mistake of "imagining that what was true of a part was necessarily
. . . true of the whole"?[16] Apparently we are not allowed to make
such deductions, according to Dr. Vickers. Yet now that it is convenient for his own presentation, he is perfectly willing to make
such deductions. In this example, though, Dr. Vickers has not
only contradicted his own "rules of the game," but he also made a
faulty conclusion. It is simply not true to say that because over-
supply may exist in the case of one commodity that it exists regarding *all* commodities.[17] This was what the classical economists
understood,[18] and what Keynes and his disciples refuse to
acknowledge.

Long ago, Mises asked this crucial question: Why should it be
that at one point in time, most of the plans of skilled forecasters go
wrong and produce losses? That a few will be wrong is inescapable, but competing forecasters will make profits at their expense.
The problem for the economist is to explain the *simultaneous* appearance of losses. His conclusion constitutes the "Austrian"
theory of the trade cycle. We must look for the one common bond
to every economic transaction in order to locate the source of the
initial confusion of the entrepreneurs. That common bond is
money. Mises then built his explanation of depression in terms of
the erroneous economic signals that are generated by the policy of
monetary inflation, and the inescapable contraction which takes
place after the public begins to forecast accurately the continuation of price inflation.[19] The depression is the phase of the cycle in
which the previous mistakes of entrepreneurs are exposed as mistakes. Only when these mistakes are realized and responded to
can there be long-term, non-inflationary recovery.

Does Say's Law hold in fact? It is obvious to any clear-thinking

---

16. Vickers, *Economics and Man*, p. 33; cf. pp. 92, 269.

17. John Stuart Mill, *Principles of Political Economy* (London: Longmans, Green
and Co., 1902), Book III, XIV:1, p. 337.

18. Thomas Sowell, *Classical Economics Reconsidered* (Princeton, New Jersey:
Princeton University Press, 1974), p. 43.

19. Mises, *Human Action: A Treatise on Economics* (3rd ed.; Chicago: Regnery,
1966), ch. 20.

person that *we have nothing to trade until we first produce something*, whether it is some visible economic good such as potatoes, or productive skills such as computer operating, or even one's personal reputation for repaying debt, which enables a person to obtain credit for present purchases. Until we actually possess these things, we have nothing which we can offer in exchange for other economic items we desire. Supply — that is, production — *does* create demand. Keynesians have merely reversed the theorem, saying demand creates supply, or that demand calls forth production, but without providing clear evidence for understanding how this is so. Hence, they insist, if only everyone had more money (demand), production (supply) would increase.

They can hold this view only by ignoring fundamental questions relating to supply and demand, and they do this by denying relationships (economic regularities) between supply and demand that exist in all circumstances. (TANSTAAFL: "There ain't no such thing as a free lunch.") In addition, they are willing to overlook empirical evidence which refutes their theory. The 1970's oil crisis resulted in reduced output coupled with higher prices. According to Keynesians, higher prices should mean more money in someone's pocket, more spending and a stimulus to industry. Instead, there was less output and the onset of stagflation in the West, that painful combination of monetary inflation and falling production. Keynesian economists had no answer, other than their tried-and-true one: *more fiat money.* That was what we got in the late 1970's, but without the promised miracle of high employment. This chain of international economic events, perhaps more than any other factor, has caused the present dissatisfaction with Keynesian theory amongst professional economists.

Competition

The meaning of capitalism, with its freedom for men to compete for limited resources, to compete for purchases of a similar item, and to compete against other laborers selling their abilities, is something Keynesians would like to see forgotten. They detest "cut-throat" competition, yet they speak as if they wanted to encourage competition. What they never want to admit is the point that Dr. North keeps hammering away at: "cut-throat" competition really means "cut-throat *opportunities*" for consumers.[20]

In the Keynesian system, however, competition has a special meaning. Dr. Vickers illustrates the theory which favors government economic activity with this example: the Australian government's national airline and bank which compete with private companies. Ultimately, though, this kind of illustrative argument depends upon how the word "competition" is defined. In the case of the federally owned airline, it is worth noting that the Australian government's airline corporation offers services against only one competitor, other companies being refused permission to enter the industry to offer competing services. Until July 1981, when some freedom was allowed the two airlines, all fares were the same by government decree, and nearly all flights were parallel — that is, the respective flights to the same destination departed and arrived within a few minutes of one another. (I suspect that had the airports been equipped with parallel runways the flights would have been at exactly the same time!) Hence, the only competition that exists between the two airlines is in areas such as airport facilities, quality of in-flight services, and the attractiveness of the hostesses. For those Australians who would much prefer to bring their own meals in sacks if the fares were lower, the government has limited their choice. (I will not even entertain the possibility of hiring ugly hostesses: no Australian would ever admit to preferring ugly hostesses and lower fares. Except, of course, the male passengers' wives.)[21]

---

20. Gary North, "Cut-Throat Opportunities," *The Freeman* (June 1983).

21. Dr. North argues privately that the deteriorating attractiveness of American hostesses since 1970 is the product of three phenomena: 1) fast jets: their increased speed over propeller-driven planes has reduced the time in which unmarried hostesses can spot potentially well-heeled husband prospects, and then strike up conversations with them; the speed also increases their work load per minute; 2) union contracts that always favor existing employees to newcomers, and which keep wage rates high, thereby encouraging middle-aged hostesses to stay on their above-market wage jobs; and 3) price competition among airlines rather than "hostess attractiveness" competition, itself a product of deregulation. He emphasizes number 2 as the main reason.

A similar situation exists with the government's competing bank. Since all interest rates are determined by government policy through the Reserve Bank, the competition is limited to service and facilities. The Australian government has been able to use the nation's Post Offices as venue for Commonwealth Bank customers to carry out limited banking transactions outside normal banking hours; therefore the competition has been strongly biased in the government's favor.

Competition? Obviously it is competition of a kind. But whether it is "proof" that governments and private industry can really compete on an open and equal basis is another question. Dr. Vickers does not suggest that these examples are "proof," but Keynesians have a distinct tendency to use such comparisons to support their thesis that governmental participation in the economy will have a beneficial effect. They are far less ready to embrace an alternative suggestion: that government participation causes many of the economic disharmonies currently exhibited in all nations around the world.

Here we have further evidence of the contradictions inherent in Dr. Vickers' book and Keynesianism in general. Dr. Vickers does not present a single cogent argument against the classical economists, nor has he proven his assertion that a free market system cannot work. His arguments are misleading, and to "refute" a misstatement of someone's position is not to refute the issue at all. Dr. Vickers' sole achievement is to lead the reader away from the truth of the matter and to a distortion of those views with which he holds little, if any, agreement. By using the device of misstatement, Dr. Vickers avoids confronting the actual theories with which he disagrees. As this is the case, there is every reason for the reader to reconsider the claims of classical and neo-classical economic theory.

Entrepreneurship

Supply does not "automatically" create its own demand (Say), any more than demand "automatically" creates supply (Keynes). Acting men plan for the future. In their capacity as producers, they attempt to produce for a *future, uncertainty-filled marketplace*, and as consumers, they plan in the present to be able to buy goods on that same *future, uncertainty-filled market*. The reality of uncertainty is basic to all human planning. Men are not omniscient.

The key element which is missing in Dr. Vickers' analysis is the central economic actor in the "Austrian School's" analysis: *the entrepreneur*. The entrepreneur's task is to predict future conditions of supply and demand. He competes against other forecasters. He may be correct in his estimates, in which case he will reap a residual: profit. He may be incorrect, in which case he will produce losses. But they key idea here is *uncertainty*. Every economic order must deal with it.

Is the profit-seeking, loss-bearing entrepreneur the best person to deal with uncertainty, or the government bureaucrat who owns no shares of the bureaucracy he is running? Is the person you think should act for you as your representative the entrepreneur (to whom you can say, "No, I don't want to buy it; and you suffer the loss") or the bureaucrat (who can say to you, "You'll take it; your taxes have already paid for it; and if you don't like it, you take the loss")? The problem of "overproduction" is always entrepreneurship. As Mises summarized Say:

Commodities, says Say, are ultimately paid for not by money, but by other commodities. Money is merely the commonly used medium of exchange; it plays only an intermediary role. What the seller wants ultimately to receive in exchange for the commodities sold is other commodities. Every commodity produced is therefore a price, as it were, for other commodities produced. The situation of the producer of any commodity is improved by any increase in the production of other [non-competitive—I. H.] commodities. What may hurt the interests of the producer of a definite commodity is his failure to anticipate correctly the state of the market. He has overrated the public's demand for his commodity and underrated its demand for other commodities. Consumers have no use for such a bungling entrepreneur; they buy his products only at prices which make him incur losses, and they force him, if he does not in time correct his mistakes, to go out of business. On the other hand, those entrepreneurs who have better succeeded in anticipating the public demand earn profits and are in a position to expand their business activities. This, says Say, is the truth behind the confused assertions of businessmen that the main difficulty is not in producing but in selling. It would be more appropriate to declare that the first and main problem of business is to produce in the best and cheapest way those commodities which will satisfy the most urgent of the not yet satisfied needs of the public.[22]

Nothing is automatic about any of this. Owners of goods must make moment-to-moment decisions to sell or not to sell. They bear the costs of making a poor decision. But the possibility that an entrepreneur will sit on a mountain of unsold goods that he could at least get *something* for if he sold his inventory, and for which he may be paying interest on inventory loans, is minimal. The possibility that some bureaucrat will sit on unsold goods that the taxpayers are financing, and which the original producers (e.g., farmers) want to see unsold and in storage, is relatively high.

When you talk about gluts, you must always add the key words, "at an above-market price." These are the words that Dr. Vickers simply refuses to discuss. This is why Dr. Vickers cannot be taken seriously.

Conclusion

Keynes misstated Say's Law. He therefore created a mythological place for himself as the scholar who at last "refuted" Say's Law. There is probably no intellectual myth so firmly implanted in the minds of modern Keynesian economists than this myth of Keynes, the "market-clearing equilibrium" slayer. That Dr. Vickers returns to this theme again and again indicates just how deeply he has been affected by this myth.

J. B. Say was no fool. He understood that in a real world of mistakes, people can and do produce items for which there is little demand, and almost none at the original asked-for price. The point is, Say and the classical economists believed, with good reason, that businessmen recognize that something is better than

---

22. Mises, "Lord Keynes and Say's Law" (1950), in *Planning for Freedom*, pp. 65-66.

nothing, that some revenues are better than no revenues. They believed that businessmen will lower their asking prices when they face situations in which they have few or no prospects of unloading their inventory. Thus, the market will eventually clear itself of produced goods, assuming that sellers are profit-seeking and reasonably rational — a not unreasonable assumption.

Keynes and the Keynesians have abandoned this faith in the rational, loss-minimizing, *price-cutting* activity of sellers. Keynesians have never succeeded in putting any other explanation of human action in its place, but they always deny Say's Law. They have never disproven it; they simply deny it endlessly. This is not argumentation; it is rhetoric.

What the reader must understand is that this denial of price-cutting, market-clearing actions on the part of sellers is the very heart and soul of Keynes' critique of free market economics. If his understanding of Say's Law *was* wrong, then his understanding of free market economics was also wrong. His understanding of the way people buy and sell was wrong. His recommended policies to "assist" the market are therefore very likely to be wrong, or at the very least, inconsistent with his critique of the free market. That, of course, is precisely what I am arguing in this book. *Keynes got everything wrong.* He returned to the errors of mercantilism — the same errors that Adam Smith refuted, and then built modern economics. Peter Drucker's analysis is on target: "Keynes not only went back to the Mercantilists in being macroeconomic. He stood all earlier systems on their heads by being demand-centered rather than supply-centered. In all earlier economics demand is a function of supply. In Keynesian economics supply is a function of demand and controlled by it. Above all — the greatest innovation — Keynes redefined economic reality. Instead of goods, services, and work — realities of the physical world and things — Keynes' economic realities are symbols: money and credit. To the Mercantilists, too, money gave control — but political rather than economic control. Keynes was the first to postulate that money and credit give complete *economic* control."[23]

---

23. Peter F. Drucker, "Toward the Next Economics," *The Public Interest* (Special Issue, 1980), p. 8.

That is what Keynes wanted: *economic control*. He was a defender of humanism's power religion, the power of State economic control. And Douglas Vickers is his prophet.

10

SOVEREIGNTY AND MONEY

This, however, brings us to the second of the two preliminary points it was desired to make. This has to do with the place of gold in the monetary economic system, and with what we noticed earlier as the claim by some Christian authors, Gary North and Rousas Rushdoony in particular, that "unbacked paper money" is immoral. . . . It is unfortunate that at this point considerable confusion has been allowed to enter economic argument from a purportedly Christian perspective. It was in order to contribute to a correction of that perspective that we have developed the entire argument of this book in the manner and in the order we have adopted. [1]

Money, as the song reminds us, makes the world go around. Some of us can at least get quite dizzy when trying to wade through the teaching of economists on this topic. Again, however, there is nothing magic about it.

If all goods were to be offered for sale in terms of all other goods, each item would have a horrendously complicated price list. The price of a plane ticket from Sydney to San Francisco, for example, would need to be expressed in all other commodities. This might mean that the return air fare could be obtained for 700 pairs of socks, 100 shirts, two-tenths of an average small family sedan, 1500 kilograms of grapes, or 200 bottles of fine champagne. Such a list would make life difficult.

What has developed historically is that one particular eco-

---

1. Vickers, *Economics and Man*, p. 241.

nomic good has been found to be most easily exchanged. This has become known as money, and allows all goods and services offered for sale to be expressed in this one commodity only. It is an economic good which people will readily accept, for they know that all others in the market place will also readily accept this good.

The best definition of money was given by Ludwig von Mises as long ago as 1912. *Money is the most marketable commodity.* That is all there is to it. No magic, no secret formulas, nothing. People through trading begin to select over time certain commodities that serve them as a *voluntarily accepted* means of exchange. Usually, these assets possess the following physical and economic features, to some degree or other: transportability, durability, divisibility, relative scarcity in relation to weight and volume, and recognizability. Money is the commodity which, apart from having other possible uses such as jewelry, if money is gold and/or silver, also serves as a medium of exchange.

All money is originally *commodity money*. But it doesn't stay purely commodity money for long. Eventually, counterfeiters take over, unless governments pass laws that require honest weights and measures, and most important of all, a law that requires 100% reserves for every warehouse receipt for gold, silver, or whatever the money commodity is.

While it is true that in different societies in different periods of history various commodities have served as money, from brass and iron to tobacco or barley, it is generally found that the monetary commodity has most often been gold, with silver also serving a valuable service as money for lower-priced items. (The use of silver avoids the difficulty of having to divide the measurement of gold, i.e., its weight, into such a small size that it is practically unmanageable.) It is only the present generation which does not fully understand the place gold and silver have had in this regard. Legislation in the 1930's in the United States and Australia, for example, caused gold to disappear as money. The movement against gold had started before this, but at this time the break was finalized. In the U.S., gold served as the official basis for the dollar in international transactions among central banks until the final tie was cut by President Nixon in 1971, but the case against gold had been decided long before this legislative act.

Warehouse Storage Receipts (Banking)

The rise of paper currency in relationship to gold is also of great interest . . . and I do mean *interest*. When gold and silver served as currency, goldsmiths and silversmiths often performed a valuable service of storing these commodities for safe keeping. They were the first bankers who issued receipts to the depositors. The recipients of these warehouse receipts in turn had a legal claim on that amount of gold or silver stock held by the banker. People soon found, however, that in transactions it was not necessary to go to the bank to get the metal to trade. Others were willing to accept the banker's receipt in the transaction knowing they could present the receipt at the bank and be paid the full value of the receipt.

This procedure operated exactly in the same manner as the check does in modern society. A check is nothing more than a receipt which entitles the holder to obtain money from someone's account. There is one essential difference between modern checking accounts and the old system of warehouse receipts: the old receipt was a receipt for something which had value as an economic good. It was not necessary for kings and governments to legislate a value for gold or silver, for it was determined in the market place by the free actions of human beings.

Fractional Reserves

The bankers got greedy. They realized soon enough that people did not keep coming to them in order to redeem their warehouse receipts for the actual precious metal. The bankers began issuing more receipts for gold than they had gold in reserve. This was the origin of *fractional reserve banking*. They did this because they could lend out the newly created money and gain interest on their money. This was the origin of the boom-bust economic cycle. Fractional reserve banking is a form of fraud. It results in painful depressions that are the result of euphoric, fiat-money-induced inflationary booms.

Politicians, unable to contain their profligate promises to attract votes, soon got into the money act. In order to prevent dishonest bankers issuing fraudulent receipts, which may or may not be actually backed by real gold or silver in the vaults, those in authority took over the issuance of warehouse receipts. These receipts, known as pounds or dollars, depending on the country of origin, were initially a piece of paper which promised to pay the bearer a certain amount of gold or silver. It did not take long for the politicians to realize they were onto a good thing—the same "good thing" the bankers had spotted. Why, if they could just issue those pieces of paper, without the necessity of actually holding the specie metal in reserve, life would be so much easier. They could increase spending without increasing taxes—*visible* taxes, anyway. It was something for nothing. In fact, once the idea was accepted that additional government spending was "good" for the economy, then those in authority searched to find ways they might not be hindered in being the benefactors to society.[2]

Prof. Benjamin Anderson has described the economic benefits of gold in these unforgettable terms: "Gold needs no endorsement. It can be tested with scales and acids. The recipient of gold does not need to trust the government stamp upon it, if he does not trust the government that stamped it. No act of faith is called for when gold is used in payments, and no compulsion is allowed." Why, if gold is such a benefit for the public, do governments oppose its widespread use? Anderson supplies the answer: *politicians hate the discipline it imposes.*

Complaints are always made about gold and the behavior of gold when there is irredeemable paper money. Under Gresham's Law, gold is hoarded, or leaves the country. It ceases to circulate, leaving the dishonored promissory note in possession of the field. Gold will stay only in countries which submit to its discipline. Gold is an unimaginative taskmaster. It demands that men and governments and central banks be

---

2. Murray N. Rothbard, *What Has Government Done to Our Money?* (Irvington, New York: Foundation for Economic Education, [1964]).

honest. It demands that they keep their promises on demand or at maturity. It demands that they keep their demand liabilities safely within the limits of their quick assets. It demands that they create no debts without seeing clearly how these debts can be paid. If a country will do these things, gold will stay with it and will come to it from other countries which are not meeting the requirements. But when a country creates debt light-heartedly, when a central bank makes rates of discount low and buys government securities to feed its money market, and permits an expansion of credit that goes into slow and illiquid assets, then gold grows nervous. Mobile capital funds of all kinds grow nervous. There comes a flight of capital out of the country. Foreigners withdraw their funds from it, and its own citizens send their liquid funds away for safety.[3]

The Resentment Against Gold

Governments love to inflate. They hate to have their inflationary policies exposed. Gold movements expose these policies. All this was going on long before Keynes arrived on the scene. His *General Theory*, however, provided apparent intellectual justification for these practices. Here, at long last, was a noted economist defending all that the politicians knew from instinct: that increasing the amount of money, stimulating the economy by government expenditure (monetary and fiscal policies, in other words), would impose great benefits on society as a whole, especially incumbent politicians. There was only one hitch. People still thought that these pieces of paper could be redeemed for the metal which backed them. Silly people.

The solution to this problem was to ban the conversion of paper money into gold. It was the abolition of a true gold coin standard and the substitution of a so-called "gold-exchange standard." The abolition of the gold coin standard took place in World

---

3. Benjamin McAlister Anderson, *Economics and the Public Welfare: Financial and Economic History of the United States, 1914-1946* (Princeton, New Jersey: Van Nostrand, 1949), p. 421. This has been reprinted by Liberty Press in Indianapolis, Indiana.

War I, when all the battling nations "temporarily" abandoned convertible currencies, so that they could impose a massive tax through inflation on their own helpless populations. The "gold exchange standard" was established by international agreement at the Genoa Conference of 1922.[4] This conference recommended a policy of "economizing the use of gold by maintaining reserves in the form of foreign balances." The words "economizing gold" meant "more fiat money issued than there is gold in reserve," and the words "maintaining foreign reserves in the form of foreign balances" meant that governments and central banks could buy interest-bearing national debt securities from Great Britain — and later, the United States — instead of holding "sterile" (non-interest-paying) gold. All nations could then "pyramid" their own money supplies on the basis of a small central core of gold held by one or two major nations.

This system led to world-wide inflation. From then on, pieces of paper were now only pieces of paper, except when governments or central banks owned the paper; by government decree they were now "money." Gold and silver were no longer money, even though for practical purposes they had not been involved directly in every transaction. By cutting the legal ties with gold and silver, governments were then able to print as many pieces of paper as they deemed necessary to govern in order that they might achieve their plans for the "Great Society." In other words, it was the fact that money was a precious metal which hindered plans for the ushering in of heaven on earth. By cutting the legal ties between gold and paper currencies, the central planners also broke the public's awareness of what long-term money is, and how crucial gold convertibility is as a means of *restricting the confiscatory practices of central governments*.

How despicable! Gold must be a terrible commodity. A barbarous relic! And what of these people who insisted that they

---

4. Jacques Rueff, *The Age of Gold* (Chicago: Regnery Gateway, 1964), pp. 4-5, 47-48.

wanted gold? Why, they, too, must be the rascals who are hindering the economic wellbeing of others. What was needed was an economic defense of why gold and silver were the great evils in society. Keynes assisted in providing that defense. Consequently, we find Dr. Vickers repeating these statements disapproving gold and silver as money.[5]

But the question of gold or silver as money is not just an economic and philosophic question. At its fundamental root it is a *religious* issue, for the question is: Who has legitimate, God-given authority to choose which commodity shall serve as money? The State, as God's delegated representative, or the free market, as the institutional creation of acting individuals? Is the State's role *creative* ("We alone create true money!") or *negative* ("You have created fraudulent money!")? Does the State have a monopoly of money-creation, or does it possess merely a monopoly of law-enforcement against law-breakers (counterfeiters)? Therein lies the heart of the matter. The issue is primarily an issue of *sovereignty*.

This provides the perspective with which we must view Dr. Vickers' disapprobation of gold and silver, not only from an economic point of view but also a theological perspective, for Dr. Vickers has gone to great lengths to argue against the idea that Scripture, as the revealed will of God, gives such explicit instruction as to which commodity should be used as money. I have already noted his defective arguments against the law of God as the source of instruction on how God shall have his creatures live. Yet it is the law of God that alone provides answers to the perplexing problems of life. Again, we have noted Leviticus 19:35-36 and its call for honest weights and measures. The Scriptures thus put parameters around man. But modern man is in revolt against the God of Scripture, as Rushdoony has argued:

> The revolt, thus, in the name of the freedom of man has been against the constraint of any law of God certainly, and also the laws of men. The

---

5. For a detailed analysis of monetary theory, see Ludwig Von Mises, *The Theory of Money and Credit* (Irvington-on-Hudson, New York: Foundation for Economic Education, [1912] 1971).

disturbances of the second half of the twentieth century should therefore be no surprise to us. When the philosophers and educators of our era have required so radical a break with established law the consequences are sure to be drastic and/or revolutionary. That men's ideas of money should be affected is a natural consequence. It was very common during the 1930's in the United States to hear progressive educators ridicule the idea of a gold standard. Anything could be money, it was said: hay, wheat, land, or goods could provide a backing for a currency, but what better backing could a paper currency have, *if* one were needed, than the credit, productivity, and taxing power of the United States?

Endless variations of this theme can be cited. Basic to all these "funny money" concepts were two essentially religious premises. *First,* man was seen as a creator, replacing God. Man's declaration of independence from God means the supplanting of God by man. This is how the Bible presents original sin, the desire of every man to be his own god, "Knowing" or determining good and evil in terms of himself (Genesis 3:5). Just as God created heaven and earth out of nothing, so man creates values out of nothing. *In Christian theology, values are what God declares them to be.* In humanism, values are what man declares them to be. . . .

Second, the logical corollary of this is that man, as his own lawmaker now, is freed from past laws. As the new god of being, modern statist man is no longer bound by the word of the old God of Scripture. . . . Re-educated man, it is maintained, will be free from past laws and will be able to prosper under fiat money.[6]

Dr. Vickers vs. Gold

Rebellious man wants freedom from God to become his own god, and Dr. Vickers plays straight into the rebel's hands. It has already been noted that Dr. Vickers makes no attempt to treat the Scriptural verses which defend the idea for a gold and silver monetary system. He argues that "Given an orderly international system, it can be said that gold, in spite of man's long history of fascination with it, should have no significance at all."[7] Such insight! We could also say:

6. R. J. Rushdoony, "Hard Money and Society in the Bible," in Hans F. Sennholz (ed.), *Gold Is Money* (Westport, Connecticut: Greenwood Press, 1975), pp. 166-68, emphasis added.

7. Vickers, *Economics and Man*, p. 237.

Given perfection, men would not need civil government.

Given omniscience, there would no longer be need for entrepreneurial profit or loss.

Given immortality, we would no longer need grave diggers.

Given basic common sense, we would no longer need Keynesian economics.

Given the ability to write in a coherent fashion, economists would no longer need editors.

It is true: *given* stable international trade, we would no longer need gold. But who is going to "give" it? Dr. Vickers knows: *international planners*. They are going to give us that—just as they have done since World War I, when the domestic gold standards were abolished, and the international gold standard was destroyed. We no longer need gold, he is forced to assume (but never is willing to admit), because we have nearly sin-free government leaders who no longer need the consumer-imposed restraints of gold-coin convertibility to keep them from confiscating their subjects' wealth through the invisible tax of inflation. How has this age-old sin been overcome? Through knowledge of Keynesian economics. Why will all these government planners be smart enough to achieve this monetary stability? Because they will all be disciples of Keynes. And why will they always be disciples of Keynes? Why, because no one can think logically about economics and not be a disciple of Keynes. "How do I know? The Bible tells me so. (Implicitly.)"

In short, Dr. Vickers has implicitly adopted the gnostic heresy: *salvation through arcane knowledge.*

It is of further interest to note, however, the manner in which Dr. Vickers, arguing against North and Rushdoony, attempts to show the impossibility of having such a monetary system.

Dr. Vickers agrees with the idea that *there is no absolute, fixed value of gold and silver,* and points out that *this is the conclusion that North and Rushdoony make also.* So far, so good. But he never knows when to stop. He makes this deduction: "But then it will not do for North and Rushdoony to embrace the magnificent inconsistency and the sparkling *non sequitur* of arguing that the country's money supply must, in accordance with imagined scriptural mandates, be 'backed' by something which is thus shown to have no necessary or stable value in itself."[8] Well, at least he thinks their *non-sequiter* sparkles. Maybe this is because it is gold-based. Dr. Vickers' *non-sequiters* have a dull green to them, either because they resemble sludge or paper U.S. dollars.

The point is, *nothing in this created world has permanent, fixed value, except the Bible, God's word.* The idea is not to search for an economic good with fixed value, and to select only this as money, as Dr. North repeats again and again. The idea is *to find a commodity which governments and bankers will find difficult and expensive to counterfeit.* But counterfeiting is of the very essence of the Keynesian solution. Dr. Vickers knows that Dr. North has said this,[9] and he resents it so deeply that he will not cite Dr. North's arguments to this effect.

A Phony Gold Standard

Dr. Vickers continues his line of reasoning with the example of gold being valued at $42 an ounce, and then concludes that if the value of gold changes to $84 an ounce, the money supply could, in this particular example, be doubled. According to Dr. Vickers, the situation may occur where market demand causes "an increase in the valuation of the stock of the monetary gold base, and an increase in the amount of money in circulation. The increased amount of money in circulation may conceivably affect the monetary demands for things in such a way that the dollar value of gold again increases. And this would permit another increase in the money supply. A self-reinforcing process of gold valuation and variations in the money supply can be envisaged."[10] Therefore, we must recognize that because "there cannot be any such thing as an *absolute* value for any commodity which it might be desired to

---

8. *Ibid.*, p. 251.

9. There are ten references to counterfeiting in the index of *An Introduction to Christian Economics*, and all ten refer to the State as counterfeiter. The reference to Keynes as a proponent of counterfeiting appears on page 135.

10. *Economics and Man*, p. 251.

use as a 'backing' for the money supply, the argument about the 'immorality' of 'unbacked paper money' falls completely to the ground."[11]

In our analysis of Dr. Vickers' reasoning at this point, notice should be taken, *first*, that Dr. Vickers has not, as observed earlier, dealt with the necessary verses of Scripture to warrant the statement about "imagined scriptural mandates." Until such a time as he offers some explanation of texts such as Leviticus 19:35-36, Dr. Vickers cannot claim to have "refuted" the North-Rushdoony argument for a commodity-based, anti-government counterfeiting, anti-banker counterfeiting monetary system.

Second, note Dr. Vickers' unwarranted conclusion concerning gold's value. He first speaks about the "absolute" value of gold, then states that because gold has *"no necessary or stable value"* (emphasis added), therefore the North-Rushdoony call for gold and silver as money falls to the ground. By this argument Dr. Vickers is implying that because gold has no absolute value, it must therefore have "no necessary or stable value." But this assumption is not necessarily true, nor warranted from the arguments he offers. Dr. Vickers would find it extremely difficult to find any evidence to support this contention that gold has no stable value. The price of gold has certainly fluctuated throughout the centuries. New gold discoveries must affect the value of gold to some extent; but a situation is possible where there is a tendency towards a stable value, *especially in comparison to fiat money monetary systems*. This is well known to anyone who has studied economic history.[12] Much of the new gold finds its way into manufacturing and other uses, and not into the monetary stream. In an imperfect world, perfect stability is a chimera which, like the mirage in a desert, may lead the unsuspecting searcher to greater disaster.

---

11. *Ibid.*, p. 252, emphasis added.

12. Roy W. Jastram, *The Golden Constant: The English and American Experience* (New York: Wiley, 1977). For a thorough review of this book, and also for a discussion of why and how the reviewers misinterpreted its conclusions, see Gary North's review in *The Journal of Christian Reconstruction*, VII (Summer 1980), pp. 206-12.

Third, Dr. Vickers fails to grasp the proposition that paper currency, being a *promissory note*, or *warehouse receipt*, or what Mises calls a "money-substitute," should by Biblical definition be *strictly* controlled by the quantity of gold in existence (if the receipts are pledges to pay gold on demand). This failure of Dr. Vickers to understand the historical relationship between paper currency and gold or silver is seen where he speaks of an increase in the "dollar value of gold." In the North-Rushdoony theoretical model of gold-coin convertibility and 100% reserve banking, because a dollar is equivalent to a certain quantity of gold, there can be no alteration in the dollar value of gold. There is no way for gold to jump from $42 an ounce to $84 per ounce. The dollar is, *by legal definition,* one forty-second of an ounce of gold (assuming that this is what Congress has determined), and changes in the physical quantity of gold *cannot* alter this fixed, definitional relationship. All it can permit is the printing of additional dollar notes in exchange for any gold which is deposited at the Treasury, on a $42 per ounce basis. Bring in $42 and buy an ounce of gold; bring in an ounce of gold and receive ("buy") $42. Take your pick.

The difference between North and Rushdoony and Dr. Vickers is essentially the fact that North and Rushdoony view gold and paper currency as a single *alternating* commodity — money — with paper currency being a one-to-one *substitute* for gold. The consumer has a choice: to store the gold (remove it from the market place) and circulate the paper, or "cash in" the paper and circulate the gold. This is not Dr. Vicker's view. He has in mind two different money commodities, enabling him to conclude that the dollar value of gold is alterable in the same manner that the exchange ratio (price) of other commodities is changeable.

More to the point, Dr. Vickers is arguing against the present fake gold standard, where the U.S. government establishes a wholly mythical value for gold ($42 per ounce) and then conducts no transactions in terms of this artificial price. It would be as if Dr. Vickers were to announce that *Economics and Man* is now worth $84 a copy, up from $42, at which price no copies were ever sold either.

It is true that under today's God-defying central bank system, if the government announced such an increase from $42 to $84, the value of the gold reserve of the Federal Reserve Bank would increase substantially. This increase in the value of Federal Reserve asset holdings would be monetized automatically by the commercial banking system unless the Fed sold half its holdings of gold or an equivalent amount of Treasury bills (debt certificates). If it did neither, then it would have to raise commercial bank reserve requirements in order to offset this inflationary effect. But all of this is simply *transaction accounts* in a world of fractional reserve banks. If Dr. Vickers does not understand the difference between this sort of rigged gold standard and the *100% redeemability gold coin standard/100% reserve bank standard* which is advocated by Dr. North, then Dr. Vickers is not a very bright fellow. But if he understands the difference, yet nevertheless went into print with such a specious (not specie) argument, then he is a knave.

As you may have noticed, he suffers from this "intellect-moral defect" dilemma throughout *Economics and Man*.

Overvalued Currency

Dr. Vickers, in his disparagement of the gold standard, endeavors to use England after the First World War as an example to "prove" that the gold standard did not work. True, England did return to a gold standard which caused economic upheaval, but Dr. Vickers, although admitting that this was because of *an incorrect ratio between the pound and gold,* never comes to the most logical conclusion that the correction of the problem was the restoration of a proper ratio between the pound and gold. Instead, Dr. Vickers raises the false question: "Should the gold parity be maintained and the unemployment and poverty accepted as the legitimate cost of doing so?"[13] Of course unemployment and poverty should not be accepted *if the cause is some government mistake,* but Dr. Vickers is misleading when he implies that tinkering with the value of fiat money is the only alternative to a gold standard. The

---

13. Vickers, *Economics and Man*, p. 247.

upheavals could have been solved by a return to a more realistic ratio between gold and the pound. England had merely made the error of restoring the gold-pound ratio to its pre-war parity, when a new ratio, reflecting the increase in the number of pounds during the war (i.e., monetary inflation) would have been the more appropriate course of action.

Dr. Vickers prefers to follow Keynes and therefore conveniently ignores the cause of England's money difficulties in the 1920's: the government's legislated insistence that the public accept at face value an over-valued pound. As Galbraith observes, "The error . . . was in restoring the pound to its pre-war gold content of 123.27 grains of fine gold, its old exchange ratio of $4.87. In 1920 the pound had fallen to as low as $3.40 in gold-based dollars."[14] The pound had been grossly over-valued. Sure enough, Gresham's Law asserted itself: the artificially overvalued currency (the pound sterling) drove out of circulation the artificially undervalued currencies (gold and foreign exchange). This is why the head of the Bank of England, Montague Norman, came to New York City and convinced the head of the Federal Reserve Bank to inflate the dollar. Norman wanted U.S. interest rates to be kept artificially low so that people would not sell pounds and buy dollars in order to invest in the U.S. at higher interest rates. The Federal Reserve Bank accommodated Norman, and the result was the inflation-fueled boom of the U.S. stock market and the subsequent collapse.[15] Who was responsible? The respective governments and their agents, the central banks (or is it the other way around?).

What Is the Issue?

The issue here is the issuing of money. Which agency is legally sovereign, the State or the market? If the market is sovereign, within the limits of the State's responsibility of monitoring and en-

---

14. J. K. Galbraith, *Money: Whence It Came, Where It Went* (Harmondsworth, Middlesex: Penguin Books, Ltd., 1976), p. 173, n.3.

15. Murray N. Rothbard, *America's Great Depression* (Princeton, New Jersey: Van Nostrand, 1963), pp. 131-52.

forcing just weights and measures, then the State cannot legally become the issuer of money. It is at most the *certifier* of honest money (and this is a dangerous precedent). What is honest money? Whatever consumers decide to use. Historically, this has been gold and silver, but it needn't be in every case. It is up to consumers to decide, not State bureaucrats.

This is what Dr. Vickers refuses to acknowledge. Why not? *Because Douglas Vickers hates the whole idea of the sovereignty of the consumers.* The idea that you and I, through our voluntary exchanges, could ever come to an agreement about the proper means of exchange disturbs him. That would mean that we are free men. Dr. Vickers does not believe that we are capable of exercising such freedom. We are in sin, he keeps reminding us.

And just what was Keynes in? Or whom?

The idea that lots of people could come to an agreement over the proper commodity to use as money, and that this decision-making process would actually produce results that would eliminate the boom-bust cycle, eliminate monetary inflation, and reduce uncertainty about the future value of the currency, repulses Dr. Vickers. That would mean that acting individuals are more capable of producing a balanced economy than State planners. That would mean that the consumers were more capable of assessing their own needs than Keynesian economists. That would mean the end of Dr. Vickers' chosen line of work. You can imagine how he resents such an idea.

Conclusion

Economic logic informs us that money is the most marketable commodity. It does not require a State decree in order for it to come into existence. It requires 100% reserve banking — the enforcement of the Biblical law of honest weights and measures. There is no need for the State to get involved in the money business. Whenever it does, the politicians eventually begin to debase the currency, so that the State can buy more than it collects in direct taxes. The State imposes the inflation tax. It fools the people who are supposed to be protected by civil government.

Gold is hated by the State officials who do not like any restrictions on their expansion of power through spending. They resent the fact that it is so expensive to produce gold, compared to how cheap it is to issue paper money and create computer entries. Gold restrains them, and they resent it. Because people can move gold from one nation to another, pressuring governments to reduce the creation of money, the politicians hate it. Gold is simply too democratic for their tastes. It restricts the elitist power of the central economic planners.

Here we have a great irony. In the name of Biblical justice, Dr. Vickers would transfer enormous power to an elite of central planners. So fearful is he of sin, that he would concentrate enormous power into the hands of a technical elite — his ideological and self-certified academic colleagues — and then allow them to decide what is best for the economy. This officially neutral, officially scientific, officially God-ignoring elite of economists — a discipline self-consciously based on atheism — is to decide what is best for us laymen. Who says this is best? Dr. Vickers. In whose name does he attempt to speak? In the name of Jesus. And who is not believed in by the elite into whose hands he would deliver us? That same Jesus, who his peers attempt to crucify daily on a cross of differential equations. In short, *Economics and Man* is a long-winded plea for a grotesque pagan idea: that sin is restrained by the concentration of power into the hands of monopolistic elitist planners who can fine or imprison anyone who fails to cooperate with their plans.

But he is not a socialist, you understand. Because he says so.

11

MUMBLE, MUMBLE

And we shall argue, moreover, that if the underlying and environmental economic conditions are such that a government budget deficit is necessary in order to support the general economic health of the country, and if there are both policy and analytical reasons why such a budget deficit should be financed by government loans from the central bank which involve the expansion of the money supply, then an increase in the money supply should most definitely be countenanced and encouraged. Too much depends on underlying conjunctures of economic forces to conclude, as North apparently wishes to do, that there is a single cause or a single cure for inflation. [1]

There is, perhaps, no more controversial topic in economic thinking today than the meaning of inflation. As someone has observed, where there are five economists you have six opinions. The error that can be made at this point, however, is the conclusion that because such diverse opinions arise, it is therefore impossible to make our way through the forest of ideas to ascertain what is, and is not, sound economic reasoning. If this is true, then the best thing to do is nothing, until we understand more. When we do not understand an economic process, then we should turn it over to the free market for resolution, not over to a bunch of bureaucrats with guns.

---

1. *Economics and Man*, pp. 178-79.

Definitions

In the long run, our understanding of any topic depends on the definition we give our terminology. This seems so obvious that such a statement should not need to be made. Yet it is a major aspect of our criticism of Dr. Vickers in particular, and Keynesianism in general, that he does not bother to let the reader know precisely how he is using particular terminology. In this, however, he is the first-born methodological son of his mentor. *The General Theory* is notorious for its unconventional and shifting definitions.

Inflation can be defined in different ways; there is no denying that fact. We need to ask: Which is the *better* definition to use? Which definition will allow us to develop our economic *theory* in such a way that it incorporates the *relevant* phenomena under consideration. This is the manner in which theories are developed. Certain happenings in the world are observed, and theories to explain those occurrences are developed. When an exception to the theory is found, the theory needs to be either discarded or modified.

Today, inflation has two basic definitions. First, there is the older and now less well-understood meaning that inflation is simply *an increase in the money supply*. The modern and newer meaning, thanks to Keynes' influence, is that inflation means *rising prices*. There is a reason for the difference in definitions. This disagreement has led to sinister implications for us, the victims of economists' definitions.

An Increase in Money

When inflation is defined as an *increase in the supply of money*, economists and voters alike are more likely to focus their attention on those agencies that control the issue of currency, coins, and checks. Anyone who wants to examine the *effects* of inflation will then have to begin with the *point of origin* of new money. By defining inflation as the creation of new money, the investigators' attention is transferred to those who have the legal right to create money. The money creators are put under closer scrutiny than might otherwise be the case.

Furthermore, if inflation is the increase of money, the investigator is more likely to ask himself: "What happens to the money after it is created? It is *spent* into circulation. Who benefits from the goods that are purchased by the spenders (or the *votes* that are purchased)? Who are the *recipients* of this newly created money? What *advantages* accrue to them, if any? Who are those who gain access to this new money later? What are the disadvantages, if any, of 'standing toward the end of the line'? What happens to *which prices* in *what sequence* from the time the new money is issued to the time that it no longer has any measurable effects?" In short, as Lenin so aptly epitomized the science of politics, *who, whom?* Who wins, who loses? If the State has the legal monopoly of issuing money, then initially the State and its beneficiaries win. At the end of the process . . . ? Revolution?

The crucial economic issue of monetary theory therefore becomes the question of *relative prices*, not the *aggregate price level*. The crucial issue becomes the economic effects of newly created money on particular segments of the economy, on certain specified interest groups. Only at the tail end of economic analysis does a peripheral and subordinate question appear: the effect of monetary inflation on "general prices," meaning *a statistical index number*.

Those who define inflation as an increase in the money supply tend to be those who examine relative prices and their effects on the way the economy functions. They examine the prices that you and I examine as we go about our task of buying and refraining from buying. Those economists who define inflation in this way tend to be in the Austrian School. The man who for half a century has called his colleagues to focus on relative prices rather than aggregate prices in their search for economic understanding is Frederick A. Hayek. He has continually criticized Keynes and the Keynesians for their unsalutary neglect of relative prices.[2] By implication, he also criticizes the monetarists and the Chicago School economists for this same neglect.

---

2. F. A. Hayek, *A Tiger By the Tail: A 40-Years' Running Commentary on Keynesianism by Hayek*, edited by Sudha R. Shenoy (London: Institute of Economic Affairs, 1972).

An Increase in the Price Level

In contrast to this definition of inflation is the one generally accepted by the Keynesians and the Friedmanites: inflation is *a rising price level*. They do not worry about inflation so defined until the index numbers selected by the government statisticians begin to indicate that *selected* "prices in general" are rising. In this sense, Friedman was correct when he announced, "We are all Keynesians now."

These economists do not believe that the issue is the issuing of money. They believe that the issue is rising prices. This means that only when monetary inflation has produced statistically measurable effects do "mainline" economists become interested in monetary policy. They do not spend time and effort in discussing the implications of the spread of newly created money through the economy *before this process affects the statisticians' index number.* They do not bother analyzing the possibility that these effects might create the dreaded boom-bust cycle of economic expansion and depression. That a boom might come without being observed in rising prices generally is not taken seriously by most economists, for most economists rely on this index number definition of inflation.[3] They rarely discuss the theoretical possibility — let alone the practical likelihood — that the effects of an increase in the money supply might be inflationary despite a stable price level, since *prices that might have otherwise have fallen*, due to increased productivity, remain stable.

This is why definitions do matter. If we define a phenomenon in a particular way, we may become blind to cause-and-effect relationships that are denied by, or de-emphasized by, our chosen definition. And since this is a book about Dr. Vickers and Keynes, let me put it a different way. If people become willfully blind to cause-and-effect relationships that displease them, they will then define a phenomenon in a way that makes it easier for them to ignore these unpleasant relationships.

---

3. One who does not is Murray Rothbard, *America's Great Depression* (Princeton, New Jersey: Van Nostrand, 1963).

An Increase in Velocity

All of the various schools of economic thought admit that if there is an increase of velocity of money, prices can rise faster than the rate of increase in the money supply. They all recognize that this happens in the final stages of a mass inflation, as it did in Germany in late 1923. The Austrian School seldom discusses the topic, however, except in these high-inflation historical contexts. It is a weakness which deserves correcting.

One major qualification needs to be made concerning the concept of the velocity of money. If people as buyers of goods (sellers of money) are getting rid of money more rapidly, sellers must also be getting rid of goods just as rapidly as *buyers of money*. Obviously, *someone* is letting loose of the goods and services. So there has been an increase in the velocity of goods and services, too. Shouldn't these two "velocities" offset each other? Why should prices of goods rise (the value of money fall) as a result of increased velocity? This question was once raised by Henry Hazlitt. I have seen nothing in print to respond to it, although there must be something in print somewhere which addresses the problem.

I think it may be a purely statistical phenomenon. As mass inflation hits an economy, owners of goods and services increasingly refuse to sell. They hoard durable goods because they expect to be able to sell them at even higher money prices for them later on. Eventually, most people refuse to sell because they do not trust the future value of money at all. Thus, the prices recorded for *those few durable goods that actually do get sold* are very high.

The government statistician then imputes the price received for the handful of actual sales to the total number of goods of this type that the statistician estimates may exist in the overall economy. This "index number" of prices is highly misleading: very few of these goods are being offered for sale *for paper money*. The high price level which is attributed to an increase in the velocity of money therefore overstates the real increase in money prices, because it "weighs" the effect of these few sales in the "money economy" *as if* a large number of these goods were actually being sold. While these goods are crucial for the *real* economy—the barter economy — they are steadily less important as a factor in the fiat money economy, where they are seldom brought to market. In other words, they are *overweight* statistics. Fat statistics get all the attention in the press and economic histories.

Nevertheless, Hazlitt's paradox raises an interesting problem which deserves a lot more attention from Ph.D.-holding economists of all schools. (Hazlitt has continued to pop the economists' balloons since about 1920, probably because he never graduated from college and has never had his thought patterns restructured by professional academics.)

If I am correct in my guess that the rise in the price level which follows an increase in the velocity of money toward the end of mass inflation is primarily a statistical phenomenon, then such an increase in velocity in the early stages of an inflation is not the cause of price inflation, but only an indication of a boom economy. Prices are rising, not because of an increase in the velocity of money, but because of the increase in the supply of money. An increase in the velocity of money merely records statistically people's increased willingness to enter into voluntary exchanges.

The Effects of Monetary Inflation

As I have already mentioned, an interesting omission in the Keynesian system is a discussion of the economic effects of increasing the money supply. Although their velocity of money concept is linked to the question of money supply increase, Keynesians generally avoid a rigorous analysis of the spreading economic effects of increasing the amount of money in circulation. Their primary reason for this is that the Keynesian system calls for an increase in the money supply, and to analyze this aspect of monetary theory in detail would expose the inherent difficulties *and inequities* that arise from this practice. It would also expose the losers in the economy, and losers might band together and call for a cessation of monetary inflation.

What if certain groups recognized what was going on? What if they began to invest in terms of taking advantage of the changes in *relative* prices created by the monetary inflation? What if their inflation-hedging investment activity in, say, gold, silver, and art objects were to call attention to the economic results of the Keynesian inflation game? What if workers then took note of this and began demanding higher wages, thereby reducing the employment "kick" which the Keynesian planners hoped to achieve for the overall economy? What, in short, if the victims should finally catch on to the essence of the Keynesian revolution, which is based on an illusion: higher employment as a result of lower *real* wages? That would be a dark day for the Keynesian planners. And so it was, in 1979 and 1980. So it will be again, when the desperate Keynesian economists recommend mass inflation to bail out the banks. (Better put, when the desperate bankers call in the Keynesian economists to justify the bankers' call for the central banks to inflate the various Western currencies, especially the U.S. dollar.)

The essence of the discipline of economics is to study *cause* and *effect* of different economic occurrences. Consider an increase in the money supply. What can cause it, and what are its likely effects? The answer to the first part of that question depends on what money is. In our era, money is regarded by most people as those pieces of paper with pictures of various politicians on them, and token coinage made up of metals such as zinc and copper. To determine the cause of the supply of these units we only need ask who controls their issuance in the first place. The answer to that is *the State*. Any increase in the money supply is thus a *deliberate* act on the part of those in civil government.

Banking

Unfortunately, it is not that simple. Men have devised a system whereby the money supply can be increased without physically increasing the quantity of pieces of paper and coinage which already exists. The method of doing this is called *fractional reserve banking*. There is nothing especially magical about this, for all it involves is certain bookkeeping procedures. We are all familiar with banks, and what they do. They take depositors' money, promise to pay them interest on it, and then lend it out at a higher rate to borrowers, pocketing the difference as reward for their service. If that were all the bank did, there would be no difficulty in understanding their place in the economic life of the community. If they were merely a storehouse for people's monetary wealth, and in addition provided the valuable service of bringing lenders and borrowers together in order that an amicable transaction might ensue, the place of banks in the economy would be highly beneficial. On the one hand, the lender would get a receipt acknowledging his deposit, while on the other hand, the borrower would sign a contract stating the terms and conditions of his repayment of the sum borrowed — a simple, straightforward contractual arrangement.

Some depositors might not want to lend their money. They may want it in the near future for some purpose, and therefore they are only putting it in the bank for safe-keeping. Under normal commercial conditions, they would pay a fee for this safe-keeping service, for the banker is not able to make any profit by lending out that particular deposit. The fact that *all* depositors get interest, whether they intend to lend their savings or not, should warn us that something is amiss. How can interest be paid when the money is not on loan to a borrower who is paying for the privilege of using that money?

We are back to the question of fractional reserve banking. Bankers have determined that at any point in time, all the depositors who have merely stored their savings for safety reasons will not turn up at the teller's cage to demand the return of their deposited funds. Bankers have thus perceived the opportunity for additional profits. If it is known that on average only a certain percentage of depositors desire the return of the finances, then the remainder could be used — *provided the depositor does not know that this is being done without permission.* So bankers have devised a scheme whereby they can use even that portion of deposits left with them that was not intended to be lent to borrowers. Their scheme runs something like this.

Fiat Money

When a depositor places money in the bank, the bank issues a receipt of some kind. In essence this is now a *liability* to the bank. But because the banker has worked out how to utilize this money for his own profit, he now perceives this deposit not as a liability but as an *asset*. Perhaps $100 has been deposited. He knows that at any one time only twenty percent of depositors want their money back, so he puts aside this percentage ($20) in his vault (non-interest-paying), and then gleefully searches for a borrower who needs $80. (Actually, the central bank collects most of this "vault money.")

He could give him the $80 cash straight out, but any time an inventory take is done, his scheme would be exposed. Why not use the bank's good standing in society and issue another piece of paper which says the borrower has access to $80? He can simply use that piece of paper as money, the receiver remaining confident that the bank will honor the obligation involved in that document. This way, the banker gets to hang onto all the money. His inventory remains full, balancing his liabilities.

Cause

If this was all he did, things would not be so bad. But there is a second banker in town. When the first bank's client (borrower) deposits the borrowed funds in his own bank account, he can then start writing checks. Someone else gets this $80, and the new possessor of the $80 deposits it. The second banker (or maybe it is the first one), rather than seeing this as a return of the loaned out capital, instead views it as a "new" deposit. He proceeds to retain his familiar twenty percent security, and determines to lend out the remaining $64. So the merry-go-round continues. The loaned-out money, each time it is returned to the bank by some recipient seller of goods or services, is dealt with by the banker as a "new" deposit. In reality, of course, it is simply a return of a portion of that original $100.

Watch the money multiply: from $100 to $500. Here is the de-

scription of the process which appears in a popular book published
by the United States' central bank, *The Federal Reserve System: Purposes and Functions*, published in 1963 on the 50th anniversary of
the Federal Reserve System. This highly revealing description is
no longer published in the more recent versions.

MULTIPLYING CAPACITY OF RESERVE MONEY
THROUGH BANK TRANSACTIONS[1]
(in dollars)

Transactions	Deposited in checking accounts	Lent	Set aside as reserves
Bank 1	100.00	80.00	20.00
2	80.00	64.00	16.00
3	64.00	51.20	12.80
4	51.20	40.96	10.24
5	40.96	32.77	8.19
6	32.77	26.22	6.55
7	26.22	20.98	5.24
8	20.98	16.78	4.20
9	16.78	13.42	3.36
10	13.42	10.74	2.68
Total for 10 banks	446.33	357.07	89.26
Additional banks............	53.67	[2]42.93	[2]10.74
Grand total, all banks......	500.00	400.00	100.00

[1]Assuming an average member bank reserve requirement of
20 per cent of demand deposits.
[2]Adjusted to offset rounding in previous figures.

This is the heart of how the modern fractional reserve (a frac-
tion of deposits *in* reserve) banking system operates. Such a practice "increases" the money supply in inverse proportion to its fractional reserve requirement: the lower the required percentage of
reserves, the more money can be created by the banking system as
a whole. In reality, nothing valuable has been created, but wealth is

steadily *transferred*: to those who gain access to the new money early, and who spend it on goods and services, from those who receive it later, and who face higher selling prices than would otherwise have been the case. It is all done by fictional bookkeeping, and therefore deserves the description "fiat money" — created out of nothing.

An economist who defines inflation to mean an increase in the money supply is thus talking about two phenomena in modern society. On the one hand, he is talking about the manufacture of notes and coins by the government, and on the other hand, he is talking about fractional reserve banking policy which also "manufactures" additional money. The fact that all modern banking systems are controlled by the federal authorities through national reserve banks is proof that even this method of increasing the money supply is ultimately controlled by State officials.

Effect

We have seen the *cause* of increasing the money supply, but what is its *effect*? The law of supply and demand, contrary to Keynesian opinion, still operates. An increase in the supply of any good, say potatoes, will result — other things remaining unchanged — in a lowering of the money value of that particular good. When we consider that commodity in terms of money, we can say its (money) price has declined. We now need less money to obtain it. Or, we could look at the same transaction and say that the value of money has *increased* because we can now purchase a larger quantity of that good with the same amount of money. Still another way we can put the same idea is to say that *as commodity sellers*, we now need to sell more of that good in order to obtain the same quantity of money (or any other economic good we wish to exchange for it).

If potatoes were money, that is, the medium of exchange in society, we would now say that prices have risen; it would now cost more potatoes to obtain any other good or service. Like a coin which can be looked at from either side or from its edge, so any transaction can be viewed from several vantage points. Money is an economic commodity, just like potatoes. Increase its supply, and its value goes down (or fails to go up) in relation to other goods and services.

But there is a difference with respect to money—a unique difference. When more potatoes are produced, consumers of potatoes are benefited. There are more consumer goods available than before. But when additional money is produced, *there is no net benefit to society.* (Or more properly put, a humanist economist cannot *say* that there has been any net increase.)[4] Holders of money are hurt, for the value of money falls. Spenders of money are benefited; they get the goods.

Although it is true that any economic good or service could rise in price owing to a change in either supply or demand, our observation here leads us to conclude that when *all* prices rise generally, what we are really observing is a lowering of the purchasing power of the monetary unit. That is, its supply has increased causing a decline in its value (its purchasing power) and this in turn creates a rise in prices. Inflating the monetary unit, therefore, is the *cause* of general price rises.

Dr. Vickers' Confusion

It is worth noting that Dr. Vickers makes no attempt to discuss the effects of increasing the money supply. He is adamant that fiscal and monetary policies are needed, and he is certain that "injections" need to be made into the economy whenever those objectionable savers withdraw their money from the national income stream. (All right, all right: savers *don't* remove money from the national income stream. They put it right back into the income stream. They deposit it in a bank, or a money market fund, or whatever, and it keeps on rolling along. You know this. I know this. Dr. Vickers honestly doesn't understand this. He lives in the shadow of Keynes.) But Dr. Vickers' call for such policies is

---

4. This is because of a crucial problem of the economics profession: they cannot, as neutral, value-free scientists, make interpersonal comparison of subjective utilities. Dr. North surveys this problem in *The Dominion Covenant: Genesis* (Tyler, Texas: Institute for Christian Economics, 1982), ch. 4.

noticeably silent on its analysis of the likely *effects* of such action. To avoid such confrontation with the law of supply and demand, Dr. Vickers, as we have seen, simply tries to argue that such a law does not always exist. On the other hand, he also hides his discussion of the topic by re-defining the meaning of inflation.

Increasing the money supply was once the meaning of the word inflation. To inflate was to inflate the amount of money in existence. Now, however, inflation means something altogether different. It is usually understood to mean a rise in prices, and that is the popular understanding in our day. To overcome this dual definition difficulty, it is necessary to speak of *monetary* inflation and *price* inflation. Such terminology allows us to clarify our words so that Dr. Vickers cannot accuse us of using "empty logomachy." Of more particular importance, though, is our observation that monetary inflation *causes* price inflation.

Theft Through Inflation

Our analysis here raises a fundamental *moral* question. If lowering the value of the monetary unit is a *deliberate* act on the part of someone, has he not *deliberately* taken the value of the monetary unit away from the holders of that unit? In other words, has there not been a deliberate act of *stealing* something from someone, in this case the *value* of their money? If this is the case, then as Christians do we not have some obligation not to defraud our neighbor? The command in Leviticus 19:35-36 contains the idea of having just weights and measures, money originally being gold and silver measured by weight.[5] Clearly this command, an application of the eighth commandment forbidding theft, also forbids defrauding our neighbor of the *value* of his monetary unit, especially when it is well within our power to maintain that value.

The Keynesians' unwillingness to see the deficiency of their analysis at this point, and their refusal to consider the moral im-

---

5. See Rousas John Rushdoony, "Hard Money and Society in the Bible," in Hans F. Sennholz, (ed.), *Gold Is Money* (Westport, Connecticut: Greenwood Press, 1975), pp. 157-175.

plications of their policies, is the cause of part of our fundamental disagreement with their system. It is not that they have departed from the older and traditional meaning of inflation. That is not such a major issue. If they were willing to discuss the cause and effects of inflating the money supply in their overall theory, there would be less reason to be critical of their system. But by re-defining inflation to mean price increases, this provides opportunity for them to *appear* as if they discuss these economic phenomena thoroughly. It builds a veneer of apparent thoroughness, but their system is devoid of any discussion on the likely effects of monetary inflation and what are the causes of general price increases. In fact, because of the weakness of their analysis, they are incapable of describing the economic phenomena that we witness today, the continual but erratic increase of all prices. Having denied the law of supply and demand in order to justify their fiscal and monetary policies, they have denied one of the fundamental tools of economic analysis.[6]

Darwinian Impersonalism

Evolutionary Darwinism has pervaded twentieth-century thought to a greater degree than we often realize. We are, to some extent, influenced by the culture which surrounds us, and a major factor in contemporary thought is the concept of evolution, which teaches we live in a world of chance, of "brute" factuality, where nothing necessarily stands in relationship to anything else. The universe is a meaningless lump of primeval matter which has, for some unknown reason, originated out of the *ylem*[7] (or some such

---

6. The pseudo-economic Social Credit theories of C. H. Douglas, which have some support in Christian circles, also fall into this category. They similarly refuse to analyze the effects of increasing the money supply. Their dislike is for the bankers whose creation of "fiat" money involves a debt burden on those who receive it. That is, it has to be repaid with interest. Social Creditors would merely like to see the creation of wealth (in their terminology "social credits") in the hands of the State to be issued to all without obligation. The *effects* of such a policy they conveniently ignore. The effects would be bad.

7. Robert Jastrow, *Red Giants and White Dwarfs: Man's Descent from the Stars* (New York: Signet, 1969), pp. 68-69.

"original universal stuff"). This leads to the unfortunate conclusion that the world is impersonal, that there are impersonal forces that bring about "whatsoever comes to pass." By denying the all-controlling God of Scripture who determines whatsoever comes to pass, men transfer predestination to some other force or object. In the mind of twentieth-century man, chance controls whatsoever comes to pass. Conveniently, this ultimately denies, unlike Biblical predestination, the validity of human choice. We are not responsible, says modern man, for our actions. ("The random, impersonal universe which chance gave unto me hath made me to sin.") This has had disastrous effects in the study of economics.[8]

The denial of the law of supply and demand has reinforced the popular notion of evolutionary Darwinism: that whatever happens is caused by chance, not deliberate human action. Consequently, price inflation is seen as the product of chance. Sometimes we have it, and sometimes we don't. After all, don't our politicians say they are doing their best to control price inflation? Don't we hear their self-adulation at bringing present (early 1986) price inflation rates down to "tolerable" levels of around five percent? Are we not promised, especially at election time, that their utmost efforts will be given to control price inflation?

Evolutionary thought thus plays into the hands of power-hungry politicians who, committed to the Keynesian fallacies, would rather impose their ridiculous fiscal and monetary policies on an ignorant and gullible public. But as Peter Drucker notes, "It is simply not true, as is often asserted, that economists do not know how to stop inflation. Every economist since the late 16th century has known how to do it: Cut government expenses and with them the creation of money. What economists lack is not theoretical knowledge, it is political will or political power. So far all inflations have been ended by politicians who had the will

---

8. The best defense, and the most delightful reading, of biblical predestination is Martin Luther's *Bondage of the Will* (various translations).

rather than by economists who had the knowledge."[9]

Mumble, Mumble

To be an economist today is not an easy life. As Dr. Vickers reminds us, "economics is no longer sure of itself." What he really means is, "We Keynesians have predicted inaccurately for so long that our younger colleagues, committed to Milton Friedman, are beginning to ridicule us. We have been blamed for inflation, and we have also been blamed for recession. Just because we have been in charge, and just because that flamboyant big-mouth Heller said the new age of Keynesian bliss had arrived back in 1966, we are now being asked unfairly to take responsibility for the bad side of the economy, as if it were the fault of Keynesian planning rather than chance, or Richard Nixon, or economics in general, or something. Furthermore, our pension benefits are not looking very reliable, and we are all getting close to retirement. So I guess we economists are all to blame. I guess all economists are wrong. I guess I'm off the hook."

What of Hayek, who began predicting precisely these bad results in the late 1930's? What of Mises, who did the same? What of the Austrian School in general? They don't count. To prove it, Dr. Vickers wrote his book.

For the average hard-working economist, Dr. Vickers' admissions (like Milton Friedman's in 1971)[10] are not so encouraging. After all, if the whole profession is not sure of itself, then what can the poor, humble economist do and say? If he is no longer sure of anything that he might propose, there seems little else the modern economist can do but mumble. To allow the dictionary to enlighten us, the meaning of mumble is "to speak indistinctly."

---

9. Peter F. Drucker, "Toward the Next Economics" in *The Public Interest*, Special Edition, 1980, p. 12. This is currently being proven to be true in Great Britain where two philosophers rather than economists, Dr. Madsen Pirie and Dr. Eamonn Butler of the Adam Smith Institute, have been influential in turning the tide against the British drift into socialism. They have effectively brought about the privatization program which the Thatcher Government is pursuing.

10. Cited at the beginning of the Introduction.

Maybe this appears a little harsh to some. Well, before making final judgment, let us take a tour of Dr. Vickers' understanding and theories on inflation. A surprise may be in store.

Douglas Vickers, Inflation Fighter?

A superficial reading of Dr. Vickers' *Economics and Man* could lead to the conclusion that there is agreement with the North-Rushdoony thesis that an increase in the money supply — that is, monetary inflation — causes a devaluation in the purchasing power of money which, in Biblical terms, is theft and fraud. "[W]e should avoid the theft and immorality of inflation," says Dr. Vickers.[11]

> Inflation, it ought to be said, is immoral, and the immorality is chargeable to those whose economic actions give rise to it, or to those who, being responsible for the right administration of the economic affairs of the nation, either adopt policies which exacerbate the inflation rate or fail to take action more reasonably designed to correct it.[12]

A closer examination of the sentence quoted will reveal, however, that Dr. Vickers has a vastly different idea of the meaning of inflation from that of North and Rushdoony. (We shall see that he has a different definition altogether than those mentioned earlier in this chapter.) Notice that he says the *failure* to take economic action can cause inflation. Now, failure to act *cannot* cause inflation in the North-Rushdoony sense (except the government's failure to enforce the law of honest weights and measures), since they define inflation as any increase in the money supply.[13] How could inaction cause an increase in the money supply? Obviously, Dr. Vickers employs this word in a different sense from those he opposes. What he refuses to accept is the definition of inflation as an increase in the money supply. No Keynesian will. If he did, he would have to abandon his entire methodology. Thus, all Keynesians cling religiously to *any* definition of inflation except the

---

11. Vickers, *Economics and Man*, p. 36.
12. *Ibid.*, p. 98; cf. pp. 175, 242, 243, 253-254.
13. North, *An Introduction to Christian Economics*, p. 20.

Austrian one.[14]

"Inflation," Dr. Vickers says, "is a condition of dynamic dis-equilibrium."[15] This means precisely nothing—or better put, it means imprecisely nothing. *Every* economy is always in a condition of dynamic disequilibrium. There never can be equilibrium in the real world. Equilibrium for economic analysis is what the philosophers call a *limiting concept*—a mental backdrop or hypothetical model by which to evaluate the real world. Once again, at a crucial point in economic analysis, Dr. Vickers is offering us another verbal smoke screen. It is another attempt to substitute meaningless phrases in order to remain safely on the sidelines while Keynesian policy-makers debauch the currency just as surely as Keynes debauched Tunisian boys.

Dynamic Muddle

But let us take him at his muddled word. What about equilibrium? *First*, if inflation is defined as "a condition of dynamic dis-equilibrium," the recurring phrase "inflationary disequilibrium" is a meaningless tautology.[16] Dr. Vickers is saying there is such a thing as a "dynamic disequilibrium disequilibrium," a phrase which does not make sense.

Second, the immorality of inflation which Dr. Vickers talks about is therefore the "immorality" of a "dynamic disequilibrium." This must mean that *any* change which occurs to upset the Keynesian concept of "equilibrium" is immoral. In other words, Dr. Vickers wants an economy that is completely unchanging to satisfy his demands for morality.

---

14. A Christian economics teacher who adhered to the Keynesian theories, and favored the ideas of Vickers, insisted to me that inflation could *not* be defined as an increase in the money supply. He just would not allow it. Even though I conceded to call it something else, he still would not discuss the crux of the matter, that increasing the money supply causes prices to rise, effectively defrauding some people in the community of the purchasing power of their money. Ignoring the *real* issues is an integral part of the Keynesian system.

15. Vickers, *Economics and Man*, p. 277.

16. *Ibid.*, pp. 15, 129, 264, 273, 274, 277, 278, 280, 281, 321, 335, 336, 340.

This is seen in his call — read: "call for the government to do something" — for stable prices. One of his stated economic objectives is "a stable level of domestic prices, or the preservation of the internal purchasing power of the economy's money supply."[17] Consequently, the nature of this world as it is, with its changes and fluctuations, must be immoral as far as Dr. Vickers is concerned. But this idea of morality is far removed from the Biblical concept that morality and immorality are in terms of the law of God.

Third, why would anyone call for stable prices? First, in a productive economy, prices should be falling. Do you really think the consumer has been hurt by electronic calculators that sold in 1985 for five percent of what they sold for in 1975? Are we dead set against a higher real income? The government does have the power to keep the money supply very close to constant. But to do this would be to allow prices to fall, as producers compete to sell us ever-increasing quantities of the goods and services we want. But Dr. Vickers is unwilling to call for *monetary stability*. That would involve no teams of central planners. That would involve no collecting of reams of price data. That would not allow the government to impose the invisible tax of monetary inflation on the public. No, he calls instead for something which the government has proven completely incapable of providing, stable prices.

Does he want price and wage controls? Does he want an increase in the money supply to match the increase of a statistical average he would call the price level? Yes, he is willing to accept either, though preferably the latter policy. The monetarists are willing to accept an annual 3% to 5% increase of the money supply, too. So are the supply-side economists. So are the Social Credit cranks. Only two groups forthrightly call for stable money — *after* a return to a full gold coin standard with 100% reserve banking — with prices adjusted *solely* by free market competition, whether up, down or sideways: the Austrian School and the re-

---

17. *Ibid.*, p. 173.

constructionists.[18] These are Dr. Vickers' declared intellectual enemies, the people against whom he wrote his book.

Fourth, with Dr. Vickers' definition in mind, his conclusion against Gary North that there is no "single cause or a single cure for inflation," is an inference that Dr. North's economic conclusions are incorrect.[19] It is, however, simply a matter of definition. Conclusions are only as good as their founding premises, and from his premise that inflation is a "dynamic disequilibrium," Dr. Vickers' claim that North is incorrect is a logical deduction. But understand: it is a logical deduction from a definition which cannot possibly have any economic meaning. It has no specific content to give it predictive or analytic value. "Dynamic disequilibrium" tells us nothing, except that Dr. Vickers has chosen not to present a logical alternative to Dr. North's analysis.

On the other hand, if North's definition of inflation is the starting premise, Dr. Vickers' conclusion is incorrect. Combine the idea that inflation is an increase in the money supply with the inescapable fact that current monetary units are controlled by State authorities, and there can only be *one* cause, and therefore *one* cure, of inflation, according Dr. North's definition.

Why Immoral?

To deliberately lower the value of money is to deliberately take away someone's purchasing power. It is theft and fraud in every sense of the word, although when conducted on the scale which is

---

18. What is really needed is several decades of monetary deflation. Without the creation of 100% reserve banking, the world will forever be at the mercy of the money manipulators. To return to a world of stable money and flexible pricing, we will have to go through the deflationary wringer. Once the various government banking insurance schemes are officially abandoned, and the thrift institutions are left on their own, there is no known way to prevent a toppling of the banks, if the central banks slowly increase reserve requirements. This deflationary policy is revolutionary, but so is the coming mass inflation (the only possible alternative to a return to sound money), which will inevitably be followed by uncontrolled deflation, or else a total destruction of today's currency, with a new currency substituted for the dead one. This is the more likely scenario, however.

19. *Ibid.*, p. 179.

currently exhibited worldwide — thanks to Keynes — it is probably better to call it grand larceny. Yet it is this precise policy which Keynesians offer as "sound" and "moral" economic theory. Biblical morality and Keynesianism are thus in radical opposition to one another at this point. How Dr. Vickers can call monetary inflation beneficial is beyond comprehension. He is aware that monetary policies cause economic recession and expansion, yet it apparently does not occur to Dr. Vickers that an obvious way to reduce expansionary-recessionary tendencies, which cause the disharmonies Dr. Vickers is so keen to eliminate, would be to do away with the Keynesian policies imposed by a central planning authority.

Monetary inflation also encourages political favoritism. When governments print money, it is given to *some* people who are now able to buy goods which were previously beyond their means. This increased demand tends to drive up the prices for those goods, thereby putting at a disadvantage those who did not get the new money early enough. Even if fractional reserve banking is used as the means of money creation, those who can borrow most will benefit at the expense of those who borrow little or nothing. Some gain, some lose. The winners in the inflation game gain at the losers' expense.

Tragic Consequences

Perhaps the most tragic consequence of monetary inflation, at least from an economic perspective, is the *misallocation of resources* which it induces. When some members of the community have their purchasing power increased, they either call for additional production in existing goods and services or for new goods and services. As this new money is spent, those receiving it are able to buy additional goods. As the new money circulates throughout the economy, however, there is a tendency for prices to rise.

Once the general price level (however compiled and "weighted") has increased, the economy is *not* back to where it was before the new money was injected into it. Expectations were induced by the prior rise in prices. The boom phase of the cycle was induced. The

misleading price signals produced by the monetary inflation—
especially, temporarily lower interest rates—led entrepreneurs to
misforecast coming economic events. The new conditions surprise
entrepreneurs. They shut down projects. They slow their spending. They stop borrowing to build new projects. They fire
employees. A recession is the result.

Monetary inflation has thus caused a misallocation of resources, including labor, resulting in a waste of some of those
resources.[20] Possibly some producers purchased plant and equipment which now sits idle, or perhaps others increased their labor
force which is no longer required. Given Dr. Vickers' requirement
that economics should concern conservation, development and
equity, nothing would appear more contrary to these ideals than
monetary and fiscal policies which create such economic upheaval.[21]

It is not only their monetary theory which creates a drastic
waste of resources; their other policies have similar effects. For example, the attempts to introduce a "just" progressive tax system
have resulted in massive tax evasion and avoidance schemes.
Each time the tax laws are altered, there is a tremendous effort in
the community to understand their effects and to find ways
around them in order to minimize any tax liabilities. How much
better off would we be if this enormous quantity of human
resources, expended in finding loopholes in the tax legislation,
could instead be put to productive use for the benefit of all? How
much better would it be if free men were allowed to compete and
innovate without bureaucratic tinkering?

Conclusion

Against this background, it is easy to see that Dr. Vickers is
mumbling. He is speaking quite indistinctly. If he cannot define
inflation in such a manner that there is some semblance of coher-

---

20. Ludwig von Mises, *Human Action: A Treatise on Economics* (3rd ed.; Chicago:
Regnery, 1966), ch. 20.

21. For a comprehensive analysis of monetary inflation and its effects, see
Henry Hazlitt, *The Inflation Crisis, And How To Resolve It* (New Rochelle, New
York: Arlington House, 1978).

ence in the message he is attempting to get across to the reader, we may readily conclude he is mumbling. But Keynes mumbled, too, and a lot of very highly placed people thought they heard something profound. What they heard was pure pragmatic balderdash. What they heard was a cry for more State intervention. They loved to hear that. His mumbling didn't matter at all.

Am I exaggerating? Consider Keynes' written reply to specific questions asked by the British government's Economic Advisory Council in July of 1930. They wanted his opinion on what should be done to counteract the growing depression. This is the advice he gave them:

> When we come to the question of remedies for the local situation as distinct from the international, the peculiarity of my position lies, perhaps in the fact that I am in favour of practically all the remedies which have been suggested in any quarter. Some of them are better than others. But nearly all of them seem to tend in one direction. The unforgivable attitude is, therefore for me the negative one, — the repelling of each of these remedies in turn.
>
> Accordingly, I favour an eclectic programme, making use of suggestions from all quarters, not expecting too much from the application of any one of them, but hoping that they may do something in the aggregate.[22]

Mumble, mumble. Spend and spend, tax and tax, inflate and inflate, elect and elect. For in the long run, we are all dead. And some of us will leave no progeny.

On the other hand, others of us will.

---

22. Cited by D. E. Moggridge, *The Return to Gold, 1925: The Formulation of Economic Policy and Its Critics* (Cambridge: At the University Press, 1969), p. 90.

12

THE GREAT UNMENTIONABLE: UNEMPLOYMENT

There are no inherent reasons in a modern capitalist or quasi-capitalist economy why the system will automatically equilibrate at a situation of full employment. [1]

In his crucially important book, *The Structure of Scientific Revolutions* (1962), Thomas Kuhn describes the way in which a particular academic discipline changes its collective mind. These infrequent major revolutions involve an academic guild's rejection of many of the truths of an earlier era, and the adoption of new insights that were considered taboo, or preposterous, by the masters of the guild prior to the revolution. This transformation, he says, seldom involves large numbers of the existing members who change their minds. Instead, they retire or die, and younger men who have adopted the new viewpoint replace them.

Why do these revolutions occur? Kuhn says that they take place when bright people, who are either outside the guild or are too young to have invested very much in developing insights (or professional papers) that favor the existing outlook, begin to take notice of certain anomalies that the guild chooses to ignore. Perhaps it is a theoretical inconsistency. More likely it is some result of experimental inquiry which cannot be explained well by the existing world-and-life view of the guild, what Kuhn calls its paradigm. As more and more bright people focus attention on the anomalies, the older masters get upset. They charge younger men

---

1. Vickers, *Economics and Man*, p. 136.

with heresy. They point to the "outsider" status of some the innovators. But if the skepticism of younger men grows, the guild is
ripe for a revolution.

Then, seemingly overnight, someone puts forth a new explanation of the anomalies. He reconstructs the guild's paradigms. A
successful theory will retain as much as possible of the received
wisdom, but the essence of the revolution is the new paradigm itself. The transformation takes about a generation. Then the guild
settles down to do "normal science" — the drudgery, puttering, and
"clearing up the doubts about the new paradigm" which character-
izes most scientific activity most of the time.[2]

Established economists are no different from other guild masters. They too have their favorite theories which they do not like
to have challenged, and will therefore avoid any discussion on
that particular area which might disprove their theory. Socialists,
for example, have yet to answer Mises' criticism that *rational* economic calculation is impossible in a pure socialist State. Without
private ownership, there is no entrepreneurship; without a competitive private market for capital goods, there is no way for central planners to impute *accurate* prices to capital goods. Calculations made by socialist planners are rational only because they
borrow from societies where prices arise in the market place.
Once they have obtained prices from outside the socialist system,
they are able to make their calculations, but without such para-
sitic activity, rational calculations are impossible.[3]

The crisis in economics which has been underway since about
1970 is closely tied to this loss of faith in the prevailing Keynesian
methodologies. I have already cited Milton Friedman's 1971

---

2. Thomas Kuhn, *The Structure of Scientific Revolutions* (2nd ed.; Chicago: University of Chicago Press, 1970).

3. Ludwig von Mises, *Socialism* (Indianapolis, Indiana: Liberty Press, [1922]
1981), pp. 97-105 (pp. 113-122 in the Yale University Press edition of 1951). There
was an attempt by Oscar Lange in the late 1930's to answer Mises, but it did not
succeed, and his proposed solution was so impractical from the standpoint of socialism that it has never been adopted by any socialist planning agency. Textbook
accounts, however, almost always claim that Lange answered Mises, in those
rare instances where the textbooks even mention Mises.

admission at the beginning of the Introduction. Things have not improved since 1971. In 1982, the *New York Times* titled an article on the president of the American Economics Association, "The High Priest of a Troubled Church" (Jan. 3, 1982). Things were no better three years later at the annual meeting. Boston University's Paul Steeton said in 1985, "Economics is in a state of disarray, more so than since Keynes." Martin Weitzman of the Massachusetts Institute of Technology (Paul Samuelson's university) said, "There's no consensus on what to do. In Europe they're totally paralyzed."[4] Yet in the classroom, little has changed. Writes Robert Kuttner:

> Today there are two quite opposite trends in economics. One is centrifugal; there is a flowering of epistemological doubt. There are anguished essays . . . in the *Journal of Economic Literature* (which, though published by the AEA, has served as a tolerant outlet for heretics) and even an occasional one in *The American Economic Review* itself. And there are those presidential addresses at AEA conventions. At the same time, there is a strong centripetal impulse. Economics *as practiced* is unchanged, and the resistance to real diversity within faculty ranks and classroom curricula is fiercer than ever. The debates are for the college of cardinals, not for the parish flock.[5]

Here is a textbook example of the conditions that prelude a scientific revolution: self-doubt at the top of the guild's leadership, and full-time blindness at the level of "normal science." Dr. Vickers is representative of Kuhn's hard-working and uncreative "normal scientist," who is always the last to find out that the revolution has come, and that he missed it.

The Keynesian Suppression

The Keynesian system, to which Dr. Vickers rigidly adheres, adopts a similar method of suppression. This system of analysis is maintained intellectually by its academic defenders by their

---

4. *Washington Times* (Jan. 2, 1985).
5. Robert Kuttner, "The Poverty of Economics," *Atlantic Monthly* (Feb. 1985), p. 83.

refusal to discuss certain aspects of market phenomena that might mitigate against their theories. Henry Hazlitt made the observation, "In the Keynesian system, the level of wage-rates and their effect on employment, is The Great Unmentionable."[6] It is unmentionable because it is closely connected to the question of wage rates in a free society. Keynesian economists despise the topic of the price mechanism, except as something to criticize.

On the surface, this seems like un unwarranted charge. Of course the price mechanism is mentioned in Keynesian literature. Why, it is even listed in the index of Dr. Vickers' *Economics and Man*. Again we are back to the problem of definition. We need to define exactly what we mean by the phrase "price mechanism." More to the point, *we need a theoretical explanation of how it functions*, and we also need cogent evidence from the world of real human action that the theory faithfully explains the events.

Objective Results of Subjective Valuations

Prices perform an essential function in the economy. They are the *result* of the subjective valuations of people acting in the market place. More particularly, prices are what buyers are ultimately willing and able to pay for a particular good or service. A price helps to inform the seller whether he is selling his goods rationally. What is an economically rational price from the point of view of the seller? A price which enables him to sell all the goods he offers for sale at a profit margin which then enables him to stay in business and achieve his other goals, including non-economic goals. Insufficient net revenues mean financial loss or hardship, whereas profits indicate that he has correctly forecast what enough buyers are willing to pay in order for him to remain in business.

Prices are the result of *subjective* valuation. Human beings have a habit, though, of changing their minds and opinions on a host of things, and on a frequent basis. Someone is willing to pay $30 for a good book today. Tomorrow he is only prepared to spend $15 on the book, and obtain a new Pierre Cardin tie with the money

---

6. Hazlitt, *The Failure of the "New Economics,"* p. 331.

which is left over. People change, they grow older, their likes and dislikes alter; limited resources and not so limited wants means a constant juggling of all desires on a scale of values. Today a new auto is on the top of a rich man's valuation scale, tomorrow a world cruise. Although a certain price will be paid for a commodity today, tomorrow may bring another price. It could go lower if something else becomes more important, or if that item climbs the ladder of our wants, what we are prepared to pay for it will increase.

Market Continuity

Consequently, there can be no such thing as unchanging prices. Surprisingly, though, in a free market prices tend to be rather stable. For mass-produced items, there is a tendency for prices to fall, especially for products that have been introduced recently, and which are now the focus of intense competition from new producers who have entered the market. Where there are a number of people acting in accordance with their scale of preferences, the price results of the very often marked changes within each individual's preference scale are levelled out across the market as a result of the large number of people in the market. There is a kind of averaging process going on. Buyers drop out of one market, and may be replaced by others who have similar, if not identical, preferences. While one buyer omits or lowers automobiles on his scale of desires, another raises autos on his list, thus mitigating against the choice of the former. In all this, the market possesses relative stability. Participants can form generally accurate expectations about what will be available tomorrow, and at what price.

This does not mean that the market cannot be subject to wild fluctuations. Anyone who follows the stock markets knows that markets can, and do, change quite dramatically and often quite rapidly. But this is because there has been a fundamental shift in valuations by a large number of people at one time. A particular gold stock plummets, possibly because the latest mining report has indicated that expected yields will not be achieved. Investors have been overly optimistic on their anticipated profits, and now

have cause to be more conservative in their expectations. Perhaps
the grape harvest this year is super-abundant, so grapes are a little easier to come by. Meanwhile, beef prices are soaring because
the supply of beef had been overestimated, and there will be some
shortage of prime beef this season. All these factors contribute to
the valuations which each person makes about the commodities
and services on his or her scale of preferences, and a free market is
one where these changing decisions are registered in the market
place as people transact their business.

Authoritarian Continuity

Suppose, though, someone were to object to these changing
valuations. He dislikes this world of changing prices and fluctuating conditions. Instead, he thinks that prices should be held constant. Suppose also that he is a government official with the authority to issue a minimum price order. "Starting today, all buyers
will pay $5 a pound for prime beef irrespective of market condi-
tions or changing valuations which buyers and sellers may make."
Such a decree looks good at first glance, at least to buyers who
were willing to pay over $5 a pound and sellers who were unable
to compete at prices under $5. Prices are regulated. Now we all
know where we are going. How much simpler budgeting will be
from now on! Right?

There is a missing factor in this equation. Our benefactor may
have noble ideas, but he is begging the question. What about
those *subjective* valuations which individual human beings make?
It may appear all very well to decree beef will be sold at $5 a
pound, but what happens if prospective buyers are willing to pay
only $4? What will happen is quite simple: they will not buy the
beef until its price goes down to the level they are willing to pay.
Each of us has his own mind, his own opinions, his own scale of
preferences for all those things which are desired. Human beings,
made in the image of God, think and act in such a way as to reflect
their personality, their individuality, and their uniqueness in the
universe which God has created. But our mysterious benefactor
wants to do away with all that. Instead, *his* valuations, *his* scale

of preferences shall be adopted by everyone else. Beef is "worth" $5 a pound because *he* says it is; therefore it must be "worth" that much.

Here, in its essence, is the Keynesian system. In the chapter on socialism, I noted how that Dr. Vickers would have the State intervene and impose one person's valuations — or at least the valuations arrived at by a committee — on the remainder of society. To recall just one example, Dr. Vickers has suggested that wage increases might be taxed to the full extent they exceed "nationally established norms."[7] This kind of system is, of course, inherently authoritarian. It would appear to the thinking person an act of gross arrogance for another to tell him how he should act, what prices he should pay for commodities, and so on. Yet *arrogance is the psychological center of the Keynesian system.* If we do not question Keynesians too deeply, and do not pressure them to answer questions which ultimately mitigate against their system, they remain content. They will not raise such questions if we don't. Like sheep, we are led to the slaughter, but as Gary North reminds us, sheep have a habit of being shorn on the way to the slaughter-house.

Vickers on Unemployment

Take, for example, Dr. Vickers' approach to the unemployment problem. It is important to remember that, from an economic viewpoint, *wages are merely another price.* Wages and salaries are the price for labor, an economic commodity. Therefore, wages need to be considered within the context of the overall price mechanism, within the context that, if left to themselves, people will make certain economic calculations and decisions which they perceive are the best for them at that particular moment.

As he develops his theories, he has this to say about wages and their relationship to unemployment. "[I]f all employers acting together, or if, that is, the economy as a whole, should reduce the wage rate it is proposed to pay to labor, then rather than there

---

7. Vickers, *Economics and Man*, p. 340.

occurring an increase in the amount of labor demanded by employers, there may actually be a significant decrease. . . . For the reduction in the prospective level of income-generating expenditure which we have seen the proposed reduction in wage rates to involve will have worsened, rather than improved, the market prospects confronting producers, and will lower the prospective demand for their output. The only course of action which economic reason then suggests is for them to reduce their level of production. And this, of course, implies a lower level of employment."[8] (Don't feel embarrassed if you need to reread this paragraph four times; the writing is at fault, not your brain.)

Dr. Vickers is saying that a general wage reduction will cause people to have less money to spend. This, in turn, results in fewer purchases, producers make fewer sales, their profits decline, so they will therefore employ less labor. A well-reasoned argument . . . *provided* you accept his conclusion that lower sales and therefore more unemployment is the *"only"* (Dr. Vickers' word) possible result.

Cause and Effect

What we really want to know is this: *Why* was there this overnight reduction in national wage rates? Sure, any employer would love to be able to cut wage rates, but none of them wants to have his workers quit and go work for his competitors. So each employer is forced to pay a competitive wage. (Yes, Dr. Vickers, these employers may be greedy. But their greed leads them to pay the going wage to laborers. They are greedy not only in relation to their workers, but even more so, in relation to their competitors. An employer dreads hearing someone who has had too much to drink tell him at the next trade association meeting: "Say, Fred, I hear you got too greedy with your work force, and they all walked off the job. I hear you had to hire a whole new crew, and your company's output dropped, and the banks didn't renew your loans, and your company is about to be swallowed up by Amalga-

---

8. *Ibid.*, pp. 269-270.

mated. What do you say to that, Fred? Ha, ha, ha. We always knew you were a loser!")

Why, then, did wage rates of an entire economy drop? A collapse of the Keynesian-operated banking system? A recession induced by Keynesian-approved tariffs? (Keynes did approve tariffs in the early years of the Great Depression. Perhaps he was just trying to lengthen it and make it worse, the better to launch the Keynesian Revolution in 1936.) The two main reasons why the wage rates of a nation drop are these: a fall in demand for that nation's production, or a fall in productivity by the nation's work force. An overnight drop in wages is historically rare, except as a result of a prior monetary inflation which at last comes to a halt during a bank panic. Short of war, or short of physical catastrophe (e.g., a volcano eruption or hurricane) in a very tiny nation, there are no overnight national wage reductions.

So, it is *not* the fall in wage rates which has reduced everyone's income. It is rather the *drop in demand* for the *output* of the labor force. To solve the problem of universally falling wage rates, we must analyze the causes of the drop in demand for labor's output. We must get economic cause and effect straight in our minds; otherwise, we might become Keynesians.

Price Competition

But, just for the sake of arguing, let us propose an alternative. Let us agree with Dr. Vickers that a general lowering of wages results in a decline in sales. People now have less spending money. They will re-evaluate their scale of preferences, reallocating their limited resources to those items deemed most important. Food, clothing, and shelter are far more important to most people than obtaining a new television set. "We'll make do with the one we have, until things get better." So television manufacturers sell less, and they don't need as much labor for their reduced production levels, and unemployment grows, according to Dr. Vickers.

But suppose — just suppose — that the television manufacturer has recognized that because there has been a general decline in wages, he is now paying less for his labor, so his production costs have been cut somewhat, and he can therefore reduce selling prices a little, yet still maintain his profit margin. What has he to lose by trying such a tactic? Absolutely nothing. His sales are already down. His wages and salaries bill is down. He has nothing to lose, *and everything to gain*, by reducing his prices. Perhaps that price reduction will be the temptation needed to induce prospective buyers to reconsider the purchase of a television. So we must disagree most strongly with Dr. Vickers when he asserts there is "only one course of action which economic reason" suggests. What we need to ask is *whose* economic reasoning is suggesting what. The manufacturer's reasoning tells him to lower his prices if he wants to sell the goods.

This may not always work. If there is simply no demand for the good at any price, it has ceased to be an economic good. Perhaps the producer has no possibility of lowering the price far enough to induce retail customers to buy. As an example, consider *Economics and Man*. After ten years, the publisher has yet to sell out the initial run of 2,000 copies, even at the low, low price of $6.95. What should he do? Sell all copies at once for a few cents each to a "remainder" book distributor? Give it away as a premium for buying five (or four, or even two) other books? Or wait for *Baptized Inflation* to create enough controversy to get the last 250 copies sold? Entrepreneurs have difficult decisions in this life. But that is the price they pay for remaining entrepreneurs.

In Dr. Vickers' hypothetical example, we can see that a lowering of the wage rate is *not necessarily* a cause of unemployment. (Economic analysis tells us that falling wage rates are almost never the *cause* of unemployment, and *never* the cause of *permanent* unemployment. Falling wage rates are the economically rational response of employers and employees to falling demand for their output. Falling wage rates are a rational attempt to *maintain* employment. They are a way to keep from going bankrupt or getting fired.) There may be some *temporary* unemployment if manufacturers and producers are slow to realize that sales will decline, since workers now have less spending money due to the general wage decline. But not all businessmen are that slow in understanding economic reality. Some of them, in fact, are quite smart when it comes to making business calculations. (In other words, they are not all Keynesians.) This is why the alert ones make higher-than-average profits. The entrepreneur who first lowers his prices in the case of a general wage decline will be at the head of the line to reap the possible benefits, assuming there is no change in consumers' willingness to buy his goods. And even if they won't buy his goods at *today's* prices, they may buy them at *tomorrow's*.

Raising Wages the Keynesian Way

So far, we have seen Dr. Vickers make the startling and inaccurate claim that his hypothetical general wage decline must result in greater unemployment. What is the result, though, if we change the situation slightly and suggest another scene? Suppose that instead of a general wage decline, a general wage *rise* occurs. Let us assume that this increase is not the result of tremendous new demand for labor's output. Let us return to our price-setting bureaucrat. Perhaps our benevolent State benefactor decides that if lowering wages causes unemployment, raising all wages and salaries will give increased spending power to the workers, so they will purchase more, and this will, in turn, stimulate production, resulting in a demand for more labor. Here, it is argued, is the possible solution to the unemployment problem. In its essence, this is the conclusion that Dr. Vickers' reasoning warrants. It should be obvious that if a lowering of wages results in unemployment (which is what Dr. Vickers argues), the solution must be to raise wages: more money in the income-generating stream, more demand, more productivity. Utopia, here we come.

If that were our conclusion, we would have fallen into the trap which Dr. Vickers has set for himself. (No, come to think of it, he has been caught for his whole career in that analytical trap. So have all his Keynesian peers. He just wants the rest of us to fall in with him.) Again, there is another possible alternative result to the one deduced above. A general wage and salary increase would result in greater expenses for employers. They would be forced to raise their prices at least as much as the wage increases in order to maintain profitability.

But wait a minute. *How* could they all raise their prices? Yes, yes, Dr. Vickers, we know: they are all incredibly greedy. But they were all incredibly greedy yesterday, too, in your view. So why didn't they all raise their prices yesterday? *Because we consumers would not have bought all of those higher priced goods they brought to market.* We will not buy them today, either . . . *unless the government creates sufficient fiat money to let us do it.* And this, my friend, is why we are back to *the* Keynesian solution. Print money.

So the government prints the money (or allows the fractional reserve banking system to create it). How will the workers be better off? The producers are still producing the same quantity, but it is being sold at higher prices. Workers have received higher wages, but they now pay higher prices on average for goods and services. How are they better off? The answer is, of course, they are no better off at all. Nothing has changed in this situation except that the dollar amounts being transacted are at higher levels than before the general wage increase was granted.

Oh, yes, now that I think of it, something *has* changed. I forgot about Dr. Vickers' enthusiastic recommendation: the graduated income tax. The higher a worker's money-denominated income, the larger the percentage of his income is taken "off the top" by the tax collector. So I was incorrect. *Almost all workers are worse off.* They will suffer a reduction of their after-tax real income.

It is the old double whammy: Keynesian-recommended monetary inflation produces Keynesian-created price inflation, which opens the door to the Keynesian-approved graduated income tax to achieve its confiscatory mission more efficiently than ever. Keynesianism increases efficiency . . . of the State to destroy freedom.

Price Controls

But our Great Benefactor may realize that prices will go up in response to his monetary policies. He knows that producers will raise their prices, thereby destroying the effects of wage increases. The obvious solution to the problem is to prevent prices from being raised by sellers. Let's have wages increased, but all other prices remain unchanged. Make it illegal to raise prices.

Now what is the situation? Wages and salaries are up, but the producers cannot raise their prices to recoup costs, so they find alternatives to the now-overpriced labor. They mechanize production (if they can buy the equipment before the manufacturers go out of business), thereby employing less labor, or they demand increased productivity to pay for the increased wages. They start firing workers who do not improve productivity. Whichever choice employers make, it involves a fundamental calculation that *the present labor rates are too high.*

So what is the result? *Unemployment.* We are right back where we started. So much for the Keynesian miracles.

Cause and Effect (Again)

Perhaps now we are in a position to inquire what causes unemployment. Is it wage reductions? Yes, it could well be, if producers do not lower prices to induce sales. But to get sales, they *will* lower prices. So unemployment goes away.

Is it wage increases? Again, it could be, if producers are not able to increase their prices to recoup production costs. So they fire workers, and unemployed workers drop their wage demands, and they get hired again, and unemployment goes away.

In reality (though perhaps not in the academic departments of tax-supported universities), *wages are paid out of productivity.* When wages levels are greater than the value of labor's output, labor is overpriced and will not be purchased.

Today's Unemployment: Compliments of Keynes

Then what is the cause of the persistently high unemployment which is afflicting the U.S., Great Britain, Western Europe, and Australia? It is not just limited to these countries, but these examples will serve our purpose here. Very simply, *the cause of unemployment is the politicians' refusal to consider the effects wage rates have within the overall context of the price mechanism.* They legislate minimum wage laws, thereby denying the employer the prerogative of determining whether labor is worth that particular price. Furthermore, trade unions are allowed to impose their demands upon employers, in order for union members to extract above-market wages from employers. These above-market wages are possible only because of State-permitted exclusion of *non-union potential employees*. If he hires some of these State-excluded workers, the employer might well have to face a government tribunal. The employer is told to deal with union members; he cannot legally replace them with non-union members. This penalizes non-union workers, and it forces them into lower-paying jobs that are made available by non-union employers. *Pro-union legislation is therefore an indirect economic subsidy to non-unionized business owners.* The new wage rates means a loss in profits for union-dominated employers. It might well force some out of business altogether. But it all adds up to one thing: less labor being employed than what an unhampered free market would support.

Keynesian economists tell us they are for the working man. They may be for him, but their recommended policies are reducing the legal employment opportunities of most of them. Most people (about 75% of them) are *not* employed by unionized businesses in the U.S. But they are not allowed to bid against union members in major industries. So they are forced to seek employment in non-union sectors of the economy. Non-union employers can then offer lower wages than they could otherwise have offered, had there been no compulsory unionization of their competitors' businesses. Here is a classic example of what Bastiat called *the fallacy of the thing unseen*. We can see the above-market wages of union members — at least of those whose companies have not yet been bankrupted. But we cannot see that these above-market wages are being paid for by the loss of freedom to bid for these high-paying jobs on the part of the average working man.

Market-Created Unemployment

We do not live in a perfect world. Unemployment can never be eliminated. There are those who would rather be unemployed and collect social welfare benefits than take on the responsibility of a job. Perhaps the preference some people have for some economic goods disappears, causing certain industries to close, thereby creating unemployment. But if people are now purchasing other goods, demanding production in other areas, this has the potential of absorbing some of that unemployment. A prime example of this is that those unemployed who were making horse-drawn vehicles at the turn of the century had the opportunity to be employed in the newly emerging horseless carriage industry as the horse carriage went out of demand. But this requires time. There would be *a period of adjustment*, meaning *a period of unemployment*. A more recent example of this aspect of economic life is the disappearance of the mechanical typewriter as electronic word processors take their place. Modern businessmen have learned a hard lesson, though. Many are no longer so slow in adapting to innovative changes and losing business to smarter competitors. Consequently, some typewriter manufacturers have become manufacturers of computers and retained their staff.

Unemployment—short-term unemployment, at least, for those willing to work—can be a sign of a *healthy* economy, one which is growing and prospering as new industries come into existence and old ones die away. People are quitting, searching for new opportunities, trying to make a better life for themselves. *There is low unemployment in jails. There is low unemployment in Communist concentration camps.* This is not to say that every form of unemployment is a delight, for it produces obvious difficulties for those who have been put out of work. Provided there are the growth industries to absorb the unemployed, in the long run we are all a little better off, even the unemployed who may now have the choice of new goods and services. Builders of horse coaches can now go places in automobiles that time and distance may have prevented prior to the advent of the car.

But what we are describing here is not the kind of unemployment we see today. Our description is of *temporary* unemployment during that period of adjustment. (Excluded from this are those who *prefer* to remain unemployed by choice.) What we see today is *longer term* unemployment of those who want to work. And there

can only be two circumstances which produce this. Either producers cannot lower their prices to meet lower wage rates (demand)
or else they cannot raise their prices to cover the labor factor in
production costs to maintain production (supply). What would
prevent them from doing either of these? *Legislation* introduced by
politicians influenced by the Keynesian economists in their employ, whose shallow reasoning demands that wages be raised
while prices are kept low, in order to "stimulate aggregate demand." This is the stupidity of Keynesianism which apparently
escapes Dr. Vickers. But Dr. Vickers has not escaped this stupidity. As Van Til would say, it is not a question of intelligence; it is a
question of *presuppositions*. It is more a moral flaw than an intellectual flaw. He who despises the law of God will soon find himself
doing stupid things and saying stupid things.

Conclusion

Dr. Vickers, following Keynes, does not tell us what we need
to know about the price system. He therefore does not tell us what
we need to know about the problem of unemployed resources,
especially unemployed people. He does not recognize how competition among all those "greedy" businessmen leads to wage rates
for laborers that tend toward equality with the value of labor's
output. Employers do not want to pay high wages, but they want
even less to lose the services of laborers who make the employers'
business profitable. This is why high wages, high profits, and low
prices go together in a free market economy. This is why Keynes
never understood either economic reasoning or the free market
economy. This is why young, highly skilled, mathematically
adept "rational expectations" economists can barely disguise their
contempt for the gray-haired "revolutionaries" of the 1930's and
1940's as they dodder toward retirement and the grave.[9] The gray
heads are now reaping what they sowed: a revolution by the people they once taught.

We have seen that Henry Hazlitt's accusation is correct: "In

---

9. Susan Lee, "The un-managed economy," *Forbes* (Dec. 17, 1984).

the Keynesian system, the level of wage-rates and their effect on employment, is The Great Unmentionable."[10] Regarding Dr. Vickers' contribution to Keynesian thought, the price mechanism in general, of which wage rates and their effect form a part, is the Great Unmentionable. Such scholarship, rather than enlightening the reader, has instead a propensity to confuse. And that in itself requires another chapter.

---

10. Hazlitt, *The Failure of the "New Economics,"* p. 331.

13

THE MARGINAL PROPENSITY TO CONFUSE

*. . . it is the economist's task so to understand the deeper deter-
minants of economic conjunctures and affairs that his policy prescriptions can be intelligently and properly shaped toward their proper
ordering, or, where it is considered necessary, their correction and resolution. This should be done in such a way as to accord with the
demands of both those deeper causal complexes now perceived in the
light of God's Word and purpose, and the requirements and basic
desiderata of economic thought and administration.*[1]

You will not be able to understand the economics of Keynes. I
know: you are waiting for me to add: "unless you first recognize
that. . . ." But I add nothing of the sort. I am saying simply that
you will not be able to understand the economics of Keynes. The
reason for this is that it is unintelligible. It has the world backward. His view of economic cause and effect was as twisted as his
view of sexual morality. The economics of Keynes is hokum, pure
but not very simple. It is, quite frankly, perverse.

If you have not recognized this yet, then this is why you have
had so much trouble in reading this book. You have assumed, incorrectly, that Keynesian economics was never meant to be understood. On the contrary, it was meant to confuse. This was basic to
Keynes' strategy. His ardent admirers admit that *The General
Theory* is exasperatingly confusing. We should not be surprised,
then, to discover doctrine after doctrine which seems to make no

---

1. Vickers, *Economics and Man*, p. 90.

sense. He bombards us with such senseless doctrines. So does his disciple, Dr. Vickers. Sadly, we have to consider several of them, just to prove to ourselves that they are nonsensical.

This is one reason why Douglas Vickers has failed to convince Christians of the essential correctness of Keynes' economic theories. Christians expect things to be clear. They would agree with Eva Etzioni-Halevy's observation that "ideas that cannot be expressed clearly are themselves muddled and therefore not worth expressing at all."[2] If we are responsible before God and men to promote a particular policy recommendation, we expect to be able to understand it before we impose it. Christians recognize this, so they have paid zero attention to Dr. Vickers (except for a handful of scholars who teach courses other than economics in seminaries or Christian colleges). We do not find Dr. Vickers cited by Christian authors. (We also do not find him cited by secular authors.) We do not find anyone arguing along the lines Dr. Vickers laid down in *Economics and Man*. The main reason for this is that *Economics and Man* is even more unintelligible than Keynes' *General Theory.*

Keynes was attempting only to refute the classical economists. Dr. Vickers is attempting to refute classical economics, plus convince his readers that Keynes' position is in essential agreement with Biblical morality. In short, he has assigned himself the unenviable task of promoting as essentially Christian the incoherent economic theories of a homosexual pervert. You may sympathize with Dr. Vickers. I don't, since I recognize the perversity of his self-appointed task, but at least I understand his problem.

So dedicated is Dr. Vickers to the incoherence of *The General Theory* that he has lost the ability to communicate. His style is stodgy at best. Usually, however, his language is so convoluted that the reader is left in the dark. *This is where he is supposed to be left.* He is supposed to read all this gobbledygook, and then think to himself, "My, this is all very complex, all very scientific, and all

---

2. Eva Etzioni-Halevy, *Bureaucracy and Democracy: A Political Dilemma* (London: Routledge & Kegan Paul, 1983), p. ix.

beyond me. But a Ph.D. in economics has written it, so I guess it must be true. I guess I will have to conclude that North and Rushdoony have misunderstood everything, since I understand them, and that means they must not be any more scientific than I am. What do they know, compared with Dr. Vickers?"

John Kenneth Galbraith, whose liberal credentials are flawless, writes clearly. His peers sometimes resent him for it, and especially for becoming a best-selling author. Galbraith understands the way the professional academic economists play the game. "Only someone who is decently confusing can be respected."[3] This is why we are supposed to respect Dr. Vickers.

The Evils of Thrift

Saving, under the Keynesian system, is a potential threat to economic growth and progress. Not always — nothing is "always" in Keynesianism — but often, especially during a depression. Dr. Vickers writes: "Does this mean, then, that saving, notwithstanding all that the Protestant ethic may have led us to believe about it, is not necessarily a good thing at all? The answer undoubtedly is yes. That is precisely what our analysis means."[4]

But how can this be? Why is the Protestant ethic so wrong, and the Keynesian ethic so correct? Because, Keynesian theory informs us, those future-oriented people who refuse to spend their money incomes are depleting the income-generating flow of money. Because one person's expenditure is another's income, according to Dr. Vickers, any time one person withholds expenditure, he is thereby denying someone else their income. Savers are therefore the cause of the economic disharmonies in society. Saving is to be despised for the hardship it creates others.

Keynesian economics teaches a peculiar (and utterly inaccurate) view of what they call the "income stream." They argue that in a free market economy, when people stop spending money, they "break" the stream of income. People's incomes fall, so they

---

3. Cited by "Adam Smith" in *The New York Times* (Sept. 30, 1979).
4. Vickers, *Ibid.*, p. 20.

hoard additional cash, which breaks the income stream more, which leads into a downward spiral of deflationary depression.

This is utter nonsense. In a capitalist economy, the stream of income never stops flowing so long as people continue to make offers of voluntary exchange that other people find beneficial. In this sense, *the "stream" is simply a series of voluntary transactions*. People exchange goods and services because they expect to derive more benefit from owning the other person's good or service compared to the good or service they now possess.

Why do the Keynesians ignore this? Because they do not believe that ordinary people — you and I, to be blunt about it — understand that by lowering the price of the good or service that they are trying to sell, they will eventually be able to sell it. People supposedly do not understand that "something" is better than "nothing," and therefore they stubbornly refuse to lower their prices and "get the stream of income flowing again." Actually, the Keynesians are even crazier than this. They actually refuse to believe that lower prices will get people to buy a scarce resource. In short, not until the good becomes free of charge — or maybe until the seller *pays* the "buyer" to take it away — will the stream of income start flowing again. Thus, the Keynesian says, the State must tax away people's money, or borrow it, or print it, in order to spend money, thereby getting Ol' Man River moving again.

Money Seldom Disappears

It needs to be recognized early that this entire argument of the Keynesians is preposterous. When someone saves money, he transfers it to someone else — to a capitalist, or to a bank, or whomever. Guess what this recipient does with the borrowed money? *He spends it.* Incredible. Fantastic. Why didn't Keynes think of this?

Let us pursue the Keynesian critique of saving. We know that hardly anybody has bought a copy of *Economics and Man*: about 200 copies a year since 1976. We can be fairly confident that the very people who might have bought a copy all had savings accounts at the bank. This has deprived Dr. Vickers of income. In fact, we might even argue that the recession of 1980-82 might have been avoided if two billion people had just bought a hundred copies each of *Economics and Man*. Dr. Vickers would then have spent this money — after all, he does not believe in saving during a recession, although your average person does, since he might lose his job, or suffer a loss in income, etc. — and the world economy would have received his personal "shot in the arm."

Or, even more true to Keynesian policy, the federal government would have taxed half his income away, and then the bureaucrats would have spent it on lots and lots of boondoggles. This is the Christian approach to economics, according to Dr. Vickers, so he would have been happy to see this money go to the State. The State can be trusted. Without the State looking over his shoulder, he, too, might have been tempted to "hoard" money in a bank account, or even worse, in a money-market fund, especially with the 18% rates they were paying briefly back then. "There hath no temptation taken a Christian Keynesian economist such as is common to man, but God is faithful and will not suffer him to be tempted above what the economist is able, but will, with the temptation, impose a progressive income tax, so that he may be able to bear it."

Thrift and Future-Orientation

Why this Keynesian hostility to thrift? Why this hostility to the formation of capital, without which there can be no long-term economic growth? Most people in the West have long understood that thrift is basic both to personal and cultural economic advancement. The more future-oriented that people become, especially under the influence of Christian preaching, the more they are willing to save at any prevailing rate of interest. Classical economic thought, having been heavily influenced by Christian morality and traditions, was built around the idea that saving is good, meaning that *future-orientation is good*. Why did Keynes think it necessary to refute this "naive idea" with his new "vision" of seeing things.

One very good reason was offered by Lewis Lehrman, the

American millionaire-scholar-politician and advocate of the gold standard. "I have five children. I have a vision of the future. Keynes had no children and no interest in getting involved in any relationship which might make possible their procreation. He was inherently short-run in his viewpoint." Keynes was famous for his dictum, used against anyone who argued in terms of economic law, "In the long run, we are all dead." Very clever. In short, there is a reason why Keynes' homosexuality is related to his economic doctrines. There is a reason why his moral perversity produced intellectual perversity. His view of time was affected.

Keynesian economists are sufficiently pragmatic to realize that people cannot be changed totally, at least not overnight. Therefore they have an answer to the problem of saving. Let there be many injections into the economy's income-generating stream of State-confiscated, State-borrowed, or State-printed money, in order to compensate for those misguided, profit-seeking private savers whose funds were (somehow, we are never told how) taken out of the stream of exchange. But let us explore a little further how the Keynesian economist twists his false theory in order to justify other proposals.

The Marginal Propensity to Consume

One of the more elaborate Keynesian theories is the Marginal Propensity to Consume. Related to this is the "multiplier process." As usual, these concepts in turn rely on the Keynesian theory of the circular flow of money. "Our earlier analysis of the circular nature of the flow of income-generating expenditure streams in the economy now enables us to make significant use of these relationships to exhibit one of the principle characteristics of multiplicative variations in income and employment levels in the economy."[5] We have had cause already to question the soundness of that particular concept. If the government spends a dollar (where did the bureaucrats get it?), the results will be a four-fold or five-fold increase in economic output. It should be of no surprise

---

5. *Ibid.*, p. 201.

by now to find there are insurmountable problems with Keynes' theorizing at this point, too.

The marginal propensity to consume and the multiplier process arguments are not so much economic theory as justification for why there should be injections of new (or taxed, or borrowed) money into the monetary stream. Keynesians, after all, do not want to be too vague about their proposals, or else politicians might not expand the power of the State with "scientific precision"; therefore, they bring mathematical precision to bear in order to illustrate the benefits of their ideas. We all know that mathematics is a precise science, so if the Keynesian can use rigorous mathematics to defend his policy prescriptions, he must be on the right track. The public is impressed. This appears to be one rationale behind their use of mathematical formulae. Certainly, their use of mathematics loses most of their potential readers. ("But, Grandma, you have such foreboding formulae!" "The better to create an elite priesthood of tenured central planners, my dear.")

It has been known to any observant person that as people's income rises, they have a tendency to save a higher percentage of that income — other things (such as morality, religious presuppositions, and lust for more toys) remaining equal. Another way of putting the same thing is to say that as disposable income increases — that is, income received after taxes — people are inclined to spend a smaller percentage of it on consumption. (These are merely two ways of saying the same thing, just as we may describe a coin from either its obverse or reverse side. Although my description appears different, in reality I am merely depicting the same process.) This phenomenon is called by Dr. Vickers, following Keynes, the marginal propensity to consume. Why it should be given that particular title, when it could equally have been called "the marginal propensity to save," is a question Dr. Vickers does not discuss, which is a real pity. He might otherwise have shed some light on a rather obscure passage of Keynesian literature. Either title could be used to describe the same observation; that people save and spend some of their income, and as incomes rise, there is a tendency for people to save more and spend less.

Dr. Vickers does not distinguish between savings invested and savings hoarded, perhaps buried in the back yard for safe keeping. Again, Dr. Vickers refuses to make the distinction between money which is taken out of the expenditure stream through hoarding, and money which, although it is not spent on immediate consumption goods, remains in the expenditure stream because it is invested in capital projects. Such a major omission is of little interest to Dr. Vickers. (It might expose the whole Keynesian system as fraudulent, or worse, being only in partial equilibrium. Dr. Vickers puts a minus on one side of the hypothetical "savings" transaction, but no plus on the other.)

Were the Keynesians to stop at this point life would not be so difficult for us. But they do not stop. Not only do they perceive that there is some propensity to consume (as well as save), but they also declare that this propensity can be measured with mathematical precision. Moreover, they are willing to accept the idea that any increase in expenditure has a "multiplier" effect in the economy.

Multiplying the Confusion

What is the "multiplier effect"? Keynes described it in his familiar style. You will need a translator. (So will Dr. Vickers.)

For in given circumstances a definite ratio, to be called the *Multiplier*, can be established between income and investment and, subject to certain simplifications, between the total employment and the employment directly employed on investment. . . . this further step is an integral part of our theory of employment, since it establishes a precise relationship, given the propensity to consume, between aggregate employment and income and the rate of investment."[6]

Please, don't feel discouraged. It wasn't meant to be understood. It was meant to confuse.

What did he mean? He meant that as someone's income goes up, his marginal propensity to save (or consume) also goes up at a mathematically fixed rate. Let's see; if I don't get more income, it

---

6. John Maynard Keynes, *General Theory*, p. 113.

will be harder for me to save more. That seems correct. if I don't get more, I can't consume more without reducing my savings. So far, so good. Not too brilliant, but not crazy.

Then it gets crazy. The multiplier "tells us that, when there is an increment of aggregate investment, income will increase by an amount which is k times the increment of investment."[7] What does this prove? "It follows, therefore, that, if the consumption psychology of the community is such that they will choose to consume, e.g., nine-tenths of an increment of income, then the multiplier k is 10; and the total employment caused by (e.g.) increased public works will be ten times the primary employment provided by the public works themselves. . . ."[8] Do not be fooled: nothing "follows therefore." This is sheer nonsense.

Now we have found the secret. Hazlitt (of whom Dr. Vickers is contemptuous) summarizes: "What Keynes is saying, among other things, is that the more a community *spends* of its income, and the less it *saves*, the faster will its real income grow!"[9] Not only are pyramids (public works) great things in the Keynesian system, but the more people spend on pyramids rather than save, the richer they become. Furthermore, thrifty societies will not benefit from pyramids as much as spendthrift societies will. Waste becomes productive; consumer spending becomes productive; even earthquakes become productive, in the land of Keynes: "Pyramid-building, earthquakes, even wars may serve to increase wealth, if the education of our statesmen on the principles of the classical economics stands in the way of anything better."[10]

If Keynes had majored in physics, he would have written a book proving the possibility of government-funded perpetual motion.

This, you understand, is what Dr. Vickers thinks we should accept in the name of Christian morality and sound economic reasoning.

---

7. *Ibid.*, p. 115.
8. *Ibid.*, pp. 116-17.
9. Henry Hazlitt, *The Failure of the "New Economics": An Analysis of the Keynesian Fallacies* (Princeton, New Jersey: Van Nostrand, 1959), p. 137.
10. Keynes, *General Theory*, p. 129.

I think Deacon is correct: "Keynes's hatred of Puritanism is important in the light of his economic theories. He was to become the man who has gone down in history as the most outstanding economist and architect of social progress of the past seventy years, though some would dispute such an assessment. But it was his hostility to the puritan ethic which stimulated and lay behind his economic theories — spend to create work, spend one's way out of depression, stimulate growth. It was also his hatred of Puritanism which caused him in early life to devote rather more time to pursuing homosexual conquests than to economics."[11]

The Vickers' Version

Here is how the world works in the land of Keynes. Someone gets some additional money, spends a portion of it, and the recipient makes a similar decision to spend a portion, and so the process continues, with the portion being spent being reduced each time it goes through the circular flow. Fortunately for the sake of our ability to spot his errors in logic, Dr. Vickers omits the algebraic formula contained in Keynes' *General Theory* to describe this phenomena,[12] but he is more than willing to agree with the conclusions Keynes makes. Dr. Vickers describes this for us.

> . . . let us *suppose* . . . that disposable income increases . . . by $100. Now this will generate an increase in consumption expenditures, the magnitude of the induced effect depending on the size of what we have just defined as the marginal propensity to consume. *Suppose* that this marginal propensity is equal to, say, eighty percent, indicating that the economy in general will spend on consumption goods eighty cents of every dollar added to its disposable income, and will save twenty cents. . . . As a result, the GNP, and therefore disposable income, rises by a further $80. But again the circular process repeats itself, and with the MPC at eighty percent the next induced increase in consumption expenditure will be eighty percent of $80, or $64. Similarly, at the next round

---

11. Richard Deacon, *The Cambridge Apostles: A history of Cambridge University's élite intellectual secret society* (London: Robert Royce Ltd., 1985), p. 64.
12. Keynes, *General Theory*, p. 115.

it will be eighty percent of $64, or $51.20. What is happening is that we are witnessing here what has become known as a "multiplier process."[13]

Perhaps it should not be drawn to attention, but he has said "suppose." So far, in other words, we have suppositions, not conclusions, drawn from either inductive or deductive reasoning. (We might even call Dr. Vickers' line of reasoning "suppository.") Dr. Vickers is not deterred, however, for "the overall increase in income which will result from the multiplier process can be simply calculated."[14]

The growth rate in our case was the MPC, *assumed* to be equal to four-fifths. What we now have, therefore, is the conclusion that what we shall define as the overall "national income multiplier" is five. Or to put it in more technical terms which we can now use comfortably, the national income multiplier is equal to the reciprocal of one minus the marginal propensity to consume. In the present case this was equal to five. We can say, therefore, that in this case the "multiplier" is equal to five, and the final and overall increase in income that results from the decision to increase the annual rate of investment expenditures by $100 will be five times that amount, or $500.[15]

If you believe all this, then how can you argue with the cartoon?

"Believe me, the whole economy profits, we rob someone of five grand. Then we buy some stuff from a fence. He gives his cut to the mob. They pay off the cops. . . ."

13. Vickers, p. 202, emphasis added.
14. *Ibid.*, p. 203.
15. *Idem.*, emphasis added.

The Biblical Response: Stewardship

Keynes argues that consumers only benefit others in the economy when they spend money, but saving isn't spending, so it doesn't count as an income-multiplier. The obvious implication is that the whole concept of the multiplier rests on the assumption that people do not put to effective, society-improving, employment-generating use 100% of their income. But they do. They *must*. God owns all the world. People are His stewards. He holds them accountable for everything they do with their lives and assets. Thus, everything which comes to man is a gift of God, and each man is responsible for the God-honoring management of every asset he owns.

The Christian economist who begins with (and adheres to) this fundamental presupposition could not possibly accept the preposterous theory of the multiplier. The person receives money, goods, and services. He then spends it, barters it, consumes it, gives it away, rents it out, hoards it, or loses it. Only in the last case has society's wealth been reduced. But losing it is an error, and these errors are not that common. With respect to conscious planning, the individual must do something with his assets. He cannot escape this responsibility before God. *He must put it to use.* There is no escape. It is basic to all creation, to man's dominion covenant with God.

Any God-fearing Christian should immediately recognize the perversity of Keynes' economics. It does not take a Ph.D. in economics to recognize such nonsense. In fact, it takes a Ph.D. in economics *not* to recognize it. *All the money spent on saving, tithing, investing, or anything else re-enters the income stream.* There is no 80-20 multiplier, or a 90-10 multiplier, or any other sort of multiplier. There is only the Keynesian *multiplication of confusion.*

Even hoarded money can be productive: the hoarder increases his sense of security, while the money is taken out of circulation, thereby reducing competition for other buyers or investors. (When I go to an auction as a buyer, I prefer small crowds. But, then again, I am not a Keynesian economist.)

Keynes on His Own Perverse Terms

Now, for the sake of argument, let us not begin with the Bible's answer to Keynes, or even common sense's answer to Keynes. Let us just examine the logic of Keynes' own arguments. What can we say about his logic?

First, we must note carefully that this illustration rests on the hypothetical assumption that people will spend eighty percent of their increased income. No factual statistic is offered, perhaps for the following reason. Let us accept the proposition at its face value, that there is a multiplier which can be determined to have an effect. Now let us ask: How is that multiplier determined? We can agree that people will spend only a portion of any income increase, but *how do we determine with some degree of accuracy just what that propensity is?* The only possible way is to get statistics from people when they receive that income. We must follow them, moment by moment, day by day, week by week, month by month, year by year, to see how they might use it.

Oh, no, says the liberal-minded "I am not a socialist" Keynesian, we would not want to do that. That would be like having Big Brother continually peering over your shoulder. True, but how else is this "magic" multiplier to be determined if we do not attempt to obtain an *accurate* account of how people are spending income? Probably the same way Dr. Vickers arrived at his supposition of eighty percent: *pull the figure out of thin air.* Think of a number; that will do just fine. If you prefer, ask the office secretary for a number which will become the multiplier. And if this slight parody of the Keynesian system offends, I would ask: In what manner does a number arbitrarily arrived at by the office secretary differ from that invented by the Keynesian economist?

The economist, you say, is a little more scientific. He *assumes* that if he can take a few representative samples, this will be enough to make judgments concerning the whole economy. How does he *know* these few representative examples have any relationship to what is happening in the economy as a whole? He does not know, of course. He merely makes the *assumption* that it does.

(Milton Friedman made his academic reputation by an empirical study of the consumption function. Sadly for the Keynesians, the evidence did not point to a stable consumption function in society. There went the "scientific handle" that Keynesians need in order to plan the economy.)

Second, what would happen to this multiplier effect if prices were to increase while this new income is multiplying its way through the economy? Several things *might* happen. People might decide to save more of their income, thus altering the multiplier effect. Today, they may prefer to spend only seventy-five percent of that income, and save twenty-five. Given the fact of the law of supply and demand, which Dr. Vickers' is not prepared to accept as operational in all cases, any increase in the volume of money in circulation (monetary inflation) has a tendency to increase prices, other things remaining equal. We would now have the situation where an increased monetary demand is being made on the same quantity of goods, and this tends to bid up prices.

So what happens to our multiplier effect? It would not remain constant. Therefore, if the economist wishes to see *accurately* how increases in income will be used, he *must* maintain a constant watch on the economy. Even if it were possible to obtain a complete statistical analysis of every conceivable transaction at one moment in time to ascertain what happens with any monetary increase, to assume life will go on unchanged from that moment is an assumption of the greatest magnitude, and flies in the face of economic reality. People change, their valuations change, and therefore statistics change.

Third, we must again draw attention to the fact that Dr. Vickers is unwilling to grant any distinction between savings invested and savings which are merely hoarded. His simple illustration of the marginal propensity to consume is not so simple after all. Why investment savings is not considered a valid "consumption" expenditure is not stated. The money has not left the income-generating stream. It is still circulating, but rather than being spent immediately on present consumption it has gone into investment for future consumption. It is then used to hire workers, buy equipment, rent space, etc. This is what saving is all about: foregoing my own present consumption so that greater future consumption may be possible. It creates jobs. But such a minor detail is not part of the Keynesian system.

Fourth, what if all savings were hoarded? What effects would this have on the economy? If people store cash in a mattress, we assume that they have their reasons. The obvious one is that they expect falling prices in the future, and they don't trust the banks. (This really doesn't sound all that stupid these days. Let us hope, however, that the mattress owners don't read *Economics and Man* while smoking in bed.)

If lots of people start hoarding cash, sellers of goods and services will have to drop their prices in order to get enough sales to reduce inventories. This is exactly what the hoarders expected, so one by one, they start spending their money again, *their expectations having been achieved*. Nobody except a utopian socialist really believes that all prices can fall to zero. At some point, people will start spending money again. In other words, *hoarded money has a legitimate economic function under certain economic conditions* — precisely those conditions (depression) that Keynesians are always wringing their hands over. Hoarded money provides fearful people with economic reserves. It is not "idle" money; it is rationally allocated money, *given the existence of people's fears of economic uncertainty, or their expectation of lower prices in the future.*[16]

Fifth, the great fallacy in this theory resides in the idea that it is by *spending* that national income is increased (and national income is, to the Keynesian, the measure of wealth). A proper understanding of Say's Law informs us that supply (if it is the product of accurate entrepreneurial forecasts and planning) creates demand, for the simple reason that it is only the fruits of one's production that enable a person to make demands in the market place. As a person's productivity increases, so too does his ability to increase his demand. Therefore, *it is through production that national income is*

16. W. H. Hutt, *The Theory of Idle Resources* (2nd ed.; Indianapolis, Indiana: Liberty Press, 1977).

generated and increased. In short, "If it ain't produced, you can't consume it."

The mistake Keynesians make here is to confuse what wealth really is. A society is not rich because it has more money than it did earlier. Adding money to the income stream redistributes wealth, but it cannot be said ("scientifically," anyway) that an increase of money increases social wealth. (Dr. North argued this in his book,[17] and Dr. Vickers fails to respond.) Money is, in the final analysis, just another commodity which serves a particular purpose in society, namely, to facilitate the division of labor.

Wealth should be defined as *all* morally legitimate goods and services (especially including *knowledge*) that members of a society can put to use to achieve their ends. As these assets are increased, so the nation may say that its real wealth is increasing. But production requires capital, and capital is made available only when people *forgo present consumption* in order to make investment possible. Long-term projects, such as building of railways, and resource exploration and discovery, are possible because people will put aside some of their present production in the form of investment to make such projects a reality. When they reach fruition, then people may or may not decide to consume their capital. But one thing is certain: *without saving, capital growth is not possible.* As Rothbard has long maintained, the great ideas that exist in any society at any point in time cannot be implemented except by means of capital. "Technology does, of course, set a limit on production; no production process could be used at all without technological knowledge of how to put it into operation. But while knowledge is a limit, *capital* is a narrower limit. . . . [T]echnology, while important, must always *work through* an investment of capital."[18]

Sixth, there is no *reason* given to substantiate that the reciprocal is the actual multiplier. Look again at Dr. Vickers' words. After stating the reciprocal is five he concludes: "We can say, *therefore,* that in this case the 'multiplier' is equal to five" (emphasis added).

---

17. *An Introduction to Christian Economics*, p. 45.
18. Murray N. Rothbard, *Man, Economy, and State* (New York: New York University Press, [1962] 1975), p. 490.

Why can we *"therefore"* say the multiplier is five? Dr. Vickers gives no reason. There is no process of reasoning from the fact given (the reciprocal is five) to the conclusion (the multiplier is the reciprocal). We will simply have to take Dr. Vickers' word that it is so.

"Spend your way to wealth!" This is the Keynesian message; the only thing hindering our economic welfare is insufficient spending power. If spending power could simply be created economic utopia would be on its way. The Keynesian system is nothing more than intellectual baggage to defend such a simple and futile idea.

Conclusion

Keynesian economics is simply one long attempt to confuse people. It is an attempt to make people believe that thrift is a liability, that spending on consumer goods is more productive than saving, and that the future-orientation of the Protestant ethic is misguided.

The theory rests on the preposterous assumption that for no reason in particular, people stop spending money. Not that they stop spending on consumer goods, but that they simply stop spending money at all. They "break" the stream of income. People hardly ever do this, and even if they did, sellers would respond by lowering their prices. Even money in hoards tends to reduce prices for other consumers. The economy can readjust to the new conditions and recover.

Keynes invented the multiplier as a means of defending his attack on thrift. It is nothing but a sham, yet the entire Keynesian system of "spend ourselves rich" rests on this foundation of sand. Dr. Vickers accepts the notion, even though he is unable to explain it.

The Biblical answer is stewardship. We are to put all our assets to work for the glory of God. God has created a world in which there can be no ownership without responsibility. Everything we own is put to *some* use, unless we have lost it or forgotten about it. We put our assets to the best use we can think of. The search for a "multiplier" between consumption, saving, and economic growth — a multiplier which multiplies wealth faster as the rate of saving drops — is about as sensible as a search for perpetual motion.

The astounding thing is that Dr. Vickers expects Christians to take his arguments, and therefore Keynes' arguments, quite seriously. He expects us to follow his logic, ignore the obvious, and jump on board the bandwagon and follow the yellow brick road to the land of Keynes. He ridicules Henry Hazlitt, ridicules the classical economists, and ridicules the "reactionary economic conservatism"[19] of his intellectual opponents. The reader should ask himself: "But what has Dr. Vickers offered as an alternative?" Confusion.

---

19. Vickers, *Economics and Man*, p. 180.

14

THE KEYNESIAN DISASTER

O what a tangled web we weave,
When first we practise to deceive.
But when we've practised quite a while,
How vastly we improve our style.

J. R. Pope

The one thing about Dr. Vickers which is not hidden from anyone is his incomparably abominable style—not his style of deception (Pope-like), but of communication. His abysmal writing style is nevertheless basic to his program of deception, just as Keynes' style in the *General Theory* was basic to his deception, as we have already seen.

We have seen enough of the Keynesian system to know that it contains inherent contradictions and difficulties. These are not mere minor faults in the thinking of Keynes, but are major flaws in economic rationality. It is somewhat surprising to find Dr. Vickers repeating most of these fallacious propositions without adding any significant thought to them. There appears to be some truth in Galbraith's observation that "economists are economical, among other things, of ideas. They make those they acquire as graduate students do for a lifetime."

Had Dr. Vickers taken the time to analyze more carefully the Keynesian system he might have been able to contribute something of value towards solving the current world's Keynesian-designed and Keynesian-administered financial fiasco—over a trillion dollars in world debt, a large proportion of which is owed

237

to American banks by countries unable and unwilling to undertake the necessary cut in life style required to pay off those debts.

The Keynesian system, as we have seen, is built on the fallacy
that "demand creates supply," i.e., that *monetary* demand creates
economic supplies. If only there could be more monetary demand
in the world, then all our employment problems would be solved.
More goods would be purchased, industries would grow, more
people would be employed — utopia restored.

The error here is the failure of Keynesians to distinguish between the *desire* which people have for goods and services, and
their *ability to pay* for such items with *productive assets*. In addition,
Keynesian monetary theory is deficient at this point. It fails to
understand the economic significance of money as a medium of
exchange *and* as an economic good. Consequently we are led to
believe we can spend our way to prosperity.

If we define "demand" as the present existence of market-
desired wealth at market-clearing prices, as J. B. Say and the
classical economists did, then of course this Keynesian truism is,
well, true enough. Demand indeed "creates" supply, just as supply
"creates" demand. Supply and demand are reciprocals. For every
buyer there is a seller; in fact, they are both buyers and sellers
simultaneously. They are *exchangers*.

What the Christian economist ought to say, however, is that
only once in history did pure, unadulterated, *fiat* demand create
supply: when God spoke His world into existence by fiat command during the first five days. He spoke, "Let there be," and
there *was*.

Humans must act re-creatively; only God is originally creative. We do not speak things into existence. We do not "demand"
things into existence. *We restructure the world*, just as Adam was to
care for the garden, by means of our minds, our bodies, and our
earthly possessions. We *recreate*. We think God's thoughts after
him. We do not create demand by supply, or create supply by
demand. We recreate as best we can on the assumption that other
people are doing the same. We *plan* our production for a *future*
market. We aim production at that *expected* future market. So do

other producers. We *forecast* the economic future as best we can. We deal with inescapable *uncertainty*.

In this sense, and in this sense only, does supply constitute demand, or vice versa. It is not that all things produced are desired by others. The ten-year flop of *Economics and Man* is proof enough of that reality. It could easily be described as a Keynesian pyramid. It did not create its own demand (contrary to Say), nor did anyone's demand for it create its production. It was an entrepreneurial venture which cost both author and publisher more than they bargained for. The publisher sat on a pile of unsalable books (at the low, low price of $6.95) for a decade, and the author attracted few or no disciples. The only beneficiary was Exposition Press, the "vanity" publisher that got Dr. Vickers to fork over thousands of dollars to print his subsequent unsalable book. I would estimate that even at zero price, for *A Christian Approach to Economics and the Cultural Condition*, there would be greater supply than demand. Dr. Vickers created a non-economic good.

The Debt Bomb

Couple this idea—that if only we had more money we could become wealthy—with the willingness of people to borrow against the future in order to obtain present temporary consumer satisfactions, and you have produced a recipe for an impending disaster. On the one hand, there is one group of people, the "haves," who are looking for opportunities to lend out their wealth in order to make more profits, while on the other there is another group, the "have-nots," whose desire is just as strong to get that money. Once this is combined with the Keynesian fallacy of *spending to create wealth*, both groups are willing to ignore common sense and undertake projects which, by any stretch of the imagination, have little chance of success. For example, to lend money on government projects that have no basis for generating the ability to make the repayments, is an exercise in futility. It is the construction of pyramids. To lend money to bankrupt nations in order for them to pay interest charges to New York banks, rather than finance the development of a viable economic project, produces a result similar to a store-owner (taxpayers) giving his customers money to spend in his store, but which they go and spend somewhere else instead (New York banks). It makes economic sense only for the multinational bankers and their hired lackeys: economists, politicians, and media spokesmen.

Dr. Vickers' failure to understand both monetary theory and Biblical teaching concerning debt causes him to assert that debt is not such a bad idea, and that national budget deficits are acceptable when related to the nation's productivity and ability to pay. He cites comparative statistics to defend this view.[1]

Howard Ruff pointed in 1979 to the manner in which national figures are manipulated to produce a result which is not, in fact, anywhere near the truth of the situation. Quoting from the September 30, 1976 Treasury Department bi-annual report "Statement of Liabilities and Other Financial Commitments of the United States Government," which tables the liabilities of the U.S. Government (which should more accurately be called a liability of the U.S. people, for they must eventually pay the bill), Ruff observes that the total debt for that year was closer to $6 trillion than the more commonly referred to figure of $650 billion. In addition, "Arthur Anderson, the largest accounting firm in the world, recently completed a study of the U.S. Government's accounting methods. They urged the government to do just like corporations do—use an accrual system that matches assets with liabilities. According to Anderson, if they used standard corporate accounting figures for fiscal 1974, it would show that the U.S. Government really ran a budget deficit of $95 billion, not the $3.5 billion they reported. This kind of accounting would highlight for the public and our legislatures, particularly the free-spenders, just how horrible the situation really is. . . . By no stretch of the imagination can the United States government be called solvent. The big question is: How long can it continue to get away with it? Only until such time as the public refuses to give them any more money, having discovered Uncle Sam is a dead-beat who has

---

1. Vickers, *Economics and Man*, p. 329-30.

already borrowed several times more than he can ever repay."[2] Dr. Vickers' defence of the nation's ability to pay the national debt rests on sleight-of-hand accounting procedures. That is the essence of the Keynesian system.

There has been a tremendous acceptance of debt as a way of life, not only on a personal level, with an average home mortgage now extending to 25 or 30 years, but also on a national and international level. In the light of this, investors are heard to demand security for their investments, and to obtain this they often purchase government bonds. But would the average person give his money so willingly to an individual if that debtor owed as much as the U.S. government? Would an investor voluntarily invest in General Motors if that company had equally little prospect of paying off any outstanding liabilities? Not likely, but that is precisely what people are prepared to do when it comes to buying government bonds. They are ready to give their finances to a government which has proved itself incapable of money management, and expect some kind of miracle that because it is *their* money which the politicians now have, they will somehow manage to hang onto it.

One can perhaps understand that most people are not professional lenders and therefore have some inexperience in determining who is a worthwhile debtor. But what about the professional money-lenders, those in the banks who have *given* the savings of millions of small investors to foreign countries that have no apparent ability to repay? It is one thing to loan to someone within one's own nation, where collateral of some kind may be secured. But when international boundaries are concerned, where no legal jurisdiction is enjoyed, it would appear to be a rather naive view of human nature to expect foreign debtors to be willing to honor debts to "Yankee imperialists" when money gets tight. Given the history of foreign financial dealings and the propensity for foreign nations to repudiate their obligations, there seems no great reason to expect the huge loans of the 1970's that were granted to Third

---

2. Howard J. Ruff, *How To Prosper During The Coming Bad Years* (New York: Times Books, 1979), pp. 100-1.

World countries will be treated any differently by those nations. What foolishness, for example, prompted Citibank to lend up to 100 percent of its net assets to Brazil alone?[3] In addition,

> The $37 billion that the six largest U.S. banks had lent to five volatile Latin American states represented an average of 190 percent of their net assets. A bank that loses 100 percent of its net assets is bankrupt, or "insolvent," to use the more sterile and less descriptive term preferred by financial specialists. These numbers mean that if 52 percent of the loans to these five countries [Mexico, Brazil, Venezuela, Argentina, and Chile — I. H.] were to go bad, the six largest banks in the United States would be bankrupt and, barring some major rescue effort, would cease to exist.[4]

How are the largest multinational U.S. banks doing as a group? Veribanc, an organization which monitors Federal Reserve data on U.S. banks, has compiled the following statistics, as of mid-1985. Seven of the ten largest multinational banks were in worse shape in 1985 than in 1984.

Problem Loans at the Nation's 10 Largest Banks

	June '85	June '84
Citibank	2.61b	2.65b
Bank of America	3.61b	3.55b
Chase Manhattan	2.48b	2.30b
Morgan Guaranty	1.05b	998m
Manufacturers Hanover	1.88b	1.80b
Chemical Bank	1.42b	1.09b
Bankers Trust	709m	598m
Security Pacific	1.34b	1.10b
First Nat. City (Chicago)	644m	862m
Continental Illinois	936m	2.98b

The total on these "problem loans" is an unhealthy $16.7 billion.[5]

---

3. John H. Makin, *The Global Debt Crisis* (New York: Basic Books, 1984), p. 134.

4. *Ibid.*, p. 136.

5. Cited by Dan Dorfman in *New York* (Nov. 4, 1985).

These are the banks, you understand, that are taking advantage of the deregulation of U.S. interstate banking and the regional bank crisis to rush in and gobble up local "problem" banks. These are the banks that the U.S. government regards as the system's long-term hope, the lenders of next-to-last resort. After that lies only the Federal Reserve System's money creation machine.

These debts amount to more than just economic theory. It is not simply that the economics profession teaches that debt is the road to prosperity, the manner in which stones will be turned into bread, to use Mises' apt description. There were other contributing factors. Debt became a way of life in the West, especially in the United States.

First, there was the incredible post-war boom in productivity. The pent-up demand after five years of monetary inflation, coupled with the lifting of price controls (repressed inflation, Röpke called it), exploded in a wave of consumer buying. Now that manufacturing was for consumption rather than war purposes, the quantity and variety of goods increased significantly. The optimism of the post-War period made Americans future-oriented in a new way: they planned to become more productive in the future, so they borrowed to buy that dream house, hoping to pay off the loan. It worked, too. As a result, the wealth of American citizens, in comparison to other nationalities, increased quite dramatically. United States citizens had more spendable income, more ability to save, more reasons to look for opportunities to turn those savings into profits. So they taught their children the same lesson. And so long as productivity increases per capita can continue to grow faster than the debt burden, the program can continue. But productivity takes capital and entrepreneurship, and debt-based consumer buying as a way of life has begun to erode the thrift impulse. So did the loss of Christian faith. So did Keynesian economics.

The result can be seen in the following chart. The ratio between after-tax income (dropping because taxes are rising) and total debt payments has more than doubled, 1950-1985. This chart graphs a revolution in Americans' thinking about debt.

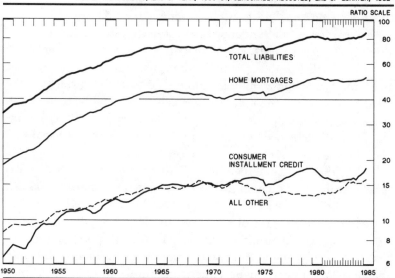

HOUSEHOLD DEBT OUTSTANDING
PERCENT OF DISPOSABLE PERSONAL INCOME
AMOUNT OUTSTANDING; END OF YEAR, 1950-51; SEASONALLY ADJUSTED, END OF QUARTER, 1952-

Second, the dramatic effects of the 1970's oil price increases, and the growing belief that natural resources were about to run out, caused people to look in areas where new resources might be found. What better source to invest in, and make loans to, than formerly backward nations that had known oil reserves, which would serve as a base for servicing the borrowed money? Then in early 1986, the "spot" (cash) price of oil fell to under $12 per barrel. The loans had been made on the assumption that $20 was the rock-bottom, and that $30 was likely. There is not a multinational bank in the United States that isn't in deep trouble because of it.

Third, the complete break from the *de facto* gold standard which Nixon achieved in 1971 allowed the free production of fiat money to finance deficit spending. The euphoria of the early part of the 1970's is hard to recall a decade later, but it had a dramatic impact on world trade.

The world was in for a shock. Productivity levels declined. Oil prices, contrary to the desires of OPEC, began to drop. Those who borrowed on the basis of being able to sell their oil at $30 a barrel or more, and who were *dependent* on that price range to service financial borrowings, now find they can get significantly less than that amount. In addition, the general productivity decline has meant that anticipated markets no longer exist, or at least exist on a reduced scale. Expected sales are simply not there. The result? The global debt crisis.

A deflation caused by a run on the banks today would bring to Dr. Vickers' attention what really "sticky" prices are all about. If he thinks that prices were inflexible on the down side in 1933, wait until he sees what happens in today's world of massive debt service requirements, labor union monopolies, price floors, and the predictable tariffs that would be passed in a recession.

The Greatest Disaster of All

But the greatest disaster of all in the Keynesian system is the *loss of moral values* that it causes. (What would you expect from an economic system designed by a homosexual?) Not only is there a casual attitude towards the use of debt, but more importantly, it leads politicians to be deceitful about the true state of affairs. As Hutt observed, Keynesians "commit themselves to the persistent deception of the public regarding monetary intentions or to disguised totalitarianism; these are the inevitable alternatives under continuous inflation."[6]

Not by any stretch of the imagination can the Less-Developed-Countries (LDC's) repay their huge borrowings without the people in those countries suffering a dramatic decrease in living standards. When an individual or a nation has to borrow in order to meet interest payments without any return of capital, a crisis of the first magnitude exists. What is it that allows lenders, with government acquiesence, to continue lending to those who have no hope of repaying? Why not face the reality of the matter

---

6. Hutt, *The Keynesian Episode*, p. 164.

and *admit* a crisis exists? Why not tell the investing public that their hard-earned funds are gone — *forever!* (The funds can be printed, of course, but the assets represented by those funds — the valuable resources that the LDC debtors have long-since *consumed* — will not return.)

Why don't we face the music, call dead loans dead loans, and start over? There is an answer, of course: multinational banks. They desperately need the legal fiction of book-value loans. They need to keep those loans listed as assets in their portfolios — assets valued at what they paid (loaned) for them, not what they are worth in the free market. Deprive them of this legal fiction by admitting that the loans are dead, and their loan portfolios will fall close to zero — perhaps even negative capital for the banks. A lot of bankers will go bankrupt. So will millions of citizens who are in hock up to their eyeballs. So the debt game goes on. For a while longer.

Monetary inflation is itself an immoral act. It perverts the financial stability of society. (And speaking of perverts. . . .) It allows one group in the community to profit at the expense of others. It is a deliberate act of taking the purchasing power out of someone's pocket, just as a common thief achieves a similar effect.

If Dr. Vickers, in the name of Christianity, is so sure that inflation and debt are moral attributes, then the *onus of proof is on him* to demonstrate that Keynesianism has not led straight into this looming catastrophe. If he cannot, then he ought to provide a solution to the current international monetary fiasco. Possibly the rest of the world has misunderstood Keynes. Perhaps the present crisis is only the result of *not* spending enough, of not putting Keynes' theories into practice to the degree that is necessary. If this is the case, will Dr. Vickers have the courage to call for *more* inflation, and *more* foreign and domestic loans? The answer to that question is somewhat obvious, at least to those who have never had the pleasure of having their economic reasoning destroyed by graduate courses in Keynesian stupidity. Unfortunately, we have modern public education to thank for the fact that although people may have been taught to read (and there is some dispute even on that fact) it has definitely *not* taught them to *think*. And if you can't *think*, you're not educated! (Then again, once you get a graduate education in Keynesian economics, you can't think either.)

More Lies, Higher Taxes

What other reason is there for the willingness of a naive public to believe the lies they are told about monetary and fiscal policy? At the time of writing this manuscript, the governments in both the United States and Australia are undertaking a major "sales" program to convince the voters of the need for tax reform. The reasons they put forward include the need for a more "equitable" system, a more even spreading of the tax burden across the strata of society.

How do they plan to do this? What the politicians in Australia are suggesting is the greatest selling campaign of all: a Tax Summit. What voters are not told is the fact that the government has only one interest in tax reform, *getting more money*. Australia's accumulated foreign debt has grown from around $7 billion in 1980 to the vicinity of $107 billion in 1985. (Anyone want to guess why the Australian dollar took such a downturn in early 1985?) The expected national deficit for 1985-86 fiscal year has grown from a projected $9 billion to an anticipated $13-14 billion. With such a large accumulation of debt, do people *really* believe the tax reform program is designed to lower their tax burden? Kangaroos might develop wings and fly, too. The reform is more likely to increase taxes as well as close current legal loopholes in the legislation which deny the government untold millions in taxpayers' earnings.

The Keynesian Legacy

If a religious revival does not occur in the immediate future, there are two possible alternatives for the future course of events. *First*, there could be a return to sound economic theory and behavior. Of all possibilities, this seems the most unlikely. Politicians are not about to give up those powers that would be necessary to re-establish the free market. Pride, human ambition, power, greed—the evils that Dr. Vickers says precludes free market economics—are all factors that must be overcome by politicians and Keynesian economists who have the arrogance, like Dr. Vickers, to believe they are capable of getting us out of this mess. The truth is that they got us into this mess by trying to get us out of one which did not have the magnitude of the present crisis. So there seems no real reason to believe this alternative—a return to Biblical economics, or even the classical economists' imitation—is about to happen. In addition, to return to sound monetary policies, to stop monetary inflation, would produce an immediate depression while the economy readjusts itself to the reality of the zero-inflation situation. There is no country on earth whose voters will accept such a scenario. They prefer to be fooled for a while longer, until the inescapable monetary crisis overtakes them.

Second, the remaining alternative is to continue the present policies, albeit with some fear and trepidation. As this seems the most likely course of action in the immediate future, it is worth considering the likely effects of such a possibility. In passing it is relevant that Federal Reserve chairman Paul Volcker has surprised most people for the past seven years and has kept reins on the money supply. He of all the Federal Reserve's staff seems most aware of the situation and the need for a check on the money supply growth. Consequently, 1980-85 produced a recessionary cycle in the market, albeit with some tendency at times to show signs of growth. With the 1980 election of Ronald Reagan, there was rhetoric to the effect that monetarism was the new policy, and that there would be severe control over monetary growth. How much longer that will last is anyone's guess. But as it was more rhetoric than substance, any financial responsibility practiced is bound to be short lived.

A recent article in *The Economist* by professor James Tobin of Yale University, winner of the 1981 Nobel Prize for economics, has announced the death of monetarism and the resurgence of Keynesian monetary and fiscal policies.[7] (Gray-headed tenured scientists desperately want to believe that the next "scientific revolution" has not already passed them by, and that they are not irrelevant after all. They always are—as irrelevant as those gray-heads they replaced so mercilessly in their youth.) Time will indicate the outcome of this prediction.[8] If it is as accurate as other Keynesian predictions, Dr. Tobin would be wise not to expect his heirs to benefit from any book royalties that he may now be receiving.

Conclusion

Given the assumption that monetary inflation is going to continue, if not for the academic reasons of economists, then at least for the pragmatic decisions of those after political votes, there are two possible outcomes for the future. Either inflation will be allowed to continue its course, which is eventually to reach the hyperinflation stage where complete economic chaos occurs, or there will be attempts to mitigate against this tendency by the imposition of government regulations. Where monetary inflation leads to price inflation, this will be held in check by price controls. Since the former alternative, hyperinflation, is politically unacceptable, we may safely predict that the controlled economy is the future state of affairs.

This being the case you might well like to prepare yourself *now*

7. James Tobin, "Monetarism's Costly Legacy," *The Weekend Australian* (May 4-5, 1985), p. 26, reprinted from *The Economist*. See especially Marc A. Miles, *Beyond Monetarism: Finding the Road to Stable Money* (New York: Basic Books, 1984).

8. Interestingly, former head of the Australian Treasury John Stone, who resigned late in 1984 over reported disagreements with the present Labor government over monetary policy, is a monetarist. It is probably no coincidence that during his period as head of this department money supply growth was held to around 11-12 percent per annum. Again, it is no coincidence that since his departure from office late in 1984, M3 in Australia has suddenly risen to 19.6 percent per annum (last quarter 1985). Interest rates have skyrocketed. Coupled with the recent decline of the Australian dollar against the rapidly declining U.S. dollar, from 90 cents to about 65 cents over a four-month period, we may be certain that prices will rise. Australians are taking a significant drop in their standard of living.

to survive in that kind of society.[9] How long it will last, and to what degree it will occur, is a matter for conjecture. It depends upon a number of variables. Perhaps there will be a religious (i.e., Christian) revival and a return to the *just* and *righteous* economic standards of Scripture, at least to some degree. Those with an optimistic postmillennial eschatology will no doubt agree this is more than "possibility thinking."[10] What is not known is how long it will take and what must be endured before it occurs. Meanwhile we live under the threat of a humanistic, totalitarian government. That is the legacy of Keynesianism which Dr. Vickers would like us to embrace in the name of Christianity.

The willingness of the public to believe the lies is, of course, a religious phenomena. "Because that, when they knew God, they glorified him not as God, neither were thankful; but became vain in their imaginations, and their foolish heart was darkened. Professing themselves to be wise they became fools" (Rom. 1:21,22). Then Paul tells us what happens next when people do this: *they become homosexuals* (Rom. 1:24-27). What is required is a return to faith and obedience to the God of Scripture because He alone is the way, the truth, and the life (John 14:6).

It is unfortunate that fallen human nature, in its stubborn rebellion against God's revealed truth, requires external circumstances to encourage it to listen to the Word of God. With all the miracles performed in Egypt as they wandered the desert, still most of the Israelites murmured against God and would not obey His Word. The seventy years captivity is another example of the necessity for external cursing before there is a willingness for people to listen to and obey the Word of the Lord (cf. Neh. 8:1-9:38).

---

9. There is no better place to begin than by obtaining Gary North's *The Last Train Out* and *Government By Emergency* (Fort Worth, Texas: American Bureau of Economic Research, 1983).

10. See David Chilton, *Paradise Restored* (Tyler, Texas: Reconstruction Press, 1985).

15

BEHOLD, OUR SAVIOR!

*At the present moment people are unusually expectant of a more
fundamental diagnosis; more particularly ready to receive it; eager to
try it out, if it should be even plausible. But apart from this contemporary mood, the ideas of economists and political philosophers, both
when they are right and when they are wrong, are more powerful than
is commonly understood. Indeed the world is ruled by little else. Practical men, who believe themselves to be quite exempt from any intellectual influences, are usually the slaves of some defunct economist. Mad-
men in authority, who hear voices in the air, are distilling their frenzy
from some academic scribbler of a few years back. . . . Not, indeed,
immediately, but after a certain interval; for in the field of economic
and political philosophy there are not many who are influenced by new
theories after they are twenty-five or thirty years of age, so that the ideas
which civil servants and politicians and even agitators apply to current
events are not likely to be the newest. But, soon or late, it is ideas, not
vested interests, which are dangerous for good or evil.*

John Maynard Keynes[1]

Keynesianism is a fact of life, if not by name, then at least in
practice. Governments everywhere are enamored with the idea
that they can spend our way to prosperity. This world is, in
Clarence Carson's description, in "the grip of an idea." "The idea
is this: *To achieve human felicity on this earth by concerting all efforts to-*

---

1. *The General Theory*, pp. 383-84.

ward its realization."[2]

This is to be achieved, according to Dr. Vickers, by the "proper regulatory function of the government. . . ."[3] "New guidelines" are to be laid down circumscribing the actions of individuals, those nasty villains who keep making life difficult for everyone else.[4] Failure to act would be "economically criminal, and against the basic objectives of conservation, development, and equity, as we have seen these adequately sustained and confirmed by scriptural data. . . ."[5]

What we have here is capitulation to the idea that man's economic problems can be solved by government action, by control and regulation of the marketplace. There is implicit faith that all problems, and especially those of an economic nature, are *political* problems and can therefore be solved by *political* action.[6] I experienced a vivid illustration of this in a discussion with the principal of a Reformed theological college who acknowledged that there were employers paying "unjust" (by that he meant low) wages, and therefore there should be legislation establishing a minimum wage. Ignoring for the moment the inherent difficulty of defining what is a "just" wage, his suggestion is that the solution to the problem is government action. An economic problem is *automatically* perceived to have its answer in the domain of politics and legislative decrees. But let us grant for a moment that there is an element of truth in this illustration. We can readily admit there are employers paying low wages. However, are minimum wage laws the solution to the problem? And what, really, is the problem in the first place?

---

2. Clarence B. Carson, *The World in the Grip of an Idea* (New Rochelle, New York: Arlington House, 1979), p. 9, emphasis in original.

3. Vickers, *Economics and Man*, p. 343.

4. *Ibid.*, p. 337.

5. *Ibid.*, p. 322.

6. See Jacques Ellul, "Politicization and Political Solutions" in Kenneth S. Templeton, Jr. (ed.), *The Politicization of Society* (Indianapolis, Indiana: Liberty Press, 1977), p. 209ff.; cf. Clarence B. Carson, *The Flight From Reality* (Irvington-on-Hudson, New York: Foundation for Economic Education, 1969), p. 351ff.

The Things Unseen

Orthodox Christianity teaches life is more than what is observed. Fundamental reality has an unseen aspect, that which is beyond more than just the physical senses of man. The inspired Word of God insists that it is out of the heart of man, the inner recess of the human being, that all things flow. "For as he thinketh in his heart, so is he" (Prov. 23:7). Scripture thus puts a different perspective on things. It says that life is not just those surface things we see but there are far deeper and more basic and fundamental realities.

It is these truths that modern man wants to deny. This has been described as a flight from reality. Modern man, in denying the fundamental truths of Biblical Christianity, has denied the reality of life. He now manufactures a world according to his own vain imaginings. In this land of fantasy, all the problems of life are perceived to have a merely physical origin. Scarcity is no longer perceived as the fundamental cause of poverty. Apparently there is now an abundance of things—behold the seemingly endless supplies at the supermarket. Poverty must therefore exist because some people are getting all the produce. Some are rich at the expense of those who do not get the goods, the poor. Employers are paying "unjust" wages and getting rich at the expense of employees; unemployment exists because some people refuse to spend their incomes depriving someone else of their livelihood. The whole economic world is interpreted in terms of an ancient fallacy: *you win; therefore, I lose.* "There has, then, been a flight from economics, a flight from economics as a discipline for study and exposition to 'economics' as a tool for social reform, a flight from economics to politics. This has been, also, a flight from reality."[7]

The Biblical View

Scripture does not agree, however, with the view that the economic problem is one of mere manipulation of physical reality.

---

7. Carson, *The Flight From Reality*, p. 370.

This is why, for example, there are material blessings offered to those who are obedient to the God of Scripture (Deut. 28:1-14). It is also why there are material deprivations promised to those who rebel against the Creator.

The Biblical perspective is that man has denied the true God in order to place himself at the center of the universe. Man is the new god who creates reality, decides what is right or wrong, good or evil, just or unjust (Gen. 3:5). As Schlossberg has pointed out, "Western society, in turning away from Christian faith, has turned to other things. This process is commonly called *secularization*, but that conveys only the negative aspect. The word connotes the turning away from the worship of God while ignoring the fact that something is being turned *to* in its place. . . . All such principles that substitute for God exemplify the biblical concept of idol."[8]

Modern man is idolatrous. He manufactures new gods to worship. But he also seeks salvation by these gods. Twentieth-century man is only too aware the world is not perfect. Deep down, he has a longing for utopia, a land of perfection, where worry, illness, and death no longer exist. Paradise lost remains in his being, and he seeks to return to it by any and every means—except one: faith and obedience to the God of Scripture.

Man is the new god who will create heaven on earth—given sufficient time and lots of taxpayers' money. What is surprising is to find Dr. Vickers endorsing such a view. Recall our college principal who wanted "fair" wages paid. Is legislative action the *only* course of action to get the employer to pay more? Orthodox Christianity insists there is an alternative. It involves a fundamental change in the way people think. In Biblical terminology, it involves the necessity of regeneration. From this fundamental change in nature, the employer might then *willingly* pay additional wages to his employees, to encourage greater loyalty and greater productivity. And if he does not do so immediately, who are we to complain to God that He has not motivated His new

---

8. Herbert Schlossberg, *Idols For Destruction* (Nashville, Tennessee: Thomas Nelson, 1983), p. 6.

subject to fit in with *our* ideas of "just" wages?

Arbitrary Humanist Definitions

Humanist man is the new god, determining for himself good and evil, right and wrong, just and unjust. To the extent that Christians adopt the *conclusions* of humanist man regarding economics, they have thereby adopted the *presuppositions* of humanist man. Dr. Vickers is a prime example of this self-deception. Consider his moralistic language. His writings abound with descriptive terms such as "justice," "equity," "exploitation," "excessive," "desirable," "sufficiently meaningful," or "legitimate." Private enterprise investment, for example, is incapable, according to Dr. Vickers, of setting a "scale of charges adequate to provide a *reasonable* or *acceptable* rate of return on capital."[9] Monetary and fiscal policy is necessary to ensure a "*satisfactory* rate and *direction* of growth" in the economy.[10]

The difficulty arises when we ask *who* is to define what "justice" means; *who* has the wisdom to determine what a "reasonable and acceptable" rate of return on capital is? If one person wants ten percent return but someone else wants fifteen, is there anything inherent in either figure which makes one more "equitable" than the other? If one employer pays $300 per week to labor, while another pays $350 for the same kind, is there something fundamentally unjust in the former case? And *who* shall be the one to decide questions such as these?

Biblical Definitions

The essence of Christianity is that *it is God through His inspired Word, the Bible, who defines what is just and unjust.* God, being the sole possessor of omniscience, is alone capable of determining these things. Man, without such divine revelation, is *incapable* of defining the meaning of words such as "exploitation." Man is only able to offer an opinion. Thus, when Dr. Vickers is calling for

---

9. Vickers, *Economics and Man*, p. 77, emphasis added.
10. *Ibid.*, p. 294, emphasis added.

State action to ensure "equity" and "satisfactory" growth in the economy, he has departed from Biblical premises, for the Bible does *not* tell us what a "satisfactory" rate of growth in the economy should be. Dr. Vickers would impose *his* opinion, or the opinions of a bureaucratic committee, on the rest of mankind. To do it in the name of economic equity and justice is to grossly mislead us away from the truth of the matter. It is to impose *his* morality on the rest of society, rather than to adhere to Biblical morality.

Biblical morality is different from that which Dr. Vickers, or our college principal, wants. For some reason, the Bible is silent on whether either $300 or $350 is a "just" wage. There is simply no verse in Scripture which gives the answer to such a perplexing question. This is why the search for a definition of "the just wage" stymied scholastic theologians, and later the first generation of colonial Puritans in New England. No matter, says Dr. Vickers, "For the economist, of all people, is, by virtue of the insight his professional training gives him, uniquely equipped to explain to society the manner in which the production of certain *more desirable* outputs could be achieved if resources were diverted away from the production of less desirable commodities."[11] The morality of the "uniquely equipped" economist must take precedence over that of other individuals or the morality of God. If you think that Dr. Vickers is talking about a *tenured, self-certified planning elite*, you are thinking what I am thinking, too.

Biblical faith finds little agreement with the Keynesian economic theories Dr. Vickers would have us accept as Christian. Where the former insists all problems, including economic problems, have their fundamental origin in the spiritual state of man, the latter says it is a matter of "lack of spending power," or some other nonsense. Dr. Vickers would seek to solve the economic problems by State decree rather than spiritual regeneration of the individual who then lives in obedience to the law of God.

Vickers on Poverty

There is one further illustration we might use to substantiate the claim that Dr. Vickers is preaching another faith than that of

---

11. *Ibid.*, p. 171, emphasis added.

Biblical Christianity. On more than one occasion, Dr. Vickers accepts the fallacy that poverty is merely the result of maldistribution of the economic resources currently available. "The abject poverty and the scandal of human distress in India cannot be evaded. And there can be no doubt that the question of the international distribution of the production of this world's goods . . . should engage the economist's thought and policy recommendations very directly."[12]

We can recall also that considerations of morality must inform our attitudes to a statistical increase in Gross or Net National Product when we confront the patent obligation of an affluent society (we spoke of the United States as an example) to consider the economic condition of the wretchedly impoverished people of the underdeveloped countries, taking, in the same context, India as a prime example.[13]

There is a strong inference that it is immoral for people in wealthy countries to be rich while the poverty of India exists. We might have less trouble agreeing with Dr. Vickers had he bothered to contextually argue from Scriptural passages that it is somehow "immoral" for some to be rich while others are poor. But as on so many occasions, we are told by Dr. Vickers that his ideas are "Christian" without any proof. We are supposed to accept his word that it is. We might have less disagreement with Dr. Vickers if he could substantiate the inference that India's poverty is at the expense of wealthy nations. His writings are singularly silent on the *causes* of poverty in that country, which really is the basis for any charge of immorality. There is no analysis of the *causes* of wealth in countries such as the U.S. That relative freedom has been granted to the individual to freely trade with his neighbor, a fact that has its foundations in the religious revivals of recent centuries and the influence of a Biblical morality that is foreign to Dr. Vickers, and the development of the market economy, provided the impetus to productivity and the growth of material wealth. That India has not had such an influence is conveniently omitted

---

12. *Ibid.*, p. 151.
13. *Ibid.*, p. 187.

by Dr. Vickers. This essential difference has been vividly described
by Edmund Opitz.

How can a society whose worldview includes such doctrines as Maya
[illusory world], karma [reincarnation] and caste produce the social
structure upon which the market economy is based? Accept the idea of
Maya and you exclude the idea of a rationally structured, cause and
effect universe. The doctrine of karma makes it virtually impossible for
individuals to have the necessary self-responsibility and will to succeed
which are essentials for a going-concern economy. And caste divisions in
a society are incompatible with the idea of inherent rights and equality
before the law. Capitalism is rooted in the cultural heritage of the West,
Christendom, and you can't have the fruits without the roots; you cannot merely *wish* an end result — to will the end is to will the means.[14]

Keynesianism Offers a Plan of Salvation

"The State loves you, and has a wonderful plan for your life."

In an earlier chapter, I suggested that Keynesianism is socialistic and authoritarian in nature. There is an inherent reason for
this, and this is why there is an inexorable move towards totalitarianism whenever Keynesian theory is adopted.

The essence of free market economic theory is this: the economy is controlled by individuals who make *subjective* valuations.
For example, a person who decides to save some of his assets does
so because he *prefers* to forgo present consumption in order to par-
ticipate in consumption at some point of time in the future. This is
the basis of the capital process. Without people's willingness to
forgo present consumption there can be no capital projects which
provide goods in the future, for example, mineral exploration.

What causes people to make the kind of decisions such as saving? Obviously there are a number of factors. There are perhaps
more obvious motives such as saving for something which is

---

14. Edmund A. Opitz, "The Philosophy of Ludwig von Mises" in *The Freeman*,
(July 1980), p. 440. Published by the Foundation for Economic Education,
Irvington-on-Hudson, New York 10533. See also P. T. Bauer, *Equality, the Third
World, and Economic Delusion* (Cambridge, Massachusetts: Harvard University
Press, 1981).

beyond the present ability of the person to obtain. But there are also deeper psychological motives which cannot be so easily explained, and in fact defy explanation because human knowledge at this point in time cannot properly understand them. As Scripture declares, "For now we see through a glass, darkly" (I Cor. 13:12). In a very real sense we may say that people's economic decisions are a product of what they themselves are. This is why Christians, those made new by the Spirit of the Living God, often make vastly different economic decisions than those who are unregenerate.

The free market economy lives with this fundamental reality and adjusts itself in terms of it. If people begin to save more than previously, others in the market place must adjust their business activities accordingly. Perhaps there are those whose goods suffer a diminished demand as consumption in the present is postponed for the future. At the same time, there are others in the economy who will benefit and take advantage of the new availability of funds for capital investment.

The Keynesian system, however, does not permit this kind of world. Instead, *Keynesianism wants a world which must conform to the expert planners' wishes and desires.* How terrible that people should save and deny someone a present income (or so they think). People, therefore, must be *forced* to conform to the Keynesian view of what reality should be. If people save, there must be policy to overcome this propensity in human beings. The economy must be made to operate the way Keynesians *think* it ought to operate. Legislation must be passed to coerce conformity from the population.

Keynesianism is therefore very much a religion. It has a theory of morality. It offers a definition of right and wrong, and offers a concrete plan to solve those wrongs. In other words, Keynesianism has a plan of salvation. But its plan of salvation is vastly different from that of the Living God who has decreed that salvation may only be obtained by faith in the atoning work of Jesus Christ and obedience to His revealed will.

To call for bureaucratic control of the individual is to deny something to man which his Creator has decreed. Man has been endowed with reason and the ability to make choices. To deny a man those choices is to deny his fundamental humanity and his inherent rights given by his Creator. To insist that "uniquely equipped" economists must make decisions for the rest of society is to say that knowledge originates in man; and that is to give credence to the serpent's lie. As the Psalmist declared, it is God who teaches man (Ps. 94:10) and God is therefore man's ultimate source of salvation — not the vague and nonsensical theories of those enlightened by the study of economics — especially the non-Biblical economics of a perverted homosexual.

Conclusion

Man is not saved by secret arcane knowledge, even knowledge with equations. Man is not saved by State power. Man is not saved by law, especially statist law. The Bible tells us that man is saved by grace through faith (Eph. 2:8-9), in order that he might walk in the ways God has planned for him (Eph. 2:10).

Dr. Vickers has adopted the first two views of salvation: salvation by arcane knowledge and salvation by statist law. He sees no way for redeemed Christians to reconstruct society along Biblical lines. We will never have a Christian society, he says.[15] That leaves only one other kind: a *non*-Christian society. He has therefore adopted his favorite brand of non-Christian society, the brand of his youth, the equation-filled, jargon-filled society of Keynesian planning. He would have us join him on the yellow brick road to the land of Keynes.

Forgive me if I try some other path. I see where this one is headed.

---

15. Vickers, *Economics and Man*, p. 45.

CONCLUSION

First, economics in a Christian perspective must accord full recognition to the rights of the individual and individual responsibility, but it cannot condone those concentrations of economic power in the hands of individuals which make it possible for the interests of others to be exploited. And full recognition is also accorded to the fact that, if left to itself, there is no inherent reason why the aggregative economic system will achieve a complete and automatic harmony of interests. Second, some intervention by the state in economic affairs is necessary, to some extent regulatory and in other instances more directly participatory. But at the same time, a Christian economist cannot countenance the exploitation by the state, or by state agencies or personnel, of the rights of individuals and the broader interests of society. And it is difficult to conceive, under scriptural mandate, of the propriety of the usurpation by the state of those economic functions and prerogatives which lie properly within the province of individual action. [1]

We have had the opportunity to pursue Dr. Vickers' ideas on the meaning of both capitalism and socialism. In both instances, we must conclude that there is a serious lack of understanding on Dr. Vickers' part about what these words mean. His definitions are either inaccurate (e.g., capitalism) or non-existent (e.g., socialism).

How, then, should we view his claim that there is a third way, an alternative to both capitalism and socialism? Essentially we should view this claim as the meandering of a mind which has made little effort to come to grips with economic history and

---

1. *Economics and Man*, p. 78.

261

theory—or which has made the effort, and failed miserably to communicate its findings in language that any reasonably alert person can comprehend.

Deliberately Ignoring His Strongest Opponents

Take, for example, the claim in his book that the reader "will find in my treatment of the relevant intellectual history the familiar names of Smith, Malthus, Ricardo, Mill, Chalmers, Jevons, Sidgwick, Marshall, Viner, Keynes, and others."[2] For one thing, he barely mentions any of these major economists in his book. More important, here is tacit admission that he is not going to make reference to at least one school of economic thought, what has become known as the Austrian School of economics. Throughout his work Dr. Vickers makes *no* reference, for example, to the writings of Carl Menger, Eugen von Böhm-Bawerk, or Ludwig von Mises, the latter having presented some of the most rigorous economic analysis of socialism to be found in economic literature. Mises thoroughly analyzes all opposing viewpoints to his own in demonstrating their inherent weaknesses. But this is something we do not find in Dr. Vickers (nor in Keynes, for that matter). Is it simply that he chose not to make reference to them? Since he knows that Dr. North and Rev. Rushdoony rely on the insights of the Austrian School, we might expect that Dr. Vickers would openly and without delay confront the fundamental tenets of the Austrian School. He does not do so. The reader is not even given an inaccurate summary of their views, let alone a fair and judicious summary.

Why not? Because Dr. Vickers knows that their views are clear and presented in English, while Keynes' views are garbled. Give an inexperienced reader the choice, and he will remember the Austrian arguments a lot better and easier than he will remember the convoluted details of the Keynesian system. The Keynesians will lose the debate far too often. So they ignore the Austrian School. They pretend it isn't there. This may be intellec-

---

2. *Ibid.*, p. vii.

tual cowardice, but that is the way the academic game is played.

The truth of the matter is Keynesianism has been refuted a thousand times over in the past 200 years. (That's right, for Keynesianism is nothing but a rehash of the old mercantile theories which the early classical economists demolished with considerable ability.)[3] The fact that Samuelson could honestly admit the language in Keynes' *General Theory* does not always seem to make sense is evidence of precisely that point: it is a nonsensical book. Yet now we have Dr. Vickers presenting Keynesianism to us first, on the pretext that it is sound economic theory, and second, that it is Christian economic theory.

The fact is, however, that his book does not make any serious use of any of these famous pre-Keynesian economists. He mentions a few of them occasionally, but his book is in no sense reliant upon the classics. We find more footnotes to an obscure and unidentified writer named H. F. R. Catherwood than to Adam Smith and the other economists Dr. Vickers parades around in his Preface. In fact, he hardly even cites Keynes' *General Theory*, which is understandable, since there is very little evidence that he has read it. Like most post-Keynesians, Dr. Vickers does not rely on its convoluted arguments and peculiar definitions when it comes down to writing his own book. It is a lot easier to quote from the post-Keynesian "crowd" than to struggle with *The General Theory*. I don't blame him a bit.

My analysis of Dr. Vickers has concentrated on establishing two things. *First*, he is prepared to misstate his opponents in order to score debate points. (Fortunately for his opponents, his style is so muddled that he never quite scores.) This is intellectually dishonest and poor scholarship. *Second*, we have seen that he tries to argue for a supposed third way in economics by denying that economics is an either-or choice between socialism and capitalism. We have seen, however, that he fails in this regard, for he categorically rejects the use of Old Testament law and history to guide us

---

3. L. Albert Hahn, *The Economics of Illusion: A Critical Analysis of Contemporary Economic Theory and Practice* (Wells, Vermont: Fraser, [1949] 1977), ch. 10: "Mercantilism and Keynesianism."

along the only conceivable and workable "third way." No matter what disclaimers he makes, what he is calling for are the initial steps down the road to socialism. To describe it otherwise would be grossly misleading.

A Pile of Errors

Our survey of the Keynesian system is completed. This analysis of some of the basic theories of the Keynesian economic system, as well as particular arguments put forward by Douglas Vickers, should serve as an aid in deciding whether Christianity and Keynesianism are compatible. As a result of this analysis, it should be possible for most readers to agree with Henry Hazlitt that the Keynesian system contains "an incredible number of fallacies, inconsistencies, vaguenesses, shifting definitions and usages of words, and plain errors of fact."[4]

Although Dr. Vickers contends that Hazlitt's work is a "shallow" analysis,[5] it is worth noting that no Keynesian economist has ever attempted a *systematic* refutation of Hazlitt's devastating critique, probably because they *cannot* refute it, and certainly because they cannot refute it in plain language. On the other hand, perhaps Dr. Vickers, in his promised longer work on economic analysis, will make the time and effort for such a refutation. Just as Marx finally gave us his definition of "class."[6] Just as Darwin finally gave us his definition of "species."[7] That is to say, fat chance. *Economics and Man* is already a decade old. It has not aged well.

---

4. Henry Hazlitt, *The Failure of the "New Economics"*, p. 7.

5. *Economics and Man*, p. 36.

6. In the posthumously published third edition of *Capital*, on the next to the last page, Marx wrote: "The first question to be answered is this: What constitutes a class?" Two paragraphs later, the manuscript breaks off. Marx, *Capital: A Critique of Political Economy* (Chicago: Charles H. Kerr, 1909), p. 1031. He built his whole theory of history on the basis of the class struggle in history, yet he never got around to defining what a class is. The joke is on us. The joke is especially on the intellectuals who still follow Marx.

7. "Nor shall I here discuss the various definitions which have been given of the term species. No one definition has satisfied all the naturalists; yet every naturalist knows vaguely what he means when he speaks of a species." Darwin, *Origin of Species* (Modern Library edition), p. 38.

Keynes' *General Theory* was a book designed to confuse. We find in Dr. Vickers a similar propensity to confuse. His "prelude" has been orchestrated as a cacophony of unintelligible, illogical, and meaningless arguments. In reality, his "prelude" is more like a theme with variations — the theme being nonsense and the variations reflecting the perverted subject. I, for one, having heard the "prelude" and paid Dr. Vickers the courtesy of attempting to understand his work, do not think it is worth the effort to remain for the main performance and the curtain call. The words of Martin Luther, although given in another context, are eminently applicable here. "And, since you cannot overthrow it by any argument, you try meantime to tire the reader with a flow of empty verbiage."[8] Or, as Howard Katz has observed, "The Keynesian economists are not true experts. They cannot *do* anything. Although they stake their prestige on their ability to predict (as part of their fraud of imitating the scientist), their predictions are a standing joke and a continual embarrassment. Neither can they explain their theories in terms that make sense. If you have had the experience of listening to one of today's economists and have come away thinking, 'I cannot make head or tail of what that fellow is saying,' then do not be alarmed. That is the response of a properly functioning mind."[9]

Why is it that Dr. Vickers can embrace such intellectual nonsense and do such violence to the Scriptures which he says he believes? The answer to that is illustrated in the joke which asks: Why are Polish cows deformed? Answer: Because they're raised in Poland and milked in Russia. Why is Dr. Vickers' thinking deformed? Because although he was raised in the Christian faith, he received his education in the schools and universities of apostate humanism. This is a disease common in too much of the Chris-

---

8. J. I. Packer and O. R. Johnston, trans., Martin Luther, *The Bondage of the Will* (Cambridge, England: James Clarke, 1957), p. 87. Or use the translation in the Library of Christian Classics: *Luther and Erasmus: Free Will and Salvation* (Philadelphia: Westminster Press, 1969).

9. Howard S. Katz, *The Warmongers* (New York: Books In Focus, 1979), p. 259, emphasis in original.

tian community. (Of course, it really isn't a disease; it is a moral failure.) And Dr. Vickers is a very good example of what can happen when we raise our children in the schools of Egypt.

If you want a good reason for Christian schools, read *Economics and Man*.

The Legacy of Keynes

We are now in a position to answer the questions raised in the introduction to this study. Did Keynes give us "a significant logical and methodological reconstruction" of economic theory? Has he achieved a "more complete understanding of the structure and functioning of the economic system"? We have found no evidence to substantiate these arguments. On the contrary, we have found substantial evidence to indicate what will happen to the present financial system, thanks to the justification Keynes gave to economic theories which have brought upon the West its greatest ever financial crisis: a mountain of Third World debt which the West's banks are unlikely ever to see repaid — at least not in dollars that are worth anything; a $200 billion annual deficit by the government of the United States; endless inflation; endless business cycles; and all of this accompanied by cries from graying Keynesian economists that they ought to be given more power to make other men's economic decisions for them, that *next time all their ideas will work*. Really. Trust them. Their promises are a lot better than gold, which Keynes called a barbarous relic. Their promises are as good as an IMF bond. Their word is their bond, and their word *is* "bond." More debt, more debt; let us spend ourselves rich.

Nor can we agree with Dr. Vickers that Keynes "gave us a new way of seeing things." Keynes' new way is in fact an old way. It dates back to the Garden of Eden and man's original rebellion against his Creator. Keynes' economics is the economics of a rebel who made no effort to submit himself to the God who made him. It is an example of man being "as God" (Gen. 3:5) in the realm of economics, with catastrophic results.

What about the claims of Dr. Vickers? Has he "redirected" the thinking of Biblical economics? Again we can find no evidence that he has. To the contrary, it is Dr. Vickers who has contributed "considerable confusion" to the economic debate.

The real issue, however, is not economic theory, as Dr. Vickers well understands. It is ultimately a matter of "ideological preferences."[10] All the arguments concerning multipliers, GNP, MPC, NNP, leakages, injections and so forth are irrelevant to the discussion. They are merely whitewash to give the Keynesian system apparent intellectual justification. Yet Dr. Vickers *knows* that what is at stake here is a matter of ideology. It is Christian thought and specific Biblical principles and guidelines versus the ideas of autonomous and rebellious man.

The Question of Sovereignty

Keynesians, generally speaking, have not arrived at the realization of this point (and neither have many Christians for that matter). Ultimately all economic theories turn upon the question of sovereignty. *Whose word is law?* God's or man's? There are no third, fourth, or fifth choices. It is that simple. Keynesians endeavor to be fence-sitters on a fence that does not exist. *There is no neutral ground.* Hence, Keynesians, and one "Christian" Keynesian in particular, oscillate from one side to the other. Witness Dr. Vickers: at one time he is quite vocal about the need for Biblical law, while on other pages he does his best to convince the reader that we cannot have Scriptural principles because we live in a fallen world.

In a more limited sense all economic theories revolve on the question of property ownership, as Mises understood so well. Will property be private or public? Again the Keynesians continually shift their base. One moment they are ardent defenders of private property, and in the next instance they will become the most eloquent advocates of public control of property. Keynesians are not epistemologically self-conscious. They have not realized, as did Marx, that by denying private property, they are at war with God and His Law, which establishes private property rights.

---

10. Vickers, *Economics and Man*, p. 334.

One of the problems of our age, as observed by Katz, has been that "by granting fame to evil men, historians have encouraged the spread of evil. . . . What is wrong with history as currently taught is that it gives primary importance to the destroyers of values and only secondary importance to the creators."[11]

Keynesian theories are destructive of values — Christian values as found in the Word of God. Therefore, "let us hope that the time will soon come when Keynes . . . will be recognized as one of the great intellectual ruiners of history — like Rousseau and Marx."[12]

Keynes and Vickers

We know what Dr. Vickers thinks of Mr. Keynes. But what would Keynes, the professional skeptic and full-time pervert, have thought of Dr. Vickers? What would he have thought of a self-professed Christian scholar who has devoted his life as a kind of acolyte to Keynes, even to the extent of writing a book fusing Keynes and the Bible? He would have been astounded, just as Charles Darwin was endlessly astounded at the stream of letters from clerics who told him that it was only *Origin of Species* which at last made sense of Christianity for them.

But would he have appreciated the effort? It is doubtful. In fact, the attempt would probably have angered him. Of what earthly use to Keynes would *Economics and Man* have been — an attempted fusion of God and revolutionary economics? Keynes' biographer Harrod describes Keynes: "His mind was highly intolerant of anything ambiguous or makeshift. Confronted with an intellectual patchwork, with an old idea and a new idea incongruously held together, he could not fail to detect the incongruity with his quick penetration, and was left with a feeling of irritation and disgust. He, like Strachey, craved for the clean sweep, the bold new idea, the crisp and lucid."[13]

---

11. Katz, *op. cit.*, pp. 271, 272.
12. Wilhelm Röpke, *A Humane Economy: The Social Framework of the Free Market* (South Bend, Indiana: Gateway Editions, 1960), p. 219.
13. Roy Harrod, *The Life of John Maynard Keynes* (New York: Norton, [1951] 1982), p. 88.

If ever there was a book which could not conceivably be described as "crisp and lucid," it is *Economics and Man*. If ever there was an incongruous intellectual patchwork, it is Douglas Vickers' attempt to fuse the Bible and Keynes. Keynes would have been appalled — indeed, as I am, but for different reasons: he for the stain of the Bible, and I for the stain of Keynes.

Final Remarks

Economics and Man never gained any influence. Conservative Christians had no use for baptized Keynesianism, and liberals had no use for Dr. Vickers' affirmation of Van Til's anti-humanist epistemology. The book is a classic example of a desperate attempt by an intellectually compromised Christian academic to synthesize opposites: his religious faith and his academic faith. As always, the academic faith won out. We have seen this story repeated endlessly in every little Christian college in the land, with their officially certified Ph.D.-holding scholars, and their vain quest for academic respectability. Faculty members have sold their theological birthright for a mess of pottage, just as Dr. Vickers sold his.

Economics and Man is notable only for its failure — intellectually, stylistically, and above all economically. It sank without a trace, except for a lecture or two at Dr. North's old alma mater, Westminster Theological Seminary. That public appearance did nothing noticeable for the sales of *Economics and Man*.

Dr. Vickers devoted his academic career to becoming a "front man" for an academically successful religion. The founder of that religion was a homosexual who had a very short-run view of life. (Given the Biblical doctrine of final judgment, he was certainly entitled to such a view.) He began his career as a logician and a brilliant essayist and polemicist. The more he wrote, the less coherent he became. We can see in his writings the earthly judgment of God. There was a progressive deterioration in his ability to communicate his ideas — not in making converts in an increasingly perverse intellectual and political world, but in setting forth his ideas in a way that his followers could repeat them, predict the economic future with them, and act in terms of them. *The General Theory* is a book filled with incoherent logic, false analogies, useless formulas, and State-enhancing conclusions. He was successful in attracting a generation of academic economists who believed that his economic system was the road to a New World Order. They joined together on a quest to the Emerald City of Keynes, where spending creates production, where money flows forever, where downward price flexibility is a myth, where government spending can cure just about anything.

And hardly anyone believes him any more. ". . . Martin Feldstein, the council [of Economic Advisors] chief recently chased back to Harvard, observes that during the 1982 recession there was hardly a call from either professional economists or elected officials for the government to do something. So, too, despite high unemployment, there was very little said about policies to bring it down during the presidential campaign. 'It's amazing how far we've come,' says ratexian [rational expectations economist] Neil Wallace. 'That hasn't happened in any of the previous presidential elections of the past 20 years.'"[14] It is not that they have all accepted free enterprise; it is that they no longer have any believable rabbits to pull out of the State's hat.

Next time they may simply impose raw power. They will not need any sophisticated economic theories to justify their actions. They will certainly not need incoherent, lackluster, unsalable books along the lines of *Economics and Man*.

In the Christian world, Douglas Vickers serves as the prime example of how a man can take the wrong path and become a propagandist for the enemies of His heavenly Savior. How could he have been so foolish? Van Til gives us the answer: the epistemological problem is not ultimately intellectual; the problem is ethical. Dr. Vicker's problem is not primarily intellectual. Dr. Vicker's primary problem is moral: he would enslave men to the State in the name of Christian ethics.

---

14. Susan Lee, "The un-managed economy," *Forbes* (Dec. 1984), p. 158.

INDEX